CECIL B. DeMILLE

THE ART OF THE HOLLYWOOD EPIC

CECILIA DeMILLE PRESLEY AND MARK A. VIEIRA

IMAGES AND ARTIFACTS FROM THE CECIL B. De MILLE ARCHIVES

PHOTOGRAPHED BY MARK A. VIEIRA

CURATED BY

Helen Cohen, the De Mille Office

Matt Severson, the Margaret Herrick Library of the Academy of Motion Picture Arts and Sciences;

James V. D'arc, Cecil B. De Mille Archives, MSS 1400; L. Tom Perry Special Collections, Brigham Young University, Provo, Utah;

Ned Comstock and Sandra Garcia-Myers, Cinematic Arts Library, the University of Southern California

RUNNING PRESS

PHILADELPHIA · LONDON

THE AUTHORS GRATEFULLY ACKNOWLEDGE
THE CONTRIBUTIONS OF:

Robert S. Birchard

Matias Bombal

Rob Brooks

Ben Carbonetto

Alfred Chico

David Chierichetti

Greenbriar Films

The Institute of the American Musical

The Kobal Collection

Betty Lasky

Lisa Mitchell

Katherine Orrison

Mark Santamaria

The San Francisco Museum of Performance and Design

Sue Slutzky

Mrs. Shirley Whitmore

Lou Valentino

Marc Wanamaker

Roy Windham

To my brother, Joe Harper, and sister, Connie Nelson, with whom I have shared this life.

—CECILIA DE MILLE PRESLEY

To the memory of my mother and my father.

—MARK A. VIEIRA

PAGES 2-3: Two of the sphinxes built in Egypt for *The Ten Commandments.*
PAGE 4: Gary Cooper in DeMille's 1940 *North West Mounted Police.*
PAGE 7: Cecil B. DeMille, wearing headphones and microphone, directs the 1956 version of *The Ten Commandments.* Charlton Heston watches from above.

 ————————————

Books published by Running Press are available at special discounts for bulk purchases in the United States by corporations, institutions, and other organizations. For more information, please contact the Special Markets Department at the Perseus Books Group, 2300 Chestnut Street, Suite 200, Philadelphia, PA 19103, or call (800) 810-4145, ext. 5000, or e-mail special.markets@perseusbooks.com.

ISBN 978-0-7624-5490-7
Library of Congress Control Number: 2014945243

E-book ISBN 978-0-7624-5537-9

9 8 7 6 5 4 3 2 1
Digit on the right indicates the number of this printing

Designed by Jennifer K. Beal Davis
Edited by Cindy De La Hoz
Typography: CycloneLayers, Bonveno, Bulmer, and Avenir

Running Press Book Publishers
2300 Chestnut Street
Philadelphia, PA 19103-4371

Visit us on the web!
www.runningpress.com

"A man is no better than
what he leaves behind."

—CECIL B. DeMILLE

CONTENTS

MARTIN SCORSESE

For many years, when people heard the words "film director," the image of Cecil B. DeMille was what came into their minds. DeMille was what a film director was supposed to be: distinguished but rugged, elegant but ready for action, decisive, imperious, extravagant, and authoritarian. This held true even after he passed away in the late '50s.

And for a lot of those people, DeMille's pictures represented a kind of essence of the movie experience. They had the simplicity of the stories we read or were told as children, the ones we wanted to hear over and over again. DeMille's storytelling still has a tremendous energy, *youthful* energy, and a visual beauty that grows from a deep love of the medium—in fact, he was one of the people who *invented* the medium.

When I was young, DeMille's pictures made a deep and indelible impression on me. The first one I saw in a theater was *Unconquered*, and there are extremely powerful images in that film, and in *Samson and Delilah* and *The Greatest Show on Earth* as well, that have stayed in my mind all these years as sense memories—really, some of the most vivid memories I have of film-going.

At some point in the '80s, I was able to see some of DeMille's silent films—most of us knew only his 1927 version of *King of Kings*, which was on television every Easter, and some stills from Richard Griffith's great pictorial history, *The Movies*, of pictures like *Why Change Your Wife?* or *The Golden Bed*. I was astonished by the sophistication and daring of pictures like *The Whispering Chorus* and *The Cheat*. They were exciting on an entirely different level from the pictures that made him a superstar among Hollywood directors.

This marvelous and beautifully designed book brings back the world over which Cecil B. DeMille reigned, throughout five decades, as the monarch of the movies. And the stills in these pages cast a unique spell. DeMille took a great deal of care with the production stills for his movies. He hired the great western photographer Edward S. Curtis, no less, to shoot the stills for the silent version of *The Ten Commandments*, and often he directed the shooting sessions himself (Robert Parrish, who was an extra in *This Day and Age*, commented that DeMille "often seemed to spend as much time and energy on the still as he did on the actual scenes."). He understood that the publicity for his films, the images that audience members would carry in their heads as they read a movie magazine or walked through a theater lobby in anticipation of the film to come, was extremely important to the movie-going experience. These still images embody and reflect DeMille and his world, the processes and dreams of the times in which he lived, just as much as the pictures themselves.

As you thumb through these pages, you'll be drawn into DeMille's world, and from there back into the glorious, colossal movies—so vast, so rich, so endless, like a story you just want to keep having told to you, again, and again.

FOREWORD
BY BRETT RATNER

ecil B. DeMille began his career directing the first feature-length movie ever made in Hollywood (*The Squaw Man*), and ended it with one of the biggest (the remake of his own *The Ten Commandments*). In between, he made his name synonymous with a kind of larger-than-life spectacle that promised to give audiences more than their money's worth and rarely failed to deliver.

Indeed, it's fitting that one of DeMille's most famous movies was about the performers in the Ringling Bros./Barnum & Bailey Circus—kindred showmen, to be sure. That movie's title, *The Greatest Show on Earth*, seemed to sum up his filmmaking philosophy. Steven Spielberg has cited that movie as one of his inspirations for becoming a director.

Has there ever been a highlight reel of Hollywood's greatest moments that didn't include Charlton Heston's Moses parting the Red Sea in *The Ten Commandments*—a movie that still shows on network TV, in prime time, every Easter? Or the train crash from *Greatest Show*, with its boxcars tumbling like dominos, sparks flying, and lions escaping into the night? You can see DeMille's influence in everything from the exploding Death Star of *Star Wars* to the flying bicycles of *E.T.*, and the sinking ocean liner of *Titanic*. Were he around today, he would doubtless be fascinated by the even more complex and realistic illusions CGI

has allowed, and the giant, towering images of the IMAX screen.

He was, above all, a great showman who put the audience first and the critics (who constantly accused him of excess) a distant second, trusting that his best work would stand the test of time and continue to enchant generation after generation. DeMille has been dead more than fifty years now, and yet he still feels incredibly present. All of us making movies today owe him an enormous debt.

"MY GRANDFATHER"
BY CECILIA DE MILLE PRESLEY

The man who raised me was my grandfather, Cecil B. DeMille. He and my grandmother, Constance, lived in the same home from 1916 until he died in 1959. It was a big home, about 42,000 square feet. Fortunately for us, it was big enough to store thousands of items from his long and successful film career. There were storyboards, paintings, costumes, artifacts, documents, scripts, photographs, and his original nitrate prints. In DeMille's lifetime, which spanned the eras of both silent and sound films, he was one of the world's most successful producer-directors. No one has had a greater impact on the history and development of the motion picture.

DeMille was an art lover. He particularly loved illustration. It told a story, just as he did. His favorite illustrator was Gustave Doré, who was famed for his engravings of Dante's *The Divine Comedy*. DeMille based some of his most famous scenes on Doré's work.

Like the Medici of old, DeMille surrounded himself with artists and craftsmen, the best he could summon. When making a film, he would first conduct painstaking research. That material alone was an impressive body of literature. Some of it has been published by university presses.

After DeMille completed his research, he would work with a team of writers and tell them the story as he envisioned it. From this narrative, he and the writers would craft a script. DeMille would give the script to his artists and leave them alone. Working from it, they created renderings of each scene. These works of art, covering seventy films and a hundred years, constitute a unique art collection, one of the most impressive and inspiring in existence.

Most of this work has never been seen before. That, to me, is a tragedy. It should be available to all who love art and film. When Mark Vieira called and said that he wanted to do a book, I was thrilled, because it meant that I could share this art.

What you will see on these pages are works from the remarkable DeMille Collection. Many of the artists will be familiar; some not. Their work is breathtaking. The way in which Mark has photographed and curated it is in itself a work of art, our tribute to DeMille and his artists.

OPPOSITE: Cecil B. DeMille directs *Samson and Delilah* with his granddaughter Cecilia at his right.

PREFACE

Colossal. Stupendous. Epic. These adjectives, used by film companies to hawk their wares, became clichés long ago. When used to describe one director's work, they are accurate. The films of Cecil Blount DeMille are expansive, awe-inspiring, and spectacular. More than any filmmaker in Hollywood history, he mastered the art of the spectacle. Using a massive canvas, he told tales that were steeped in Victorian morality yet unmistakably of the twentieth century. His films were grand but never lost sight of their characters. He made intimate spectacles. One hundred years ago he made film history.

In November 1913, a group of enterprising New Yorkers became filmmakers. They called themselves the Jesse L. Lasky Feature Play Company. When they were ready to make their first film, the partners sent Cecil B. DeMille to Los Angeles. Once there, he chose to shoot in Hollywood. Motion pictures were no longer in a kindergarten stage, running less than twenty minutes. DeMille made his film as long as a short play. Released in February 1914, *The Squaw Man* is acknowledged as the first feature-length film made in Hollywood.

The Squaw Man was also a hit. It established DeMille and his partners—Jesse Lasky, Samuel Goldfish (later Goldwyn), and Arthur Friend—as Hollywood filmmakers. Their success drew more companies and led to the founding of Paramount Pictures. Ten years later, Hollywood could call itself the "film capital of the world." DeMille continued for over forty years, making a total of seventy films. Most were hits; some were box-office champions. DeMille remains the most commercially successful director in history.

C. B. DeMille died on January 21, 1959, aged seventy-seven. The press accorded him the respect due an elder states-man. "Pioneer of movies," said the *New York Times*. "The greatest creator and showman of our industry," wrote the *Los Angeles Times*. "The founder of Hollywood," said the *Guardian*. There was no doubt: DeMille would be remembered. Or would he?

Less than a month earlier, on December 28, 1958, CBS Television had aired a one-hour program, *Small World*, hosted by Edward R. Murrow. The show contrived to interview politicians and celebrities separated by thousands of miles. This episode featured a three-way conversation—between actress Vivien Leigh (in London), critic Kenneth Tynan (in New York), and producer Samuel Goldwyn (in Los Angeles). While discussing Orson Welles, Goldwyn mentioned the filmmaker with whom

OPPOSITE: A 1929 portrait of Cecil B. DeMille by M-G-M photographer Ruth Harriet Louise.

he had partnered forty-five years earlier. "No one likes Cecil DeMille's pictures," said Goldwyn. "I mean the critics, they don't like him. The public seems to like him. And, after all, the public, they have the final word."

Tynan was determined to have the final word. "I would be very interested to hear," said Tynan, "if anybody will be seeing Mr. DeMille's pictures in, say, fifty years' time. Millions of people are seeing them all over the world now, but will they last, as for instance, *Citizen Kane* will last?"

"May I answer that?" said Goldwyn. "Cecil produced a picture thirty years ago. It was a biblical picture. I forget the name of the picture."

"*The Sign of the Cross*!" exclaimed a smiling Vivien Leigh. "*The Sign of the Cross*!"

"*The King of Kings*," remembered Goldwyn. "Mr. Tynan, it's still being shown."

"Really?"

"All over the world."

"Where?" asked Tynan. "In outlying islands in the South Pacific?"

Tynan's supercilious attitude was lamentable, and more so his ignorance. DeMille's 1927 silent film *The King of Kings* had a unique distribution arrangement. In defiance of talking pictures, this biography of Jesus Christ had played continuously since its premiere and had verifiably been seen by close to *800 million people*. Likewise, in defiance of Tynan and his critical compeers on both coasts, *Samson and Delilah* (1949) and *The Ten Commandments* (1956) had joined David O. Selznick's

Gone With the Wind in the list of the top ten all-time box-office champions. As Goldwyn said, nobody liked DeMille's movies. Nobody but the public.

We are not writing this book as apologists for DeMille. His work speaks for itself, and it is seen. Tynan's tart predictions were made in a time of sporadic reissues. In the era of instant availability, DeMille's films are ubiquitous. *Samson and Delilah*, *The Greatest Show on Earth*, and *The Ten Commandments* continue to earn revenue for the De Mille Estate. We are writing this book so that other aspects of his work can be seen. Anyone writing a book on DeMille has encountered these aspects, but telling his story accurately has been a task of words, not images. There are excellent DeMille books. In 1994, Sumiko Higashi used the DeMille holdings at Brigham Young University to affirm his

relevance with *Cecil B. DeMille and American Culture*. In 1999, Katherine Orrison vividly described the production of DeMille's greatest achievement with *Written in Stone: Making Cecil B. DeMille's Epic The Ten Commandments*. In 2004, Robert S. Birchard examined each DeMille film in his eminent, intensely readable *Cecil B. DeMille's Hollywood*. In 2010, Scott Eyman wrote the definitive DeMille biography in his masterly *Empire of Dreams*. Although these authors had access to the De Mille

OPPOSITE, LEFT TO RIGHT: A costume rendering by Ralph Jester for the 1956 *The Ten Commandments*. • A concept painting by Dan Sayre Groesbeck for *The Plainsman* (1936).

ABOVE, LEFT TO RIGHT: A cape designed by Gilbert Adrian for *Madam Satan* (1930). • A costume sketch by Natalie Visart for *The Sign of the Cross* (1932).

Estate, their books were not pictorials. There has never been a large-format book on DeMille or the art he commissioned.

On the occasion of *The Squaw Man* centennial, it is fitting that we pay tribute to DeMille's achievements with a photographic showcase. His films contain commanding images. The art and artifacts that helped create these images have been lovingly preserved by the De Mille Estate. For the first time they can be seen in an art-format book. *Cecil B. DeMille: The Art of the Hollywood Epic* presents a panoply of magnificence—concept art, costumes, props, and an array of photographic imagery—plus an illuminating text written by his granddaughter, Cecilia de Mille Presley. Raised by C. B. DeMille and his wife, Constance, Cecilia both observed and participated in the making of his later films.

C. B. DeMille was the first film director to forge a bond with the visual artists of his day. He created the title of art director for Wilfred Buckland, who was a fellow pupil of theatrical impresario David Belasco. DeMille utilized the concept paintings of Dan Sayre Groesbeck and Boris Leven to illustrate in-progress scenarios. Designers Mitchell Leisen, Natacha Rambova (Mrs. Rudolph Valentino), and Gilbert Adrian all benefited from their association with DeMille. He hired fine-art photographers, such as Karl Struss, William Mortensen, and Edward Curtis to shoot on his sets. Few Hollywood directors gave the unit stills photographer sufficient time to capture his setups. DeMille did. There is a painterly quality to these photographs, and he had them mounted in sumptuous albums. These survive in the estate's collection.

The focus of this book is to present unseen treasures. We also want to present an unseen DeMille. He did not surround himself with "yes men" whose frightened reply to his every utterance was "Ready when you are, C. B.!" This oft-quoted phrase turned up nowhere in our research. Cecilia de Mille Presley recalls her grandfather's sense of humor, especially about

himself. He kept an album of DeMille caricatures. His favorite was cartoonist Al Capp's "Cecil D. Mildew." One day Yul Brynner came to DeMille in a fury because Capp had turned him into "Jewel Brynner." DeMille took Brynner aside and showed him the album of cartoons. "You need to develop a sense of humor about yourself," DeMille told him. This is the DeMille whom his granddaughter knew, and whom we present here.

In 1968, when Andrew Sarris was populating the auteur pantheon with fourteen directors—including D. W. Griffith, Howard Hawks, and Alfred Hitchcock—he pointedly omitted DeMille. We are not here to right that wrong, but we do show that DeMille was the author of his films. We do not analyze or deconstruct them. We do not criticize them. We review DeMille's films with production highlights, with impressions, vignettes, and tableaux. We hope these will encourage viewings of his work and lead to a renewed appreciation of it. This book is a celebration of his films. They are seductive, powerful, and transporting, as are the images and artifacts that were created for them. We hope this volume is as desirable an object as the golden calf in the De Mille Collection.

As you go through this book, imagine that Mr. DeMille has displayed the collection in a great hall. You are walking with him and his granddaughter, Mrs. Presley. The artifacts are arranged in chronological order, beginning with the Underwood typewriter that transcribed *The Squaw Man* scenario in December 1913. One by one, DeMille and Presley point out significant items. I draw on his photographic expertise to explain DeMille's effects. I also quote DeMille artists such as Edith Head, Claudette Colbert, and Charlton Heston. DeMille shares an anecdote. Presley gives it a fuller context by recalling a story he told her. She has contributed to previous DeMille books. Here, for the first time, she tells the story herself, recalling script conferences, visits to sets, and her grandfather's thoughts on various films. She relates details of the Egyptian expedition to

film *The Ten Commandments*, a remarkable experience by any estimation. No one knows DeMille and his films better than Presley. No one has devoted as much time to maintaining his legacy and his archives. With *Cecil B. DeMille: The Art of the Hollywood Epic*, the legacy and the archives, the artists and the art are showcased in a tribute to an extraordinary filmmaker.

MARK A. VIEIRA
MARCH 2, 2014

ABOVE LEFT: Cecil B. DeMille was born on August 12, 1881, under the astrological sign of Leo the Lion. This behind-the-scenes shot from *Samson and Delilah* (1949) shows him with Jackie the Lion.

ABOVE RIGHT: A promotional statuette of the golden calf created for *The Ten Commandments* (1956). Photograph by Mark A. Vieira.

INTRODUCTION

ow is history made? Sometimes in the most unplanned, effortless way. A casual conversation brought Cecil B. DeMille to Hollywood. On November 23, 1913, he was sitting with his friend Jesse L. Lasky in the Claridge Grill, a restaurant in the newly opened Claridge Hotel at Forty-Fourth and Broadway. DeMille enjoyed going to the Claridge. He would leave his mother's literary agency at 220 West 42nd Street and walk two blocks to join Lasky. The ritual lunch gave his spirits a much-needed lift.

DeMille was living with his wife, Constance, and his five-year-old daughter, Cecilia, in a small apartment at 241 West 108th Street. "I had been married for eleven years," he recalled. "Eleven years of almost unremitting struggle to keep our heads above water."

Cecil spelled his name *DeMille*, not *de Mille*, because he felt it would look better on a marquee.* He fully expected to see it there. His father, Henry de Mille, had been a successful playwright. His mother, Beatrice, was an influential literary agent. His brother, William, was a prosperous playwright. At thirty-two, Cecil had achieved little. He was a sometime actor trying to be a play producer. "I was at an age," he said "when most men have found their groove in life, even if the groove is only a rut." He had yet to see two hits in a row. "Cecil's world looked dark," recalled William. "His latest play had followed its predecessors into oblivion." Lasky knew this. "A change of scene," DeMille said to him. "That's what I need."

As a child, Cecil de Mille had a secret. He had created a mythical character: "In my imagination, fed with the heroic tales my father read us, I was the Champion Driver, a Robin Hood whose Sherwood Forest was the world." This superhero was a fearless gallant charging to save the day, slashing villains with his sword until the forest was red with blood. In the fall of 1913, the only red was in his finances. "Cecil's bank account," wrote William, "suggested the deep, red glow of a western sunset."

William had given Cecil work as an actor in his hit play, *The Warrens of Virginia*. He had invited Cecil to collaborate on other plays, but they failed to draw. He had lent Cecil money.

OPPOSITE: Henry Churchill de Mille was remembered by his son, Cecil, as "a very great playwright, a very successful one. I grew up in that atmosphere. I absorbed it. He kept on his desk a saying of Dion Boucicault, 'Plays are not written, but rewritten.'"

Cecil used the spelling DeMille in his professional life, and de Mille in private life. The family name de Mille was used by his children Cecilia, John, and Katherine. It was also used by Cecil's brother, William, and by William's daughters, Margaret and Agnes. It is also used by his granddaughter, Cecilia de Mille Presley.

ABOVE: Beatrice de Mille was a great influence on her son. When Henry was courting her, she was known as Matilda Samuel. He began calling her by her middle name, alluding to Dante's "Beloved Beatrice." To marry Henry, Beatrice converted from the Jewish faith to the Episcopal religion. After his sudden death, she drew on her own resources to support her children. She ran a girls' school, and then a literary agency that promoted female writers. She was America's second female play broker.

Cecil persevered. In 1910, he was commissioned to write a play for the theatrical impresario David Belasco. Years earlier, Cecil had watched his father craft plays with Belasco. The dark, angular Belasco was a character in his own right, making grand entrances, wearing capes and a clerical collar, even though he was Jewish. "Belasco was flamboyant, bigger-than-life, almost operatic," says Cecilia de Mille Presley. "He became a kind of uncle to William and Cecil. He bought them gifts and asked their opinions of scenes he'd written with their father." Henry encouraged his sons to seek truth in writing. "The dramatist is a camera," he said. "His photography of life must be true if he would reach men's hearts." Henry was a deeply religious man. His collaboration with Belasco ended in 1891, when the director became involved with the notorious divorcée Mrs. Leslie Carter. Henry disapproved. Belasco stopped visiting.

Cecil was sorry to see Belasco go, even though the director had hurt the boy deeply by promising him a pony for his birthday and then forgetting his promise. Cecil loved both animals and the grandiose David. "It was a bitter experience," DeMille wrote later, "as only a childhood sorrow can be." As an adult, he took care never to break a promise to a child.

In 1892, Cecil was eleven. William was fourteen. Their sister, baby Agnes, was a year old. The boys doted on Henry. All through 1892 he indulged them with a nightly reading. "Father had a beautifully modulated voice and a fine sense of dramatic values," wrote DeMille. "There would be a chapter from the Old Testament, a chapter from the New, and often a chapter from American or English or European history, or from Thackeray or Victor Hugo." The tone was not didactic; in fact, far from it. "Father liked to have his head rubbed while he read. Bill and I used to take advantage of that to prolong the evening's reading."

In February 1893, Henry was stricken with typhoid fever. In a few days, he was dead. Two years later, while Beatrice worked to support her children, three-year-old Agnes fell mortally ill with spinal meningitis. Once more there was a sudden death.

Years later, when Cecil wrote a play for David Belasco, it dealt with life after death: *The Return of Peter Grimm* was the tale of a sinful man who returns to earth seeking regeneration. It looked like the thing to establish Cecil. He was twenty-nine, with a wife and child. He needed a hit—and an ally. In 1910, Belasco was a power on Broadway. Power can corrupt. Belasco took advantage of an artfully worded contract and rewrote enough of the play to present it as his own. At the January 1911 premiere of *Peter Grimm*, DeMille read the cover of the play program in disbelief. Belasco had taken credit for writing the play, claiming that he had based it on his own psychic experiences. The only credit that Cecil got was in small print at the bottom of the cover. "This was worse than a bitter pill," says Cecilia. "It hurt Cecil very much."

Beatrice could not let her younger son slide into failure. She hired him for her agency and taught him agenting and playwriting. In time, he was managing the agency and was a junior equity partner with Beatrice. In October 1911, she introduced him to a vaudeville producer named Jesse Louis Lasky. "The Lasky vaudeville companies ruled the nation's circuits," says his daughter, Betty Lasky. "My father had introduced a form called the 'miniature musical comedy' or 'American operetta.' It was a one-act piece, about forty minutes long, and it featured pretty, expensively costumed actresses singing bright new songs."

When Lasky met DeMille, it was not a case of love at first sight. Lasky had come to Beatrice for her playwright son, not for his manqué brother. For his part, DeMille had no interest in musical theater. Beatrice held the two men in her office until the ice melted. Lasky began a halting description of his project, an operetta called *California*. Like Belasco, he was a San Francisco native. He grew enthusiastic in the telling. DeMille watched warily, and then warmed, suddenly interjecting, "Say, I like that!"

"The minute he said, 'I like that,'" wrote Lasky, "I liked *him*. And I've never stopped." It helped that he and DeMille shared a love of fly-fishing. It also helped that Lasky was bright and spontaneous. "The world was new to him every morning," said DeMille. "For Jesse, life was a sparkling road full of unknown curves, round any one of which might lie untold adventure." *California* was written and staged by DeMille and produced by Lasky. It was very successful and allowed them to develop other projects. But DeMille's plays flopped and Lasky's *Folies Bergère* was indeed a folly. The oversize restaurant lost $100,000 (more than $3 million in 2014 dollars), of which Lasky's partner, Henry B. Harris, bore the most. Lasky continued with his vaudeville shows, so he needed more "miniatures." For DeMille, these writing assignments meant both income and the promise of royalties. He would sit with Lasky at the Claridge Grill, swapping ideas.

DeMille spent his evenings with his wife and daughter. The marriage was a happy one. Cecil had met Constance in a Washington, DC, theater. They were both acting in a play called *Hearts Are Trumps*.

DeMille and Lasky supped at the Claridge with Arthur S. Friend and Samuel Goldfish, two pals who were not in "the show business," as it was called. Friend was an attorney with theatrical clients. He talked of "moving pictures," but neither DeMille nor Lasky was interested. "They're crude and jittery," said Lasky.

"Is it *art?*" asked DeMille. "Yes, like a trained dog that plays a piano."

Samuel Goldfish was an affluent glove salesman. "DeMille was impressed by Sam's cleverness," says Cecilia. "Sam would order a shipment of right-hand gloves, which were orphaned when customs saw they were incomplete. Since they were unclaimed, he would bid on them for a cheap price and not have to pay the import duty. Then he would do the same thing with the gloves for the other hand. Grandfather would shake his head and laugh at this story." Goldfish was married to Lasky's sister, Blanche. It was with Blanche that Lasky got his start in show business. Ten years earlier, Blanche and Jesse had toured vaudeville doing cornet duets. Jesse Lasky was one of the most likable men in show business. He even got along with his brother-in-law. Few people did. Sam Goldfish was contentious and brusque.

One day in 1911, Goldfish wandered into the Herald Square Theatre on Thirty-Fourth Street, a legitimate house that also showed moving pictures. "Going into a nickelodeon wasn't considered entirely good taste," recalled Goldfish. The audience was lower class, noisy, and smelly. But the images he saw on the screen were arresting. One of the short films featured the cowboy actor Broncho Billy Anderson. "The image of this performer brought me into a whole new exciting world," said Goldfish. "I wanted to be a part of it." Arthur Friend shared Goldfish's enthusiasm for the new medium, but when they tried to convert DeMille and Lasky at the Claridge one day, they were met with skepticism. DeMille and Lasky thought movies were a fad, something to beguile immigrants. If you wanted that market, why not grab it with food? Lasky had grown up in San Jose, California, with Mexican food. "If we tied up the tamale concession in the East, we could make a fortune," said Lasky, joking.

Goldfish was serious. He took Lasky to dinner at the Hoffman House on Broadway and appealed to his ego. "The Lasky Feature Play Company," he said grandly. "That sounds better than 'Lasky's Hot Tamales,' doesn't it?" Why waste Lasky's name on food when it meant so much in show business? Goldfish and Friend took Lasky and DeMille to see a couple of movies. "Well," said DeMille on the way out of the theater, "I don't know anything about pictures, but if I can't do better than that, I ought to be shot at sunrise."

Back at the Claridge, Friend cited the roadshow presentation of "the Divine" Sarah Bernhardt in *Queen Elizabeth*, the film made by Adolph Zukor's company, Famous Players. Lasky agreed that the number of attendees was impressive.

In July 1913, Lasky and DeMille turned over a Claridge Grill menu and started making notes. "Jesse would head the company," recalled DeMille. "I would make the picture, or pictures, if the company survived the first one. Sam Goldfish would sell them. Arthur Friend would handle the corporate and legal side." Shortly thereafter, they announced the formation of the Jesse L. Lasky Feature Play Company. This was in name only; they could always incorporate later. First the company needed $20,000 to capitalize. While his partners looked for investors, DeMille wrote more miniatures for Lasky, cowrote a play with William, and produced another flop.

If DeMille had been working in vaudeville or on the Broadway stage, he might have met with success, but he had been raised to write a specific kind of play. It was not serious or experimental, nor was it crudely physical. It was crafted for the middle class. That branch of the theater was dying, in spite of hits like Belasco's *The Girl of the Golden West*. Melodrama relied on formula (the ingénue rescued from the villain by the hero) and on complicated stagecraft (ships, trains, chariot races). DeMille's middle-to-lower-class audience was literal-minded. It preferred a real train on a movie screen to a plywood train on a stage. Nickels were going to movies, not to melodramas. DeMille watched twelve years of work go down the drain.

In late August, DeMille wrote William that he intended to make movies. His brother was less than pleased. "You come of a cultured family," wrote William, "two of whose members have made honorable names in the field of drama. I cannot understand how you are willing to identify yourself with a cheap form of amusement which no one will ever allude to as an art." His argument was valid. "For more than a generation," wrote a critic, "the name of de Mille has been closely linked with that of Belasco, both synonymous with high altitudes of dramatic art." In the fall of 1913, DeMille made a last-ditch effort to save his theatrical career. He produced two plays. They both failed. In late November he was fired from a directing job. "I'm sorry, C.B.," said producer Arch Selwyn. "But you won't do. You haven't enough in you—here." Selwyn pounded on his chest to indicate a lack of heart.

"I had been directing," said DeMille, "according to my usual quiet method of suggestion, rather than raving and ranting. I left the theater and sought the Claridge Grill for solace. And who should come in but Jesse Lasky. We were real friends, friends such as are formed by tramping the woods and shooting your daily meal side by side."

"Jesse, I'm pulling out," he said. "The show business is all right for you. You're doing well. But I can't live on the royalties I'm getting. My debts are piling up. I want to chuck the whole thing."

"What?" asked Lasky. "What'll you do?"

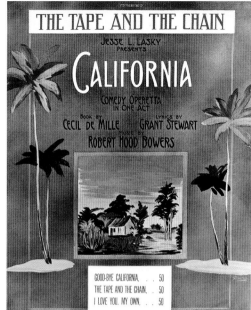

"There's that revolution in Mexico, I'm going down there. I'll get in on it, and maybe write about it."

"If you want adventure," said Lasky, "I've got a better idea. Let's make some movies!" Lasky had an ace up his sleeve. A week earlier, he had met with the playwright Edwin Milton Royle and asked to buy the screen rights to his long-running hit, *The Squaw Man*.

The Squaw Man was a western with a message. Henry Wynnegate, an English nobleman, takes the blame for his cousin's theft of charity money because he loves his cousin's wife, Diana. Disgraced, Wynnegate goes to Montana, where a "squaw" named Nat-U-Rich kills a cowboy to save his life. Wynnegate and Nat-U-Rich live together and have a child, a scandalous situation. Then Diana, still in love with Wynnegate, shows up with the news that her husband has confessed to the theft and died. Wynnegate must choose between her and Nat-U-Rich. And what of the child? If Nat-U-Rich has to give him up, she will die. *The Squaw Man* was a sensation, and a good bet for a film.

"I have been honored with numerous propositions," said Royle. "I cannot take this movie madness seriously. Every emotion in the raw, every situation since the fall of man, is being grabbed with coarse, unskillful, and sometimes thievish hands and smeared pell-mell into pictures. It is all so crude and formative."

Perhaps it was because Royle knew the de Mille family. Perhaps it was Lasky's track record. Perhaps it was the increas-ing number of quality films being made. Whatever the reason, Royle accepted Lasky's offer of $10,000. Lasky had a valuable property. "Cecil," he said, "let's make some movies!"

DeMille thought for a moment. Then he reached across the table and grabbed Lasky's hand. "Let's!" he said. With that, they were out of their seats and out the door of the Claridge. The Champion Driver was on his way.

CECILIA DE MILLE PRESLEY

"Henry de Mille, in addition to being a lay minister in the Episcopal Church, was a playwright, one of the earliest successes of this country. He collaborated for five years with the acclaimed David Belasco. Henry was a tremendous influence on the boys. He involved himself in their lives. He taught them to honor nature and respect animals. As soon as the boys were old enough to understand any story at all, he read to them—from the Old Testament, the New Testament, and from a history book or classic. What he instilled in them was a love of drama played out in a religious setting."

ABOVE, LEFT TO RIGHT: This family album shows Henry de Mille (center, top), his wife, Beatrice (center, lower), their older son, William (lower left), his wife, Anna (upper left), Cecil (lower right), and his wife, Constance (upper right). • Sheet music from DeMille's first collaboration with Jesse Lasky.

CHAPTER 1

HOLLYWOOD PIONEER

THE SQUAW MAN

Cecil B. DeMille and Jesse Lasky strode down Forty-Fourth Street, gaining momentum. "We were charting a new course," recalled DeMille. "The future lay in 'feature plays,' pictures several reels long, telling a well-constructed story, well-acted; intended not as conglomerate items on the daily changing programs of the nickelodeons but as 'feature' attractions which could stand on their own as a new form of drama."

Drama requires actors. The budding filmmakers were passing the Lambs Club, a theatrical society. Inside, there was a hubbub. A stage star was displaying the wounds he had acquired the night before. Dustin Farnum and his wife, Mary, had been hit by a drunk driver. Farnum's leg had been hurt and his wife's wrist had been crushed. "That wasn't a stage automobile that struck Dustin Farnum," confirmed a reporter. In spite of his injuries, Farnum had managed to chase and subdue the felon.

Besides being a real-life hero, Farnum was a matinee idol. He was thirty-nine, tall, and burly, the star of western plays like *The Virginian*. He had just returned from Cuba, where he had made his first movie, *Soldiers of Fortune*, for the All-Star Feature Corporation. DeMille and Lasky buttonholed him. "Listen, Dusty," said Lasky, "we've formed a company and we're going into moving pictures. We've got *The Squaw Man*. We're going to make a feature, five, maybe six reels."

"It's a good play," said Farnum. "I've done it myself."

DeMille moved forward. "I tell you, Dusty," he said, "features are bound to sweep the country. All they need are men from the theater who know real drama. Why, just look what the pictures can do that the stage can't. Listen. I can make a picture out of this play. I've seen pictures, but I've never seen one that did what I want to do, which is to take a great story and put it on the screen."

"Here's the point," said Lasky. "We feel we've got a great chance here. All we need is a big Broadway name. We want you to play the part. What do you say?"

Farnum was inclined to say no. Lasky was offering a salary of only $250 a week, plus 25 percent of the profits. Farnum was not impressed. William Faversham, who had originated the role, was getting $2,500 a week on tour. But there were other things to consider. Farnum was thinking of retiring from the stage. He owned land near San Diego. He wanted to get away from New York, and especially from his wife, actress Mary Conwell. He had enjoyed filming in Cuba. While there, he had fallen in love with his leading lady, Winifred Kingston. He wanted to be near her, far from his wife. If he could have Winifred as his leading lady, *The Squaw Man* would serve his needs. On that condition he said yes.

Before DeMille committed himself to the new venture, he asked Constance for her approval. "Do what you think right," she answered, "and I will be with you." For the time being,

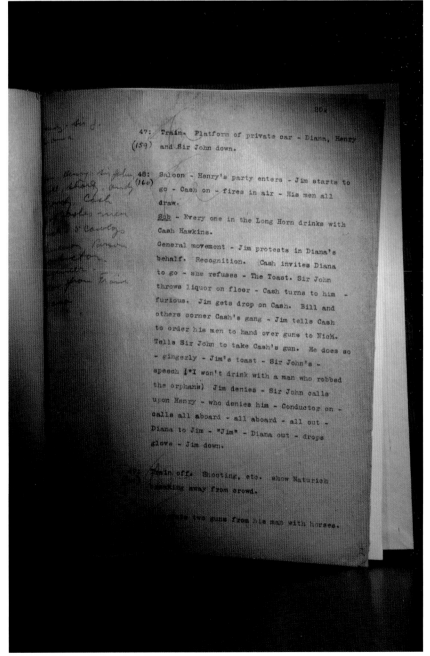

OVERLEAF: Cecil B. DeMille and the Jesse L. Lasky Feature Play Company used this Pathé camera in December 1913 and January 1914 to shoot *The Squaw Man*, the first feature film made in Hollywood. DeMille had a sentimental attachment to it and rarely started a film without using it to get a token shot. In later years, it occupied a place of honor in his office, where this photo was made. The De Mille Estate has lent the camera to the Autry National Center in Los Angeles.

CLOCKWISE FROM TOP: DeMille subleased this "moving-picture studio" to make *The Squaw Man*. "Unmistakably, it was a barn," wrote DeMille in his memoirs. The barn belonged to realtor Jacob Stern, but had been converted to a studio and film laboratory by L. L. Burns and Harry Revier, two of the new filmmakers in 1913 Los Angeles. This view is from Vine Street looking into Selma Avenue. • The scenario of *The Squaw* Man was simple. In 1913, directors relied on ideas carried in their heads—or on last-minute inspiration. • This Underwood No. 5 typewriter was used to type the scenario that Oscar Apfel and Cecil B. DeMille had written on the train from New York to Los Angeles. It belonged to a hired typist-bookkeeper named Stella Stray. Photograph by Mark A. Vieira.

though, she would stay in New York with Cecilia. Constance had been a steadfast, supportive wife, never complaining about the rigors of life on the road traveling with shows.

The Jesse L. Lasky Feature Play Company had recently incorporated. Its offices were in the new Longacre Theatre Building on West Forty-Eighth Street. Goldfish and Lasky were investing $10,000 each. To come up with his share, DeMille importuned his brother. William responded with a predictably opprobrious no. The Lasky partners were aware of DeMille's failures. They also saw his potential. The investment was waived, as it was for Arthur Friend. The two partners were given 10 percent of the Lasky Company, and DeMille was put on a salary of $100 a week. He was given the title of director-general. He had research to do.

"I had never been inside a motion picture studio," said DeMille. "Sam arranged for me to spend a day at the Edison Studio in the Bronx." Edison? Wasn't that the company that headed the malevolent Trust? If a film company used equipment that had not been patented by the so-called Trust, the Motion Picture Patents Company enforced the domain of Thomas Alva Edison via lawsuits and raids—and violence. This was a reality for Lasky and his partners, and they expected to dodge the Trust. One way of doing this was to keep away from the East

ABOVE, LEFT TO RIGHT: After filming more than a week in Hollywood, DeMille took cast and crew to several locations. This photo shows the bundled-up company at snowy Mount Palomar. • DeMille (right) posed with his pet wolf, Sheba, and cameraman Alfred Gandolfi.

CECILIA DE MILLE PRESLEY

"My grandfather told me about Sheba the wolf. He loved his wolf. She cared for him and never left his side. She had a habit of pacing and watching over him like a bodyguard. He said that he never, ever saw her sleeping. One day a cowboy encountered her and didn't realize that she was my grandfather's pet. He pulled out a gun and killed her. Grandfather felt terrible. His first friend in Hollywood was gone. The de Mille family had many dogs through the years, but Grandfather never again had one of his own."

Coast, although a number of Trust companies—Selig, Vitagraph, and Essanay—were operating in California. The plot of *The Squaw Man* was set in Wyoming, so the Lasky Company would be going west. "We hoped that Flagstaff might escape the notice of the Trust's strong-arm squads," wrote DeMille, "and that we might finish the picture with our Pathé camera intact." Just in case, DeMille packed a revolver.

Lasky found a way around the Trust. He followed the lead of Adolph Zukor, who had paid the Trust to leave him alone. "You can make your cowboy picture," they told him, "but you can't sell it. There's no one to sell it to but us." That remained to be seen. In any case, DeMille could visit the Edison Studio without fear. On the appointed day, he went with the crew and their cast of two to East 188th Street, by Bronx Park. The camera started turning. The Edison actress looked over her shoulder in terror as the Edison actor approached. "They talked, in pantomime of course, with much emotive gesticulation," said DeMille, who was incredulous at the crude technique. "If that's pictures," he told Lasky, "we can make the best pictures ever made!"

Goldfish expected DeMille to spend a week learning production methods. When he called and said one day was enough, Goldfish looked for a director to understudy him. William F. Haddock had just directed Farnum in *Soldiers of Fortune*, so he was interviewed. "The night before Thanksgiving," recalled Haddock, "I was in Jesse Lasky's office from a quarter past five 'til a quarter past seven. Lasky, DeMille, and Goldfish wanted me as a director. I had 'til Monday to make up my mind. But I took some bad advice. I was told that they'd make only one picture, close it up, and I'd be held responsible." Lasky hired Oscar C. Apfel, who had gone from an impressive stage career to make films for Pathé and Edison.

On December 10, the Lasky Company paid the Southern Pacific ticket agency $307.45 for five tickets to California. Cecil wanted to say good-bye to William. "I had spoken my piece before," wrote William. "Cecil knew my doubts and fears. If he chose to disregard them, well, he would find in me only a brother who wished him well, and who would help him pick up the pieces later."

On December 12, Cecil DeMille boarded the Broadway Limited. He was accompanied by Dustin Farnum, his road manager Fred Kley, Oscar Apfel, and an Italian cameraman named Alfred Gandolfi, who was carrying raw film stock. The Eastman Kodak film was unperforated. It was cheaper than raw stock that

had sprocket holes. The film could be perforated by a laboratory in Flagstaff, or better yet, by one of the crew. DeMille was used to cutting corners; he could cut sprocket holes, too.

The United States whizzed by the coach windows, but DeMille ignored it. He had seen the scenery many times. He concentrated on writing the scenario with Apfel. "By the time our train was chugging over the last miles of Arizona desert," wrote DeMille, "Oscar and I had perhaps twenty pages of penciled script and the hope that we could find a typist in Flagstaff, cheap." They envisioned a dramatic landscape against which to stage their cowboy saga. In Chicago, they changed to the Santa Fe California Limited. When the train pulled into Flagstaff on December 16, they saw something else.

Jesse Lasky would later tell his son, Jesse Jr., that there was a sheepman-cattleman war going on. William heard there was snow. Another story said there was pouring rain. Flagstaff was cold but there was no war, and the scenery was neither white nor wet. It was muddy. "There were high mountains," recalled DeMille. "I didn't want high mountains. I wanted plains with mountains in the distance." DeMille was also put off by the quality of light. It had no direction. "Somehow," said DeMille to Farnum, "this doesn't strike me as the perfect spot in which to make moving pictures."

"Well," replied Farnum, "I think we ought to go on to Los Angeles, where all the other companies are, and have a look." The Lasky party climbed back on the train. The "other film companies" included the Lubin Studio in San Diego, Keystone in Edendale, the Universal Film Manufacturing Company at Oak Crest Ranch in the San Fernando Valley, and Thomas Ince in Santa Monica. There were a dozen companies in Southern California.

The Lasky troupe arrived in Los Angeles on December 18 and checked into the Alexandria Hotel. This was the hub of the city's filmmaking. "Casting was carried on in the bar," wrote historian Kevin Brownlow. "Deals were made in the lobby, on the carpet called the 'Million-Dollar Rug.'" In this charged environment, DeMille was approached by owners of rental studios, but

Fred Kley was already looking. He went to Santa Monica, Boyle Heights, and Edendale.

Six years earlier, DeMille had acted in *The Warrens of Virginia* with E. Allen Martin. The actor was in Los Angeles making films. DeMille looked him up. On December 20, Martin introduced DeMille to L. L. Burns and Harry Revier, who owned a studio in the neighboring district called Hollywood. Burns managed both an Indian curio shop and a small film company. Revier had been an exhibitor. Their first studio had been in East Hollywood, at 4500 Sunset Boulevard. In March 1913, they had leased that to the Kinemacolor Company and moved a mile west. Their new studio was well equipped, with a laboratory and a stage. This was where Martin had filmed *Opportunity* for the Efsco Film Company.

In August, the veteran actor Hobart Bosworth had been to the Hollywood facility, seeking to rent it for his feature film *The Sea Wolf*, but when he met young Revier, he was put off by the sight of his crippled hand and went instead to the J.A.C. Studios on downtown Court Street. *The Sea Wolf* was the first feature film made in Los Angeles. It was released on December 7.

Fred Kley had also noticed the studio. It was in the wilds of Hollywood, in the middle of a lot of orchards. The streets were unpaved and there were no stop signs; telephone poles were painted red at their bases to indicate an intersection. Rustic or not, it sounded like a good deal. DeMille wanted to see it.

Burns and Revier drove him the seven miles to Hollywood. The district had become a city in 1886. In 1910, its orchards needed water so badly that it rejoined Los Angeles. In 1913, its population was 7,500. "After a long drive through the straggling outskirts of Los Angeles, and then through a stretch of open country, they delivered me to the somnolent village of Hollywood," wrote DeMille. "Turning off the sparsely-settled main thoroughfare, grandly called Hollywood Boulevard, we drove down a broad, shady avenue more appropriately named Vine Street; and there it was. It was a barn. Unmistakably, it was a barn. To its credit, it was a surprisingly large barn. L-shaped, one of its

yellowish, heat-beaten wings ran along Vine Street and the other stretched back, parallel with Selma Avenue, into an orange grove."

The barn that was now a studio had been built in 1901 by Colonel Robert Northam for his citrus farm. In 1904, when he was gambling, he lost the land to a real estate developer named Jacob Stern, who used the barn to house his horses and carriage. In March 1913, Burns and Revier leased it from him, with the agreement that the animals remain. "When we went in," wrote DeMille, "the horses looked me over with mild curiosity."

DeMille liked the studio. On December 24, he signed a lease contract for four months at $250 per month, and a three-year renewal option. Outside the barn there was an open-air stage with a framework for white muslin diffusers. Burns and Revier would expand this stage to dimensions of forty by seventy feet, add a second stage to share with the Lasky Company, and turn the horse stalls into dressing rooms. DeMille thought the film processing rate of 1.5 cents per foot was exorbitant. There were other labs in town, so Burns and Revier dropped the fee to .75 cents per foot, which included tinting and toning of release prints.

DeMille moved to a rental house at 6136 Lexington Avenue. His only roommate was a prairie wolf named Sheba, a domesticated animal he found in a *Los Angeles Times* ad.

TOP TO BOTTOM: A photographer named J. A. Ramsey came from the Dingman Studio to make this panoramic group portrait of the cast and crew of *The Squaw Man* on December 29, 1913, the first day of shooting. • Another group portrait on the auspicious first day shows DeMille and Apfel holding a loving cup in front of Dustin Farnum. The banquet scene was probably the first to be shot.

CECILIA DE MILLE PRESLEY

"Grandfather told me that he ended up in Los Angeles instead of Arizona (as planned), simply because he found the terrain boring. The stories about bad weather were all untrue. He wanted mountains, valleys, and lush green. So they reboarded the train and ended up in Los Angeles."

The scenario was complete. Someone had to type it. Kley was working as studio manager, so he hired twenty-two-year-old Stella Stray as "secretary-bookkeeper" at a weekly salary of $15. DeMille saw her sitting "behind the kitchen table, perched on a straight wooden chair, with a couple of city directories added so that she could reach the typewriter keys." One of his New York partners decided that Stray was being overpaid, so she was told to leave. She slid the heavy Underwood No. 5 off the table and started out the door. "Stella," said DeMille, "where are you going with that typewriter?"

"It's my typewriter," she said. "I'm taking it with me."

"Well, if it's your typewriter, we can't fire you." It was only then that Stray told the story of the typewriter. On a previous job, a western film, the company had gone broke, owing a great deal of money to both her and the Native Americans who were acting in it. In lieu of payment, she accepted twenty cow ponies and two mules. The Indians inexplicably accepted a typewriter. After her first trip to a feed-and-grain store, Stray had second thoughts about the deal. She went back to the Indians. They got the beasts. She got the Underwood. *The Squaw Man* got an expert typist.

Stray spent more time on correspondence and accounting than on the scenario. It was a mere thirty-five pages long, with only 284 scenes, most of which were brief summaries.

> 1. *Mess room – Henry prepares the fund – Jim and Henry made trustees – end of dinner.*
>
> 2. *Maudsley Towers – library – Diana – Lady Elizabeth – Lady Mabel – Henry and Jim on – Henry's affection for Diana – Jim's Explanation of Fund . . .*

Stray also had to type casting records. Only two actors had come from New York: Farnum and Kingston. Every other role had to be cast in Los Angeles. "The number of motion-picture actors and actresses living in the city now numbers upward to 200," reported a *Los Angeles Times* article in 1910. Three years later, with six companies in Hollywood alone, there were many more actors. Kley posted a sign on a telephone pole. Within hours, the street outside 6284 Selma Avenue was crowded with eager applicants. DeMille used a small red notebook to list interviewees. They included:

> *J. G. Harper, strong old Kentuckian*
>
> *Dick Palace, Indian, hair to shoulders*
>
> *Horses, Mr. W. H. Stratton, $2.50 per horse, $3 per man*
>
> *Miss Jane Darwell, Heinzeman Hotel, 620 South Grand*
>
> *H. E. Roach, Telephone: West 2376, $5—O.K.*

Darwell was rejected because she wanted $10 a day. Roach was hired. (He later found fame as the comedy mogul Hal Roach.)

The important role of the squaw Nat-U-Rich was cast by the film's star. DeMille was considering a short, stocky Native American actress named Red Wing. Her Winnebago name was Ah-Hoo-Sooch-Wing-Gah. Twenty-nine and a graduate of the Carlisle Indian Industrial School in Pennsylvania, she had been working in films for five years. DeMille thought she was too short. "Don't go any farther," Farnum called out. "She'll do." This was a wise decision. Red Wing would bring conviction to the scene in which she surrenders her child.

Every day the barn looked more like a studio, even if it retained a horsey aura. The actors were troupers, accustomed to cross-country tours. Even Winifred Kingston was agreeable. "She didn't ask what performer last used the dressing room," recalled DeMille. On Broadway, it might have been a rival actress; in Hollywood, it was a horse.

The weather on Monday, December 29, 1913, was warm and sunny, a far cry from New York. "The sun was California's

great asset in the making of early films," wrote DeMille. "Rain meant that work stopped, while the payroll kept rolling along. But our first day was a good day." The sun shining on the white diffusers created a soft illumination for the dining room of the English mansion. It looked odd facing acres of orchards. "When I went out that glorious morning," DeMille recalled, "to take the first 'stills' and begin posing the artists, it felt to me just like it must feel to a prisoner leaving solitary confinement for the open air."

DeMille started to direct the actors but stopped short when Apfel reminded him to consider the camera. "I felt lost," DeMille admitted. "At first I couldn't get the stage idea out

of my head. I looked skyward for sets of lines, borders, and drops. Then I seemed to enter into the spirit of the thing. I was enamored of the way Mr. Apfel went about focusing his camera, getting the actors and actresses within range of the lens. He

ABOVE: A freshly painted sign tells the story in this photograph. Except for Red Wing, who is standing in front of Farnum (and Iron Eyes Cody, who appeared in other scenes), most of the Native Americans in *The Squaw Man* were portrayed by performers of other races. Among them are Noble Johnson, an African American; Guillermo Calles, a Mexican; and Joseph Singleton, an Australian. The cast was on location at Oak Creek Park, which is now Forest Lawn Cemetery in Burbank.

went through this, my first picture, with me until I had gotten the technique of motion-picture direction. I learned the art of directing all over again, but this time with the universe as a working basis."

Much of *The Squaw Man* was shot under muslin on sets behind the barn, but there were exterior scenes, so the company traveled to Mount Palomar to shoot in the snow. There was a good deal to learn. "We didn't see dailies," said DeMille. "You looked at the film in your hand. You looked at the negative, to see what was there." After the company returned from Palomar, they made an unhappy discovery. "After we took a wild Western scene of an Indian lost in the snow," said DeMille, "static in the camera killed almost every foot of it. The static was from the cold mixed with the friction of the film being drawn across the velvet on one side of the film gate. The static looked like lightning coming in from the sides of the frame. We only got one usable scene out of all that Palomar stuff. That was really heartbreaking."

There was no time to lament lost scenes. Each location excited DeMille more—Hemet, Chatsworth, Oak Crest Ranch. "Imagine the horizon is your limit and the sky your gridiron," he said. "No height limit, no close-fitting exits, no conserving of stage space. Instead of a 'set' mountain with the paint still wet, a real, honest-to-goodness mountain looms in the background." He was responsible for an entire production in an unfamiliar setting and with a huge amount of capital invested. He had to be careful. One day he saw a player touch his lit cigarette to a coil of discarded film stock—nitrate film stock. "Puff!" wrote DeMille. "It was gone, in a vanishing whiff of smoke. Was that how quickly our investment, not to mention the cash we were already taking in from exhibitors, could literally go up in smoke?" From then on, every shot was taken twice. After the negative was processed, he separated the two takes and carried one set home.

DeMille wrote to Constance every day. "The tales that drifted back from the West were hair-raising," wrote William's daughter, Agnes de Mille. "Uncle Cecil had bitter rivals who

were intent on doing him in." DeMille was receiving anonymous letters, warning him to shut down the production. "I was riding along homeward in the dusk," wrote DeMille, "when—zing!—a sharp, whizzing sound passed by my head, followed soon by the crack of a shot from somewhere back in the thick growth beside the road. I turned my horse and drew my gun, ready to shoot. Not a leaf was stirring. There was nothing for me to do but go on home."

It was hard to believe—then and later—that such things could occur in a sleepy little town. "These were not press stories," wrote Agnes de Mille in her 1951 memoir *Dance to the Piper*. "These were Uncle Ce's letters to his anxious wife." In 1957, when DeMille was preparing his autobiography with interviews on a reel-to-reel tape recorder, he said that he had fired a lab technician—and that the unnerving incidents might have been perpetrated by this individual. After DeMille died, his ghost writer blamed the Trust for the incidents; it made a better story.

DeMille hired a "cutter" named Mamie Wagner, who created a "first assembly" work print as it came from the lab in the other wing of the barn. "The cutting paraphernalia consisted of a pot of film cement, an electric light bulb behind a piece of ground glass, and two rewinds," said DeMille. There were

distractions. Water ran through the rooms when Jacob Stern washed his carriage, so DeMille put his feet in a wastebasket. Starting January 16, heavy rains halted filming for three days. DeMille moved inside to edit with Wagner. He had to hold an umbrella over her because the roof was leaking.

Back in New York, Goldfish was hard at work, selling exhibition rights to the in-progress film. His ad in *Variety* highlighted the title and star, plus the novelty of feature length. "In those days pictures were sold on what was called a 'states' rights' basis," recalled DeMille. "This meant that the distributor acquired the exclusive right to arrange the exhibition of a picture in a given state." The first to buy was a New York exhibitor named William Sherry. "Almost immediately letters from theater managers began to pour in," Goldfish wrote. "The swiftness and volume of those first orders overwhelmed me." Fourteen states' rights buyers committed cash. The pressure was on.

DeMille and Apfel finished shooting on Tuesday January 20, 1914, with the English manor exteriors. These were made in the fashionable West Adams district, at the mansion of a businessman named John J. Haggarty. "It looked like a castle," recalled DeMille. "I was sitting there, and I happened to be thinking about my mother because it was her birthday. I was thinking how lovely and sunny it was and that she was in New York and she ought to be out here where she could have the sun." Yet he did not send for Beatrice. He sent for Constance and Cecilia. When they arrived, he took time off to drive to the station and meet their train. "It was the Santa Fe Limited," DeMille recalled. "It came in around five. Cecilia was wearing a coat with a brown fur collar and carrying a brown muff. I came for them in an Oldsmobile with big wheels, like a truck, and I'd bought two dollars' worth of violets, and filled the back of the car. The whole back of the car was a mess of violets." Winifred Kingston

OPPOSITE: Cash Hawkins (Billy Elmer) intends to kill Jim Carston (Dustin Farnum), but Nat-U-Rich (Red Wing) intervenes. "Me kill 'um" was the famous quote from *The Squaw Man*.

ABOVE, LEFT TO RIGHT: "The minute a man marries a squaw, he is taboo," Dustin Farnum told a reporter. "Yet this scenario creates such a situation that no man with a heart in him can fail to forgive. And Red Wing was splendid in her portrayal." The Winnebago actress was so steeped in her character that she went into hysterics during the scene in which her child is taken from her. • Red Wing tends to the near-frozen Jim Carston, assisted by Tabywana (Joseph Singleton) and Grouchy (Dick Le Strange), who is dressed as a medicine man.

had tidied up a cottage in the Cahuenga Pass. "The house was a hundred yards or so from the road," recalled DeMille. "It was a very grown-over place. There was a little lost vineyard back there, too." DeMille brought Constance and Cecilia there to live.

The Squaw Man took eighteen days to shoot and cost about $15,000. (The final cost would come to roughly $47,000, which included Farnum's profit participation, pro-rated overhead, and DeMille's pro-rated dividend distribution.)

Hours after shooting finished, DeMille started editing with Wagner. By Thursday, the 22nd, a rough cut had been completed and a print made, so they had an early evening screening for Apfel and Gandolfi. This was the first time that the film had been projected on a screen. It should have been a thrill. Instead, it was a shock. "The title of *The Squaw Man* went on the screen," recalled DeMille. "And it promptly skittered off. The actors appeared, and as promptly climbed out of sight, sometimes leaving their feet at the top of the screen and their heads peeking up from the bottom. We checked the projector; it was in perfect order. We checked the film; nothing wrong that we could see."

What the filmmakers could see with the film partially unspooled told them nothing. But when a stretch of it was laid next to a stretch of another film, the problem became apparent. The other film had sixty-four sprocket holes per foot. *The Squaw Man* negative had *sixty-five* holes per foot. When printed onto positive stock that had the standard perforations, there was an accelerating mismatch of sprocket holes. This was causing the image to levitate. The raw stock had somehow been perforated incorrectly. It was incompatible with American printers—and projectors. How did this happen? Did an unknowing DeMille do it? He knew too little of film handling for such a task. Who perforated the stock? Was it an errant lab technician? Or was it Gandolfi, who never worked for DeMille after the completion of *The Squaw Man* . . . and who was trying to sabotage the production? A century later, there are no records to tell us. All that survive are a few terse telegrams.

At this juncture, the film was not considered a total loss. The problem was intermittent, appearing in certain shots and certain reels. "Our operator was alert to where it came and was

ABOVE, LEFT TO RIGHT: Filming concluded on January 20, 1914, with scenes of Monroe Salisbury and Winifred Kingston at J. J. Haggarty's mansion. York Castle was situated at 3330 West Adams Boulevard in Los Angeles. • This paper contact print was made from an outtake of *The Squaw Man*'s credit sequence. Baby De Rue can be seen exchanging smiles with Red Wing and Dustin Farnum. This credit sequence does not survive in existing prints, which come from a reissue.

ready with the framing," said DeMille. "You could frame it quite easily, you know. Then it would run all right for a while. But then it would go off again." The next morning, DeMille had pondered the problem sufficiently to wire Goldfish for help, but in a way that would not alarm him. He asked for more positive stock and a perforator with settings for both sixty-four and sixty-five. Goldfish would not be able to send a perforator for several days, which would not help the immediate crisis. DeMille decided to cut the negative. Maybe the problem could be fixed in New York. The important thing was to send a print there for an exhibitor screening. "Sam had already sold exhibition rights to *The Squaw Man*," said DeMille, "and sold them for cash—which we had used in production."

On Saturday, January 24, DeMille covered himself by wiring Goldfish that *The Squaw Man* was "a great picture." Then he started cutting the negative. As he most likely discovered, editing is at first hypnotic, then addictive. Walking away after a ten-hour session is an admirable goal, but there is always one cut that needs to be adjusted just once more. "Have not been to bed for sixty hours and still up," DeMille wired Lasky early on the morning of January 27. "Proper cutting takes a great deal of time. You may be satisfied you have good picture." At midmorning on the 28th, it looked like he was going to make his self-imposed deadline. "Just completed our eighty-seventh consecutive hour of assembling and cutting. Without sleep."

DeMille was in no condition for a cross-country trip. Dustin Farnum agreed to carry the six reels of answer print to New York. He left that afternoon and arrived on Sunday, February 1. The print was screened that evening. This time the projectionist was flummoxed by the rolling image. Lasky, Goldfish, and Farnum were thunderstruck. They were facing ruin. "Not only ruin for the Jesse L. Lasky Feature Play Company," wrote DeMille. "Perhaps for the whole idea of feature plays on film. More than that: personal, disastrous, irremediable ruin, and quite possibly jail terms, for Jesse, Sam, Arthur Friend, and me."

Ruin was averted, not by DeMille, but by the fractious Sam Goldfish. He remembered Siegmund Lubin, a veteran producer and lab owner in Philadelphia. A steely-eyed Goldfish and a nervous Jesse Lasky walked into Lubin's lab and set the reels on the counter. Then they told Lubin their tale of woe. "Let's look at the film," said Lubin with a smile. Then he walked through a door and disappeared into the recesses of his lab.

Lasky and Goldfish waited a frightening fifteen minutes. Lubin could have emerged with bad news about the sprocket holes. Instead, he returned with a broader smile and said, "There's nothing wrong with your film. We'll fix it." His technicians glued clear celluloid over the negative and then used a sixty-four-hole perforator to make new sprocket holes. Even though the film was thicker, it would run through a printer. In gratitude, Lasky and Goldfish awarded Lubin the contract to make the *Squaw Man* release prints and all future Lasky Company prints. Then they did a victory dance on a Philadelphia sidewalk.

There was another scare. The negative was being printed in the barn by Burns and Revier because forty prints were needed to fill states' rights orders. DeMille picked up a freshly printed reel and threaded it on the hand-cranked projector in the outer room. "I saw scratches on the film," he recalled. The scratches were white, which meant that the negative had been damaged. "I examined the negative. It was scraped, pitted, and disfigured. It looked as if someone had set it on the floor, put his heel on it, and dragged it between heel and floor. Whoever did it was operating from the printing room. He didn't do it until we began to make our final prints. And whoever did it had been very careful to wrap the negative back onto the reel so that nobody could tell that it had been scratched. Two reels were completely ruined. So would our company have been, if I had not had the extra negative at home."

On February 17 at the Longacre Theatre, Lasky and Goldfish hosted a trade screening of *The Squaw Man*. For a Tuesday morning event, it had an air of elegance. Theatrical celebrities and film exhibitors attended. When the lights dimmed, an orchestra accompanied *The Squaw Man*. William de Mille, the principal naysayer in Cecil's life, was present, ready to judge the results. There was plenty to judge, at least in the presentation. "A makeshift projection machine with sprocket holes constantly obtruding themselves, reinforced by a cracked condenser, did not contribute to otherwise good effect," wrote a *Variety* reviewer. "Nor did the sheet, a piece of muslin. There were half a dozen breaks in the film, necessitating the flashing of the 'One Moment, Please' slide more often than the average."

The film proceeded. William tried to remain impartial.

> *Much to my amazement, I found myself first interested, then held, and finally moved. When I felt a tear in my eye and a catch in my throat, I knew something important was taking place. Never before had a motion picture affected me as a depiction of real people with genuine emotions. The whole audience was under its spell as much as they could have been in the living theater. In spite of the film's faults, limitations, and silence, I saw unrolled before my eyes the first really new form of dramatic story-telling which had been invented for some five hundred years.*

The review in *Variety* was succinct. It called *The Squaw Man* a "genuine masterpiece in moving picture production."

A masterpiece is one thing; a hit is another. The trade screening caused a surge in sales. *The Squaw Man* was officially released on February 23, 1914. Within three weeks, every state had bought it. This, of course, was the company's goal. What the partners had not anticipated was the film's runaway success. Everyone was seeing it. This gained the attention of the same Adolph Zukor who had imported Sarah Bernhardt. He had been at the Longacre screening. It showed him that the Lasky Company was a real entity. DeMille's mother had also been at the screening. "I'm proud of your movie," Beatrice cabled him. Then she went to Simpson's Pawn Shop, retrieved the family silver, and shipped it to Los Angeles. No, not Los Angeles—Hollywood, where Cecil B. DeMille had made his first feature film. And Hollywood's first feature film.

CECILIA DE MILLE PRESLEY

"Grandfather was getting ready for his cross-country trip to make *The Squaw Man*. He was drawing a salary, but was in debt. He and Grandmother took all their silver to Simpson's Pawn Shop on Forty-Second Street to have money for the trip."

OPPOSITE: *The Squaw Man* was recognized as an important film, and many of the stage actors who appeared in it found careers in Hollywood. Thus Jesse L. Lasky, Sam Goldfish, Arthur Friend, and Cecil B. DeMille launched an unknown district as the film capital of the world.

FOSTER KNOX AS SIR JOHN.

MONROE SALISBURY AS SIR HENRY.

JOS. E. SINGLETON AS TABYWANA.

BILLY ELMER AS CASH HAWKINS.

WINIFRED KINGSTON AS LADY DIANA.

DUSTIN FARNUM AS JAMES WYNNEGATE.

RED WING AS NAT-U-RITCH.

FRED MONTAGUE AS MR. PETRIE.

BABY DERUE AS HAL.

DICK LARENO AS BIG BILL.

DICK LE STRANGE AS GROUCHY.

LEARNING HIS CRAFT

Nothing succeeds like success. *The Squaw Man* was born of a need to create one career and diversify two others. In February 1914, it was accomplishing that. As it propelled its new-fangled entertainment to forty-eight states, it also beckoned Cecil B. DeMille, Jesse L. Lasky, and Sam Goldfish to follow. They wasted no time. While DeMille edited, his partners secured literary properties for him and Oscar Apfel to direct. They began with *Brewster's Millions*, a comedy about a man who must spend a legacy of $1 million by a certain date in order to inherit a second legacy of $7 million. Then the team made three more films. By April, DeMille was ready to direct his own, a Dustin Farnum western based on Owen Wister's *The Virginian*.

Lasky and Goldfish wanted a better way to get their films to the public than the time-consuming states' rights deals. In May, the Jesse L. Lasky Feature Play Company joined the Hobart Bosworth Company and Adolph Zukor's Famous Players Company to sign with a producing-and-distributing combine. The Paramount Pictures Corporation was managed by a distribu-

tor named William Wadsworth Hodkinson. "On his way to establish his new company," wrote DeMille, "W. W. Hodkinson passed a building called the Paramount apartments. That struck him as a good name. During the conference, remembering the Wasatch Range of Utah, where he made his start, Hodkinson drew on a desk blotter a picture of a snow-capped mountain. Paramount had a trademark." Paramount would finance and distribute 104 films in a year. The Lasky Company would supply thirty of those, and, beginning in August, would receive $17,500 from Paramount for each film.

DeMille was feverishly busy in early 1914, codirecting a new film every few weeks, and also managing, supervising, writing, editing, casting, and hiring. He was taking control. In late February, he purchased the Burns and Revier laboratory and then assumed their lease, signing a three-year agreement directly with Jacob Stern. By the end of 1914, the Lasky Company would own the Stern property, plus 1,200 acres in the San Fernando Valley, the Lasky Ranch.

As DeMille geared up to meet the Paramount quota, he engaged a number of artists, creating a repertory company behind

OPPOSITE: This portrait of Cecil B. DeMille was made in his office at the Lasky Feature Play Company in the spring of 1914. Looming above him is a poster for *The Squaw Man*. The elements of his image were already in place: open-necked shirt with rolled-up sleeves, corduroy pants, and boots to support his calves and ankles. The legendary whip and pistol do not appear in this photo, but in the early days of Hollywood, he did need the complete ensemble. "The taking of outdoor love scenes was sometimes interrupted by the unexpected entrance of a scorpion, a centipede, or a rattlesnake," wrote William de Mille, "and much of the vegetation was either thorny or poisonous."

the camera. Alvin Wyckoff was a middle-aged actor who had just become a cameraman. He was hired in time to shoot *Brewster's Millions*. Wyckoff, like every other cameraman in 1914, adhered to the soft, dull look that overhead diffusers created. "The cameraman was rated by how clearly you could see under the table," said DeMille, "and how clearly you could see the back corner of the room. Both corners." That would change with DeMille's next artist.

Wilfred Buckland had history with the de Mille family. He had taken playwriting courses from Henry de Mille. William and Cecil had both taken Buckland's makeup classes at the American Academy of Dramatic Art. And he had been David Belasco's lighting and scenic designer for twelve years. "Belasco's productions were something nobody in the world could equal," said DeMille. "That was because of Buckland." The Lasky films had been criticized for their painted backdrops. Beatrice recommended Buckland. He had a lofty goal, "to picturize in a 'painter-like' manner, supplying to motion pictures the same rules which govern the higher art of painting." He was hired in May, and worked on part of DeMille's second film, *The Call of the North*. Shortly thereafter, the Lasky studio was enhanced with electric lighting fixtures. To better use this equipment, a partially enclosed stage was built. The Lasky Company would be the first to move away from the monotonous flatness of diffused light. Buckland also used miniatures, forced perspective, and foreground objects. In allowing these liberties, DeMille created the post of motion-picture art director.

DeMille needed scenario writers. Lasky and Goldfish were buying ten David Belasco plays. This transaction said a great deal about DeMille's improved status, and it might salve his old Belasco wounds, but the plays would have to be adapted. Why not hire the playwright who had coauthored one of them? On July 30, DeMille sent his brother an offer. "Come on in," wrote DeMille. "The water's fine." He was taken aback when William de Mille asked $200 a week. Both brothers thought it over. "I had never seen a moving-picture camera," wrote William, "nor had I the faintest idea how pictures were made." William arrived on September 29. In three months, he had completed six feature scripts and put up a shingle that said "Scenario Department," probably the first one in Hollywood.

DeMille found a writer by accident when he hired an actress named Jeanie Macpherson. She was twenty-seven, trained in musical theater, and had acted for no less a film director than D. W. Griffith, already a towering figure in the industry. She was writing and directing films for Universal. She also possessed as fiery a temperament as any Broadway star. Her first five encounters with DeMille, all intended to land a job, ended in slammed doors. "I am not interested in the Star Macpherson," said DeMille. "I'm interested in the Writer Macpherson." When mutual respect broke through the storm clouds, DeMille began teaching Macpherson to write, but his way. He needed an outline for his next film. "When Jeanie brought it in," recalled DeMille, "it was full of mistakes. I told her that she wrote like a plumber. I was frightfully insulting to her, but the kid took it and plugged along. During the rewriting of the play, I fired her regularly, but it did no good. She would always come back with another version of the script. She would not give up the work. She was like a tarantula. When she got her fangs into anything you could not shake her loose." The training paid off. By late 1915, Macpherson was working shoulder to shoulder with DeMille.

CECILIA DE MILLE PRESLEY

"Nineteen fourteen and fifteen were years of learning for Grandfather. He was learning what could be done on film that could not be done on stage. There was so much to learn, and then he had to teach what he'd just learned. Actors could no longer stride across the room. They had to simply walk across the room. In this new medium they had to look natural. As he got the camera gradually closer, he filmed nuances that an audience in the second balcony of a stage play could never have seen."

On March 2, Jesse Lasky came to visit the studio that bore his name. He learned that fame is a sometime thing. "I arrived at the Santa Fe depot," wrote Lasky, "called a taxi, and told the driver I wanted to go to Hollywood. He gave me a puzzled look but said, 'Get in, boss. We'll find it.'" Seven miles later, Lasky was at the desk of the Hollywood Hotel, which was situated at Hollywood Boulevard and Highland Avenue. He asked the clerk for directions to the Lasky Company. "I'm sorry," said the clerk, "I never heard of it."

"The director-general of the company is Cecil B. DeMille," Lasky said.

"Never heard of him," said the clerk. Then he brightened. "I tell you who might help you. Drive down this main road 'til you come to Vine Street. You can't miss it. It's a dirt road with a row of pepper trees right down the middle. Follow the pepper trees 'til you see an old barn. There's some movie folks working there that might know where your company is." When Lasky saw the hitching post and the sign with his name on it, he was relieved. And warm. The temperature was seventy degrees.

"Vine Street was one of the most beautiful streets in the world," recalled DeMille. "There were pepper trees and great stands of eucalyptus, magnolia, and jacaranda trees." William's wife, Anna George de Mille, and their daughters, Margaret and Agnes, arrived in the fall of 1914. They also found Hollywood

CECIL B. DeMILLE

"Jeanie Macpherson and I had rather a unique method of operating. She was more creative, more inspired in conversation than she was at her typewriter. She would give you great ideas but if you had her write them out, she was considerably at a loss to match what she had when she told you those ideas originally. So we would transfer from her mind to my mind what she wanted to say, and then I took that and built on it. But she was a very brilliant woman."

picturesque. "Vine Street had palm trees and pepper trees lining it," said Agnes de Mille. "Those were very beautiful, graceful trees. And in the grass would be tangled the lupins, the poppies, the brodiaea, all of them exquisite, and all of them just blooming wild and in the gutter. The streets ran right into the foothills, and the foothills went straight up into sagebrush, and you were in the wild, wild hills, with rattlesnakes, and coyotes, and the little wild deer that came down every night."

Lasky had to be pleased with DeMille in 1914. The director-general made seven films of his own and supervised a total of twenty-one. In 1915, he made fourteen and supervised thirty-six. The films featured well-known players such as Blanche Sweet and Thomas Meighan, and attractive titles such as *The Warrens of Virginia*, but nothing could really explain why a film costing $28,000 could gross $86,000. The modest *Wild Goose Chase* cost $10,000 and grossed $60,000, perhaps because Ina Claire was a Broadway star.

In two years, Cecil B. DeMille had moved from a lackluster stage career to a spectacular run in a medium that he had once doubted. The Lasky Company was receiving a constant stream of revenue from *The Squaw Man*. DeMille would later quote a gross of $244,000. This is unbelievably high, and may be a combination of related numerous incomes, including the 1918 remake, but there is no denying that the film made a huge profit and was the primary factor in DeMille's newfound prominence.

Ten-year-old Agnes de Mille often visited the Lasky lot to watch "Uncle Ce" and her father at work. "Cecil was in his early thirties," wrote Agnes, "with the dynamism of a young bull, his head lowered, his beautiful teeth flashing. Father, the older brother, was thoughtful, intelligent, practiced, waiting slightly to the rear." Seeing the brothers in this environment was exhilarating; the work was pioneering. "Every picture broke boundaries," she said. "Some new thing would be done, a new way of handling the camera, a new way of cutting, a new way of lighting, and they'd be so excited about it." Sometimes the new things did not come quickly enough.

OPPOSITE, TOP TO BOTTOM: A hay wagon was often in the sight line of Lasky actors in 1914, when the open-air studio faced Jacob Stern's orchards. • Even though this snapshot breaks the cardinal rule of photography and obscures its subjects' faces, it conveys the excitement of working in a new medium.

CLOCKWISE FROM TOP LEFT: The hay wagon at work. • C. B. DeMille's first solo directing credit was *The Virginian*, which he began in April 1914. Dustin Farnum was reprising his stage role, and his wife-to-be, Winifred Kingston, was his leading lady. • On any given morning at the southeast corner of Selma and Vine, there was evidence of the Lasky Company's prosperity. Everyone wanted to work for them. • DeMille went with cast and crew to Big Bear for the making of *The Call of the North*.

⸻ CECILIA DE MILLE PRESLEY ⸻

"Constance and their nine-year-old daughter Cecilia joined Grandfather in 1914. Since money was in short supply, both wife and daughter went to work acting any part that was needed. Constance was very beautiful and had been on the stage, but what she really wanted was to be a wife and mother."

In late 1914, when DeMille was starting *The Warrens of Virginia*, he was becoming frustrated. "I could not be satisfied with indoor night scenes that showed California's celebrated sunshine streaming in at the windows," said DeMille. "Nor did I feel that realism was helped by bathing the entire set of every scene in uniformly brilliant light." Wilfred Buckland was stymied, too. "A man who had made the sun rise and set on a theater stage was not likely to leave our early films to the whims of weather," wrote Jesse Lasky Jr.

The Warrens of Virginia was an important project because of DeMille's connections with the play. "The story was based on the incident of our grandfather's capture by the enemy during the Civil War," said DeMille. His brother had written it. Belasco had directed it. DeMille had acted in it. "We were determined to do our very best." To tell the story properly, they had to break new ground. This drama could not look like every other film shot under muslin diffusers. It had to be different.

DeMille and Buckland began by hanging black velvet outside the windows of the sets, something that had not occurred to

anyone before. "What I was after was naturalism," said DeMille. "If an actor was sitting beside a lamp, it was crudely unrealistic to show both sides of his face in equal light. With some portable spotlights borrowed from the Mason Opera House in downtown Los Angeles, we began to make shadows where shadows would appear in nature."

The first scene shot with this radical technique showed a spy creeping through a dark mansion. As he came from behind a curtain, he moved into the light projected by the Kliegl spotlight. "I lighted half of his face," said DeMille. "There was just a

ABOVE, LEFT TO RIGHT: Comedy of contrasts was as sure to please movie audiences as stage audiences. This scene shows the bowery "tough" Moore encountering the real thing in *Chimmie Fadden Out West*. • Ina Claire was famous for her naturalistic, elegant performances on Broadway. She made a huge hit of DeMille's 1915 *The Wild Goose Chase*, even though no one heard her voice. "All I remember about that little picture," said Claire later, "is running around and around one dusty block in Hollywood and getting more hot, dirty, and sore by the minute."

smash of light from one side, the other side being dark." The film was "slow," about ASA 24. There were doubts that it could capture the subtlety of this lighting scheme. The doubts were mostly Wyckoff's. He started putting more lights. The director-general had to assert himself. "You mustn't make this part so light," said DeMille. "It should be dark and the back corner of the room shouldn't be light. It should be dark!" Wyckoff deferred to DeMille's authority, as would many others in the years to come. When the results were viewed in the screening room, the contrast was startling and effective. DeMille was vindicated. "We carried out that idea of lighting all through the rest of the picture," said DeMille. "A smash of light from one side or the other."

Sam Goldfish thought *The Warrens of Virginia* looked *too* different. "Cecil, you've ruined us," cabled Goldfish. "You've lighted only one half the actor's face. The exhibitors will pay only for the half they can see." DeMille had already been chided by Goldfish for spending too much money; now he was accused

of burning it. "I was really desperate," recalled DeMille. But he found his footing and pushed forward. "A director has to go through. He has to *do* something. So Allah was very kind to me and suggested the phrase 'Rembrandt lighting.'" DeMille sent a return cable. "If you and the exhibitors do not know Rembrandt lighting, it is no fault of mine."

"Cecil, you are wonderful," replied Goldfish. "The sales department can charge double for art." And so they did, as "Lasky lighting." The Champion Driver had chalked up another victory.

ABOVE, LEFT TO RIGHT: In March 1914, Jesse L. Lasky was photographed on his first visit to the company that bore his name. • *The Warrens of Virginia* starred Blanche Sweet, whom DeMille had lured away from D. W. Griffith's company to star in a play that had special meaning for him. "A good part of Belasco's magic on the stage was his marvelous use of lighting effects," wrote DeMille. "Trained in that school, Wilfred Buckland and I decided to experiment, as D. W. Griffith and Billy Bitzer were doing, with special light effects."

SOCIAL DRAMAS

n 1915, Cecil B. DeMille, Jesse L. Lasky, and Samuel Goldfish were an unbeatable team. After making two dozen films, they had yet to have a flop. Lasky was visiting from New York more frequently, but DeMille was the director-general, running the studio and making a film a month. DeMille was fluent in both business jargon and film technique. He had directed westerns, comedies, and melodramas. He could say what he wanted, and say it well. He needed something worth saying. While Lasky looked for stage stars to bring the company prestige, DeMille adapted a play by Charles Kenyon called *Kindling*.

Social realism was not a cinematic genre in early 1915. Moving pictures had left the nickelodeon too recently to aspire to anything beyond entertainment. *Kindling* was a grim look at slum life. "In this environment," says Heine, a laborer, "children burn up like kindling." DeMille's film walks into that environment. "Where the devil wins," says the intertitle for a shot of a slum street. The camera moves closer. Heine and his wife, Maggie, see a shocking sight: "Two children—a girl and boy eating from a garbage can which is full of all sorts of decaying food and flies." Heine is outraged. "I'd rather kill a child of ours the day it was born than send it up against a game like that," he tells Maggie. She has a secret. A child is coming, and she is desperate

to leave the slum. She falls in with a petty thief and robs her rich slumlord. DeMille's script punishes Maggie for her crime but not for her plight. As the film ends, she and Heine escape the slum.

As might be expected, *Kindling* got harsh reviews. The post-Edwardian era did not countenance children eating garbage. "This scene is so strong as to cause one to become ill," wrote a reviewer in *Variety*. There were favorable reviews. *Moving Picture World* compared DeMille's street scene to "anything that ever came from the hands of Hogarth or Rembrandt." DeMille had studied audiences from the stage for years. He felt they were ready for strong meat. He was right. *Kindling* cost $10,000 and grossed $66,000.

In the fall of 1915, after directing three star vehicles (to be discussed in succeeding pages), DeMille returned to adult themes. *The Cheat* was an original scenario written by playwright Hector Turnbull and adapted by Jeanie Macpherson. It was a departure from the usual 1915 plot. Edith, an extravagant socialite, diverts $10,000 in charity funds to a stock speculation.

OPPOSITE: In Cecil B. DeMille's 1915 film *Kindling*, Thomas Meighan and Charlotte Walker see a drunk stagger out of a bar and force a waif to drink from a pail of beer.

She loses it. A Japanese art collector named Tori offers to replace the stolen funds—if she will grant him "favors." Edith is so desperate that she agrees. Before Tori can exact payment, Edith has a windfall. When she tries to renege on her promise, Tori attacks her, pulls a branding iron from a red-hot brazier, and presses it into her shoulder. Crazed with pain, Edith shoots him. Tori survives but lets Edith's husband, Dick, take the blame. To save him, Edith shows the courtroom her branding scar. While interracial tension was not new to DeMille's canon, the collision of sex and violence was. This was a risky project.

DeMille asked the stage star Fannie Ward to portray the social butterfly with the singed wing. "But Mr. DeMille, I am a comedienne," said Ward. "I have never played emotional roles."

"Which is exactly the reason I want you to play in *The Cheat*," he said.

"That put me on my mettle," recalled Ward. "I was determined to do that role better than anything I had ever done before." Ward was forty-four but mysteriously ageless, a society darling with a collection of jewels worth half a million.

Her fiancé, Jack Dean (who played her husband in *The Cheat*), had a similarly smooth face. They later admitted to cosmetic surgery. To cast the role of Tori, DeMille turned to Lasky, who had signed a twenty-six-year-old Japanese actor named Sessue Hayakawa.

The Cheat went into production on October 20, 1915. DeMille found Hayakawa to be conscientious but determined to play the character his way. "I was raised in the traditions of a Japanese boy of the Samurai class," said Hayakawa. "I was always taught that it was disgraceful to show emotion." DeMille tolerated this, as well as the actor's barking bulldog, Shoki. DeMille also had to deal with Ward's behavior. She mandated that her wardrobe be purchased from Martial et Armand of Paris. "Fannie Ward was very temperamental," recalled Hayakawa. "She complained about everything, and she treated Jesse Lasky like a prop boy."

When it came time to deliver the goods, though, neither Ward nor Hayakawa held back. The actress proved that comedy prepares an actor for tragedy. And Hayakawa's restraint was

as powerful as a shout. "I purposely tried to show nothing in my face," said Hayakawa. "But in my heart I thought, 'God, how I hate you.' And, of course, it got over to the audience with far greater force than any facial expression could." There was conviction in the actor's hatred; he was tired of Ward. "It was a pleasure to brand Fannie Ward," he said later.

If Hayakawa was tired of Ward, DeMille was just plain tired. Three weeks after starting *The Cheat*, he began directing a second film at night, *The Golden Chance*. "From nine until five, I directed *The Cheat*," wrote DeMille. "Then my secretary, Gladys Rosson, served me dinner on my desk and I lay down to rest until eight, when it was time to direct the fresh-as-a-daisy

cast of *The Golden Chance*." The second shift lasted six hours, after which DeMille slept in his office and then started all over again. He did this for about three weeks.

The Cheat was released in December. There was an angry outcry from the Japanese community in America. (Nothing was done to soften the story until 1918, when the film was re-released. Its intertitles were rewritten to change the Japanese art collector to a Burmese "ivory king.") *The Cheat* became an international hit, and more. The French novelist Colette wrote that artists and writers were viewing the film repeatedly in order to study and discuss it. "In Paris this week," wrote Colette, "a movie theater has become an art school. A film and two of its principal actors are showing us what surprising innovations, what emotion, what natural and well-designed lighting can add to cinematic fiction." American critics were equally enthusiastic. "Features like this one put the whole industry under obligation to the Lasky Company," wrote W. Stephen Bush in *The Moving Picture World*. Neither DeMille nor Lasky had gotten reviews like this on Broadway. Within a few months, *The Cheat* had established them as the country's foremost filmmakers, and made stars of both Fannie Ward and Sessue Hayakawa.

The Golden Chance was also a success. "There is a new force in this moving picture play," wrote Bush. "I speak of the wonderful lighting effects which seem to lend an indescribable charm and lustre to numerous scenes." Lighting effects would not be worthy of comment had they not told the story. In years to come, *The Golden Chance* would be acknowledged as a minor masterpiece. *The Cheat* would be recognized as a cinematic milestone.

OPPOSITE: *The Golden Chance* featured Wallace Reid and Cleo Ridgely. "The master hand of Cecil B. DeMille is evident throughout the whole picture," wrote a critic. "His is the bigness of vision that can see and appreciate the value and importance of little things."

ABOVE: This dramatically lit scene shows Horace B. Carpenter in *The Golden Chance*. "Never before have the lighting effects, this skillful play with light and shade, been used to such marvelous advantage," wrote critic W. Stephen Bush. "The highly critical spectators who saw the first display of the film were betrayed into loud approval by the many and novel effects."

ABOVE: DeMille introduced this scene in *Kindling* with the intertitle "Where the Devil wins."

OPPOSITE: *The Cheat* was another showcase for DeMille's effects. "I was known as the man who likes everything contrasty," said DeMille. "There were some terrible battles because of that, because to me it only means making the blacks blacker and the whites whiter, and putting the shading in the right place." In later years, the term "Lasky Lighting" would be attributed to cameraman Alvin Wyckoff as much as to Cecil B. DeMille. Yet Wyckoff had no understanding of chiaroscuro. DeMille had to force it on him. They would eventually come to a parting of the ways because of Wyckoff's limitations. Without DeMille, his career faltered.

THE SILENT DIVA

The Santa Fe Station in Los Angeles was abuzz with excitement on June 11, 1915. There was a band. There was a chorus of a hundred from the municipal show *Fairyland*. There were fifty boys from the Young Men's Institute, fifty boys from Page's Military Academy, and a gaggle of giggling girls. As a train pulled into the station, the chorus began to sing "O Kami! O Kami!" from Giacomo Puccini's *Madama Butterfly*. As Geraldine Farrar emerged from a private Pullman car and stepped onto a red carpet, the girls threw roses. "Welcome to California!" they shouted. Farrar blew kisses to them. "Never was a queen of old welcomed more royally than the beautiful star of the Metropolitan Opera Company," wrote Grace Kingsley in the *Los Angeles Times*.

Nine years after her Met debut, Geraldine Farrar was more than an opera star. The thirty-three-year-old was a cultural phenomenon. Two hundred thousand American homes had Victrolas, and Farrar had sold several million records. There was even a name for the teenage girls who idolized her: "Gerryflappers." On April 23, Jesse Lasky had gone backstage at the Met to meet Farrar after her performance in *Madama Butterfly*. Farrar regarded Lasky as "a theatre man of taste," so he was able to broach a delicate subject. "Stars are sometimes afraid that

acting in a movie will hurt their stage prestige," he said. "But I can see by the ovation you just got that whatever you do, your public will accept."

Like Dustin Farnum a year earlier, Farrar had numerous reasons to consider Lasky's offer, even if some of her peers would say: "Oh, Geraldine! How can you?" She had strained her vocal cords in the 1914–15 season. Her European summer engagements had been canceled because of the Great War. And she could earn $35,000 for eight weeks of work. Farrar was the greatest American prima donna. She was also a level-headed professional, the daughter of a baseball player. "I was enthusiastic," wrote Farrar. "The opportunity for acting, the charm of summer in California, the vocal repose—all seemed to point to a happy adventure of interest and novelty." For Samuel Goldfish, it was more than a happy adventure. The Lasky Feature Play Company had arrived. "There would be no more pinching and scraping," he recalled. "No more wondering whether we could

OPPOSITE: Geraldine Farrar had star quality. Even a child like Agnes de Mille could see it. "She had jet-black hair with blue lights in it," wrote Agnes. "Her hair was naturally chestnut, but she dyed it. She also had glowing skin, blue Irish eyes, a figure superbly held, a lovely provocative voice, and the most dazzling smile we had ever seen."

afford a new star. We were firmly on the road to success." All he needed was for DeMille to get them there. The Champion Driver was ready.

"The first step," said DeMille "was to forget that Miss Farrar had had any connection with opera. I had had enough experience directing actors from the stage to know that there is a great difference between stage technique and film technique." For all the celebrity of Sarah Bernhardt's films for Adolph Zukor, there was a problem. The "Divine Sarah" overacted. "On the stage, an actor is trained to project himself," said DeMille. "The people in the last row of the top gallery must be moved by his voice and gesture. They cannot see the actor's eyes. But the camera can, ruthlessly, infallibly. You cannot lie to a camera." Actors like Ina Claire had been experimenting with more natural styles

ABOVE, LEFT TO RIGHT: Jeanie Macpherson took a break from writing scenarios to play in *Carmen*. • Playing opposite the great Farrar contributed to Wallace Reid's stardom. And his experience with D.W. Griffith helped her.

OPPOSITE, CLOCKWISE FROM TOP LEFT: This shawl from *Carmen* has been preserved by the De Mille Estate. Photograph by Mark A. Vieira. • In 1964, Geraldine Farrar told filmmaker Kevin Brownlow: "The Lasky studio was no bigger than a pie plate, yet Lasky and DeMille managed to do these big pictures. Extras got five dollars a day. They'd come panting in from the streets: 'Any work today?'"

of delivery, but opera singers were still declaiming. "At every performance," said Farrar, "I cut myself open with a knife and give myself to the audience."

Farrar's debut film would be a silent adaptation of her favorite role, Georges Bizet's *Carmen*. Lasky had promised this to secure her services. To DeMille it looked risky. Farrar was used to playing Carmen in a big way. Better that she learn screen technique in a lesser vehicle, and then play Carmen, which could be released first. The lesser vehicle was a play called *Maria Rosa*, with settings reminiscent of *Carmen*.

There was concern that the diva might display temperament. "Opera stars are reputed to be notoriously temperamental," wrote DeMille. "Geraldine exploded the myth. She was always gracious, always cooperative, always worked hard. She might be billed as 'Miss Farrar,' but it was not long before everyone on the lot was calling her Gerry." She took direction well and liked making movies. "Most things were shot outside," said Farrar. "They were spontaneous. There was a great feeling of life. I hadn't any cinema technique, so I didn't have to alter it! I wasn't conscious that we were to do anything but the natural thing."

There were three films to be made that summer. *Maria Rosa* was shot in two weeks. *Carmen* was shot in a little more, and *Temptation* in a little less, as befit a minor project.

Carmen premiered at Symphony Hall in Boston on October 1 with Farrar and her parents in attendance. "The audience had their snoot a little bit in the air," she recalled, "but they took it very well. I was pleased with the results. I was very flattered seeing myself moving." The film was praised by critics and went on to gross, with *Maria Rosa* and *Temptation*, a total of $352,000.

In June 1916, Farrar returned to make one film, *Joan the Woman*. It took four months to make, cost $302,000, and gained the distinction of being the first historical epic made by Cecil B. DeMille. D. W. Griffith's *The Birth of a Nation* and Thomas Ince's *Civilization* had been epic successes, inspiring numerous companies to tackle the format. DeMille almost succeeded. *Joan the Woman* was excellent; but its grosses, though high, were insufficient to make a profit. Farrar's last two films with DeMille, shot in the summer of 1917, were historical dramas, but scaled down. All in all, the two-year collaboration had been a rewarding one. An opera star had become a movie star without singing a note. And DeMille had created his first epics.

CECILIA DE MILLE PRESLEY

The Lasky Company was prepared for a high-maintenance diva. Geraldine Farrar was anything but. Grandfather said that she was one of the hardest-working stars he'd ever directed. Gerry loved the fight scene in *Carmen*. Grandfather talked to me about that scene several times. He could not believe that those two women fought like they did. They really went at it, the scratching and pulling hair. You can see where Jeanie's wig is starting to come off and she's holding it on with one hand and pummeling Gerry with the other."

GERALDINE FARRAR

"I thought Cecil DeMille was a genius, and I was very fond of him. He would never shoot you in close-up against white, and he would never allow a moving background behind a close-up. He wanted all the attention focused on the expressive moment."

OPPOSITE: Geraldine Farrar posed for a photo after her fight scene. "I hate things that are prettified, that are not truthful," said Farrar. The next time she sang *Carmen* at the Metropolitan, she added the fight to the cigarette factory scene.

ABOVE: In this scene, DeMille gave Farrar a close-up that ran long enough to catch her subtle expressions. "The motion picture has the ability to photograph thought," said DeMille. "An actor learns to use his eyes and the slightest flickering change of facial expression to project what is in the mind of the character he is playing."

OPPOSITE, CLOCKWISE FROM TOP: 'William de Mille's wife and daughters watched this scene from *Joan the Woman* being shot at the Lasky Ranch. "We sat around in open cars with picnic baskets," wrote Agnes de Mille. "It was like an English hunt breakfast. The French came charging across the field with Joan at their head carrying her standard. They jumped the stockade and fought the English, and they won. It was the most beautiful scene." • This chain mail headdress from *Joan the Woman* has been preserved by the De Mille Estate. • "I want everybody who has the unhappy habit of chewing gum to throw it away," DeMille said to his cast. "And do not put it in your armor or anywhere like that."

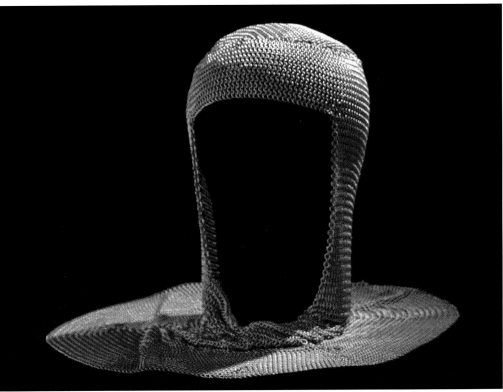

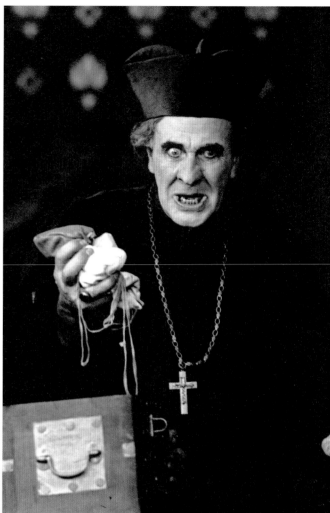

OPPOSITE, TOP TO BOTTOM: "We were allowed free action as we felt it," said Farrar. "For this reason, we had real expression and feeling." • "With *Joan the Woman* we were all so impressed," said Farrar. "We gave everything. There was an aura of mysticism attached to the film."

ABOVE, LEFT TO RIGHT: Farrar recalled: "Mr. DeMille was worried about my safety in the battle scenes and particularly about the effect of all the smoke on my throat and on my voice. At one point I was up to my waist in mud, in heavy armor. It was made of aluminum silver and weighed eighty pounds." • Theodore Roberts played Bishop Cauchon in *Joan the Woman*. "Our characterization of some churchmen as the villains caused flutterings of resentment in some religious circles," wrote DeMille.

LEFT, TOP TO BOTTOM: "Before shooting the burning of Joan of Arc, Uncle Cecil stood at her stake for hours trying out smoke," wrote Agnes de Mille. "He never asked an actor to do what he would not do himself." • "Then Farrar stood at the stake until she was obliterated by smoke and flame," wrote Agnes. "But when they burned the dummy and its hair caught and flaked off in a single shower of fiery cinders, Farrar turned sick and had to go to her dressing room and lie down."

LEFT, TOP TO BOTTOM: In 1917, Farrar played an Aztec queen in *The Woman God Forgot*. In 1938, she wrote: "No idea can be obtained from black-and-white photography of the lavish splendor provided by Mr. DeMille's imagination, of the feathered attire, riotous in exquisite colors." Fortunately for us, DeMille had a still photographer make photographs with the Autochrome Lumière process. • "Theodore Kosloff of the Russian Ballet was an exotic figure at the head of the Aztec soldiery," wrote Farrar. "My boudoir was hung with ropes of magnolias. This floral magnificence was an incentive to passionate action."

AMERICA'S SWEETHEART

n 1916, Cecil B. DeMille was no longer broke and in debt. He was getting rich off the movies. So was Los Angeles. "Film making means millions to Los Angeles," announced the *Los Angeles Times*. "Twenty producing companies spend over $1 million a month. They employ 12,000 people. They produce eighty percent of the films made in America. These 'movies' are seen by 50 million people, twenty-four hours of every day, all over the world." This was why Geraldine Farrar had braved her friends' scorn. To be seen by millions. To court immortality. "For every member of the paying public who will see a play," said DeMille, "there are two thousand who will see a picture. Whereas one country will see my play, practically all the countries in the world will see my picture."

The movies paid better than the stage, too. DeMille had been able to honor his debts because of an ever-increasing income. In December 1913, he had started at $100 a week. By the end of 1917, he was making $300 a week [more than $9,000 in 2014 dollars]. In early 1916, he moved Constance and Cecilia into a handsome home overlooking Hollywood. Later that year he bought property in a box canyon twenty miles way. This became the setting of his ranch, the very private property he named Paradise. These oases of quiet were necessary. Running a studio and creating product was more than a full-time job.

"I have been working until one, two, and three o'clock every morning, trying to make up for the gaps in our programme," DeMille wrote Sam Goldfish. "A director is a man who never sleeps. If he endeavors to please the exhibitors, the critics, the censors, the exchange men, and the public, it's a perfect cinch he won't have time to sleep." It was a pressure-cooker existence. DeMille thrived on it. He was the Champion Driver. He was Director General. "It is really harder to see you than the U.S. president," wrote Dick Le Strange, who had acted in *The Squaw Man* and was in need of work. DeMille established a precedent by lending the actor money and by keeping him employed at the Lasky Feature Play Company. Numerous actors who started out at the Lasky barn would continue with DeMille, and for years.

In 1907, DeMille had appeared in *The Warrens of Virginia* at the Belasco Theatre, playing the older brother of a Canadian actress named Mary Pickford. Ten years later, they were thrown together again. Pickford was under contract to Adolph Zukor's Famous Players. "The first of the great film stars, Mary's rise had been sensational," wrote Zukor, "and a little frightening. We

OPPOSITE: *The Little American* starred Mary Pickford. Directing her was a major step for Cecil B. DeMille. When he filmed Pickford and Jack Holt in the bombing of a Belgian church, the figure of Christ survived the blast.

were building the star system, but there had never been anything like the adulation showered on Mary. It was barely possible for her to go shopping without being accosted and mobbed. In Chicago a dozen policemen were required to break a path for Mary when she left her train. In another city a crowd ripped the top from her taxicab. Many penalties are attached to movie fame. Mary paid them with good grace." Pickford could afford to pay them. She was earning $10,000 a week. Translated into current terms, she was earning a million dollars every three weeks, and without the bother of income tax.

Zukor had control of this aspect of the company, the production, but not of distribution or exhibition. In his quiet, resolute way, he began to acquire them. His first step was to merge with the Lasky Feature Play Company. "Mr. Zukor was never entirely happy with the terms of the releasing arrangement with Paramount," recalled DeMille. "Neither was Sam Goldfish. Both those titans felt that we would all be in a stronger position to deal with the Paramount distributing organization if our two companies, Famous Players and Lasky, merged." This took place in July 1916.

Zukor's next step was to take control of Paramount. "Adolph was quietly buying up Paramount stock," says Cecilia de Mille Presley. "When W. W. Hodkinson went into what he thought was a routine meeting, he found himself fired from his own company—by Zukor, the major stockholder." Zukor next created a releasing division called Artcraft. In September, Mary Pickford incorporated her own production company. Both she and DeMille would release their films through Artcraft. In late 1917, Zukor made his big move. He pulled seven companies— Artcraft, Bosworth, Cardinal, Cohan, Famous Players-Lasky, Morosco, and Paramount—into one. Jesse L. Lasky and Cecil B. DeMille suddenly found themselves on top of a vertically

ABOVE: In 1916, DeMille bought this home in the Laughlin Park district of Los Angeles, a neighborhood now known as Los Feliz.

OPPOSITE, TOP TO BOTTOM : This group portrait was made to commemorate the creation of the Famous Players-Lasky Corporation. Left to right: Jesse L. Lasky, Adolph Zukor, Samuel Goldfish, and Cecil B. DeMille. • The company's logo included its distribution outlets, Artcraft and Paramount.

 **FAMOUS PLAYERS~LASKY CORPORATION**

ADOLPH ZUKOR *Pres.* JESSE L. LASKY *Vice Pres.* CECIL B. DE MILLE *Director General*
·NEW YORK·

integrated corporation. Famous Players-Lasky had become the cinematic equivalent of the Ford Motor Company.

Lost in the shuffle was Sam Goldfish, who had rubbed Zukor the wrong way. Goldfish cashed in his company stock for $900,000 and joined with a playwright named Edgar Selwyn to create Goldwyn Pictures. Before long, Sam legally changed his name to Goldwyn. No one lamented his departure. Pickford detested him, and Lasky resented his treatment of Blanche, who had sued him for divorce on grounds of infidelity. "This was a terrible thing for the Lasky family," says Cecilia de Mille Presley. "Before the 1920s, you just did not divorce. It was a shameful thing. A woman could be ruined. So Jesse had no problem voting Sam out of the company." Goldwyn held a lifelong grudge against Lasky and Zukor, but remained friends with DeMille. "Sam and Grandfather loved being together," says Cecilia. "As difficult as Sam was to work with, he was fun in private. I remember them being together. They were telling stories constantly and laughing. They had a great friendship."

When the merger dust cleared, DeMille had a new responsibility, a two-picture deal with Pickford. "I agreed very readily," recalled DeMille. How could he not? Directing Pickford would be even more prestigious than directing Farrar. There was a catch. "Mr. Zukor had given Mary the privilege of selecting the writer of her scenarios and approving the script," said DeMille. "I put my foot down. It is the producer-director's job to produce and direct. If he divides that authority with anyone else, the result is almost certain to be a bad picture."

Pickford was scheduled to depart New York on February 10, 1917. "This much is certain," Lasky wrote DeMille on January 11. "We will not allow her to go to the Coast unless she consents to be managed and guided by you." Lasky gained the upper hand when Pickford's latest comedy, *The Poor Little Rich Girl*, caused a screening room full of executives to sit in humorless silence for ninety minutes. Coming on the heels of two unpopular films, this made Pickford look vulnerable. Zukor, who had maintained a paternal role with her, grew stern and ordered her to send DeMille a telegram.

"I have no desire," wrote Pickford, "to interfere in the choice of stories, in the casting of different actors, including myself, and in the final editing. I am placing myself unreservedly in your most capable hands. Obediently yours."

CECILIA DE MILLE PRESLEY

"Adolph Zukor wanted DeMille to do two pictures with Mary Pickford. She was a trouper, the biggest star of films, but she'd made a bad marriage with an actor named Owen Moore, and her last two films weren't doing well. She needed help. Mary believed that she had to run the set in order to make good films. DeMille wanted it known that no one ran his set. Mary backed down, and when they met, it was tense. DeMille, being smarter than anyone I've known in dealing with people, gained her confidence. He did make two good films for her. She was grateful and they became friends. Years later, when she wrote her memoirs, she asked him to write the foreword."

CECIL B. DeMILLE

"The director of a symphony orchestra does not allow the French horns to improvise flourishes of their own ad lib. A commanding general does not allow the supply corps to decide all by itself when and where to deliver the needed material. I have never allowed script approval or any other such major authority to anyone who works in any of my pictures."

OPPOSITE: "I was absolutely terrified of Cecil B. DeMille," Mary Pickford said. "It was like being in an iron cage. I decided I would not again appear under his direction. We were simply not compatible professionally."

MARY PICKFORD

"DeMille was a great producer, but I don't think he had any heart. He was a very commanding person, but he wasn't a great director. However, I loved him."

DeMille had hoped to film the topical story of an American girl who goes to Belgium and faces the reality of the war, but American films were still playing in Europe, so he chose a story of vigilantes in the Old West. *A Romance of the Redwoods* began shooting on February 17. Meanwhile, to everyone's surprise, *The Poor Little Rich Girl* was doing very good business, and Pickford regained the upper hand. She did not like DeMille's style of direction. He did not cater to her, as many of her directors did. She threatened to quit. DeMille cabled Lasky for support. "If Pickford refuses to work, we have a perfect law suit against her for heavy damages," wrote DeMille. "We will instantly stop paying her immense weekly stipend, which will be a relief. She has eight months under this contract and we could get an injunction so that she could not work for anyone else for that period. We can get along without her and prefer to do so rather than give her an increase of her salary which is of course the main object of her kicking up a row." Faced with the prospect of legal action, Pickford complied. Even with location filming in the Boulder Creek district of the Santa Cruz Mountains, *A Romance of the Redwoods* was completed in a month.

After a three-week break, Pickford was ready for her second DeMille film. It would be the Belgian war story, and it was brutal, as brutal as the war that was coming closer and closer. Four American ships had been sunk by Germans in 1917. On April 6, Congress declared war on Germany. *The Little American* began shooting a week later. One scene showed a passenger ship torpedoed by a German submarine while neutral Americans enjoyed a party. "We built almost an entire deck of an ocean liner and mechanically tipped it so that the passengers were seen slipping into the water," wrote DeMille. "I had to flounder in the ocean at San Pedro," recalled Pickford. "In those days I couldn't swim more than two or three feet—but I did the scene. I tell you, that was some experience. It gets very cold at night in California, and I was wearing only an evening dress." Pickford was not happy to see a $400 ball gown destroyed, but she was otherwise uncomplaining. "She took the dousing with the same good will

that marked her wholehearted devotion to her job and to taking my direction, in keeping with her promise," wrote DeMille.

"I lived up to my word to Adolph," recalled Pickford. "If I didn't agree with the way Cecil was doing a scene, I didn't let him know. I was determined to give the very best performance possible, so that he could have no criticism of me." Curiously, the formal, forced collaboration resulted in two highly profitable films. Pickford went on to a distinguished career as "America's Sweetheart." After big productions with her and Geraldine Farrar, DeMille looked forward to a change of pace.

CHAPTER 2

AN ARTIST
MATURED

A NEW ERA

our years had passed since Cecil B. DeMille came to Hollywood. In that time, both he and the city had changed. He was still friends with Jesse Lasky, but their conversations were no longer about an exciting future. They were about a pressing present. Every project involved thousands of dollars. Even the conversations were costly. "We were daily increasing the profits of the Western Union and Postal Telegraph companies," recalled DeMille. They could afford to. Famous Players-Lasky (FPL) was part of a powerful new industry. Paramount alone was making $5 million a year. Hollywood was evolving from an expanse of orchards to an industrial hub. When DeMille and Lasky opened shop on Vine Street, the lovely, lacy pepper trees dropped berries onto the automobiles parked below and stained them. This posed no problem for Lasky. "Dad rode on horseback from our house at 7209 Hillside Avenue down to his studio at Selma and Vine," said Jesse Lasky Jr. By 1918, Lasky was driving a shiny sports car, as befit a captain of industry. The pepper trees were chopped down.

In December 1917, Cecil B. DeMille started *The Whispering Chorus*, his twenty-ninth film. He had made the transition from playwright to filmmaker with an eclectic series of projects, going from westerns to comedies to urban dramas and back, and then slowing his pace to accommodate two stars, Geraldine Farrar

and Mary Pickford. Big films did well, but their budgets created a problem. *Joan the Woman* was a lesson. Because its production had been so costly, even a gross of $600,000 was insufficient to yield a profit. DeMille heard complaints from FPL's New York offices. "A modern story would have gotten over bigger," publicist Carl H. Pierce wrote him. "What the public demands is a modern story with plenty of clothes, rich sets, and action."

DeMille's response was to make two modern stories. True to form, his projects fit no existing category. He invented his own. In so doing, he created a new type of film, a modern morality tale. Old standards looked pallid in the face of a new prosperity—and a new decade. DeMille was the child of Victorians. He was also a hearty young man living in the twentieth century. He was ready to lead his audiences to a new era. He started in—of all places—the bathroom. "In *Old Wives for New*, the scene of a husband trying to shave in the messily littered bathroom was designed to establish the character and habits of his wife," wrote DeMille. "Because of her, the bathroom never looked nice. There was always a ring around the tub, or something. That was

OVERLEAF: Gloria Swanson in *Don't Change Your Husband.*

OPPOSITE: In *The Whispering Chorus* (1918), the aptly named John Tremble (Raymond Hatton) is a mousy accountant taunted by entities. He heeds their advice and embezzles.

the first 'DeMille bathroom scene.' Its purpose was to help tell the story." It did more than that.

The East Coast partners of FPL were scandalized by the sight of a bathroom on the screen. "They had just come out with a long and expensive campaign of advertising," said DeMille. "Everything was going to be sweet and dainty in their pictures. When I came up with *Old Wives for New*, they came to the conclusion that I'd pretty well ruined them. They nearly severed connections with me." DeMille would not be put off.

> *I put the film under my arm, took it down to a little town, and previewed it at a theater there. The house had a few people in it, probably a third full. By the time the picture was half over,*

CECIL B. DeMILLE

"Everybody who's ever been married will agree that after a certain number of years, different traits start to develop that you didn't know were there perhaps. And little irritations come in. I took the little traits that can be cultivated into divorce. In *Old Wives for New*, there was a slight uncleanliness on the part of the wife. Little things at first, but then, after a while, just uncleanliness. And it was unpleasant. This man she was married to was a very wonderful man. He didn't like it. That led to his finding a woman who was different, who was dainty and sweet."

the men in the audience started going out and coming back, going out and coming back. And I said, You know, that's great! They're telephoning their wives! The manager came to me and said, "We've got to keep this for a second showing!" So I said all right. Well they ran the picture all night.

They didn't stop. And the man begged me to let him keep it a second night.

Old Wives for New grossed four times its cost and set DeMille on a new path.

OPPOSITE: Jane Tremble (Kathlyn Williams) prays for her husband, John, whose crime has pulled him into a maelstrom of guilt. To escape the consequences of his embezzlement, he has dressed the corpse of a transient in his clothes and disfigured its face. Then he is convicted of murder, but under an assumed name. Only Jane knows that the condemned man is really John Tremble.

ABOVE: John Tremble's last hours are tormented by the whispering chorus. "The still small voice never comes to us from the lips of ghostly faces," wrote a skeptical Antony Anderson in the *Los Angeles Times*. Other critics called the film "morbid." Although *The Whispering Chorus* grossed three times its modest cost, for some reason it acquired the tarnish of failure. "*The Whispering Chorus* was not a big success financially," DeMille said in a 1958 interview, one of several in which he inexplicably repeated this untruth. "The picture was released at a time when it was the darkest hours of the war for us. It was the first psychological drama. People didn't know really just how to receive it. They were at a loss."

GLORIA SWANSON

"I am the star mill," said Cecil B. DeMille in 1922. "They come to me as grist and I turn them out as stars." For this vanguard of producer-directors, it was easier to make new stars than to suffer established ones, who could be expensive and temperamental. In Gloria Swanson he found his raw material, an artist who pursued success as avidly as he did. He called her to his studio in early 1918. She had been with the Essanay, Sennett, and Triangle studios for three years, a teenager learning a craft. "When I first noticed Gloria Swanson, she was simply leaning against a door in a Mack Sennett comedy," wrote DeMille. "I saw authority, as well as beauty." For her part, Swanson was awed. "Mr. DeMille's paneled office was vast and somber, with tall stained-glass windows and deep polar-bear rugs. Light from the windows shone on ancient firearms and other weapons on the walls. The elevated chair resembled nothing so much as a throne. When he stood up behind the desk, he seemed to tower. Not yet forty, he seemed ageless, magisterial." Swanson did not know that the imposing office was a copy of the room where DeMille had faced his own fears. In recreating David Belasco's sanctum, DeMille was confronting demons of helplessness and resentment.

DeMille's first film with Swanson was a follow-up to *Old Wives for New*, but more daring. *Don't Change Your Husband* (1919) showed a woman leaving her husband because he neglects his appearance. She is driven to this drastic measure by not only his slovenliness but also by fantasies of unattained sensuality. These fantasies were shown in sequences that were dreamlike but not literally dream sequences, which was a departure from an established convention. DeMille called these sequences his "visions." Along with his newfound worldliness and bathtub scenes, these visions would become a signature.

What caused the most comment was the credo espoused by DeMille and Jeanie Macpherson. A woman had a right to sexual satisfaction; if denied it, she had a right to end her marriage. "I believe in divorce as an institution as much as marriage," Swanson told an interviewer. "It has formed the foundation for many a moving-picture plot. Without it, we would go back to that old milk-and-water hokum." *Don't Change Your Husband* was too clever to caricature the husband as a boor. DeMille shrewdly cast the appealing Elliott Dexter as the gentle, self-neglecting spouse. "Of all the scenes Elliott Dexter played in *Don't Change Your Husband*," said Swanson, "the best was the one in which he realizes I have left him. He looks stunned, absolutely miserable. I love that scene. I could watch it over and over without

OPPOSITE: Between 1918 and 1921, Gloria Swanson made six films with Cecil B. DeMille. "Mr. DeMille has chosen Gloria Swanson to represent the typical society woman in his exquisite satires," wrote *Motion Picture* magazine in 1919.

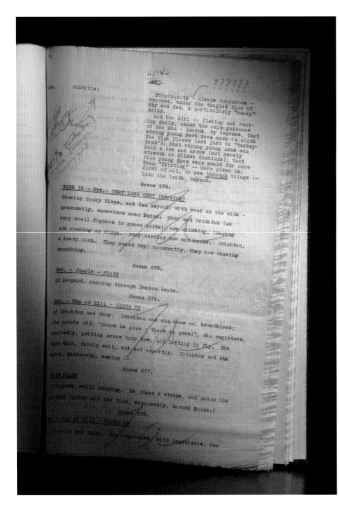

ABOVE: Page 114 of the shooting script for *Male and Female* (1919) shows doubt over the word *propinquity*. At the time, intertitles were called "subtitles."

RIGHT: Before Sid Grauman opened the Egyptian Theatre or the Chinese, his flagship was the Million Dollar Theatre in downtown Los Angeles. In February 1919, Gloria Swanson's first film for DeMille broke attendance records at this house.

OPPOSITE: "Mr. DeMille made a practice of inserting into many of his films special episodes which he referred to as his 'visions,'" recalled Gloria Swanson. A fantasy sequence in *Don't Change Your Husband* featured the famed dancer Ted Shawn and a stage full of semiclad performers. There was no Production Code in 1919. Regulation was left to local censors, who had their work "cut out for them."

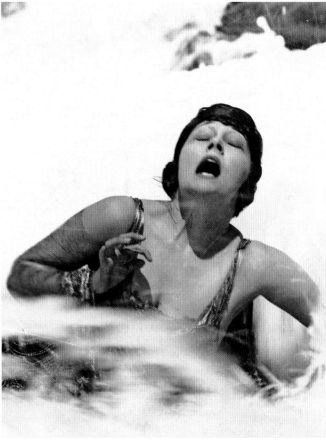

THIS PAGE: DeMille took his cast and crew to Santa Cruz Island and wrecked a full-size yacht to make these scenes for *Male and Female*. "I had to wade out of the surf in a beaded gown and crawl up an incline of slippery rocks," recalled Swanson. "When I finished the scene my knees were bloody, my hands were scratched, and pieces of crushed beads had dug into my thighs. Mr. DeMille began to call me 'young fella,' as if I were one of the boys."

ABOVE: Karl Struss was a "Stieglitz Secession" photographer whom Cecil B. DeMille hired as a second cameraman, but Struss also shot stills, both portraits and scenes. Struss made this photograph under trying circumstances, because the scene itself was tough.

"*The Lion's Bride* by Gabriel Cornelius Ritter von Max was inspired by the story of a woman lion tamer," said Swanson. "When she was about to be married, she went to bid farewell to her pet. She had raised him from a cub, and he was jealous that she was going to be with a man. He killed her. When I went to Lincoln Park in Chicago as a child, I used to imagine myself as the bride of the lion in the cage.

"When the scene was taken, there was a trainer on each side of the cage, and they put canvas over his claws so that they wouldn't scratch me. And there he was with the weight of his paws on my bare back. To make the lion roar, the two trainers lashed at him with their whips. The feeling of having the lion's weight on my shoulder, his hot breath on my neck, and the vibration when he roared was a thrill that I cannot describe. My father was visiting the set when the scene was being taken. After I had gone through the episode, he took me in his arms as if I had come back from the dead."

tiring of it." The film was released two weeks after the Armistice, and it created a sensation. "I have had hundreds of letters," said DeMille, "from wives and husbands, thanking me for showing them their mistakes in *Don't Change Your Husband*. All that I picture is true." Not everyone was convinced. "Here is life," sneered Julian Johnson in *Photoplay*, "as it grows in gardens fertilized with gold."

DeMille's next film with Swanson was *For Better, For Worse*, the timely tale of a wife whose husband returns from the war with a face disfigured and an arm missing. "The skill of the director fairly makes the heart cry out," wrote one critic. In *Male and Female*, DeMille's third film with Swanson, he orchestrated his customary elements—romance between classes, the spoiled rich, bathing scenes, anthropomorphized beasts—to play an elemental theme. "The theme of man and woman stripped of the position which civilization has given them has always thrilled me," said DeMille, "just as Auguste Rodin's powerful sculpture *The Hand of God* is one massively modeled hand in which are posed two handsome miniature figures, a man and a woman. Their problems are the most fascinating that a workman can toy with."

Male and Female became DeMille's biggest hit, grossing ten times its cost. It was widely considered his first film to gross a million dollars. It was a star-maker, too. It paved the way for

CECILIA DE MILLE PRESLEY

"Gloria Swanson was between husbands when she started working with DeMille. She was twenty and he was thirty-seven. After working with him for a time, she developed a major crush. A fixation, really. One night they were alone in a screening room, watching rushes. And she came over and sat in his lap and put her arms around him. He stood up and put her back in her seat. 'That was the hardest thing I ever had to do,' he told me. 'I had a star who thought I was a wonderful man, a god. I didn't want her to make me human. I would have lost a star.' He wouldn't give in. She was good-natured about it and they remained friends. Great friends. To the end of his life he called her by the nickname he'd given her at Santa Cruz Island, 'Young fella.' (He used this name for her in the 1950 film *Sunset Boulevard*. The DeMille in that film was the man I knew.)"

three more Swanson vehicles. He had made her a star, and he was overtaking Griffith as Hollywood's most successful director. The Champion Driver had come a long way from *The Squaw Man*. When he was interviewed in his office one day by *Motion Picture* magazine, he pointed to the barn. "Just a few yards from this spot, I produced the very first Lasky picture. Six and a half years ago. And look at the place today!"

CECILIA DE MILLE PRESLEY

"Gloria Swanson became a star for Cecil B. DeMille and partly because Mary Pickford came to Adolph Zukor with an outrageous salary demand, one that would have hurt Paramount. Zukor called a meeting with DeMille and Jesse Lasky and said, 'What do we do about this?'

"Lasky had never subscribed to the star system. 'The play is more important than the star,' he said. DeMille thought that stars were important but he was beholden to no one. 'We can make pictures without stars,' said DeMille. 'We can be *making* stars.' Not to mention that DeMille himself was becoming a star. D. W. Griffith had originated the idea of the star director. There were Maurice Tourneur, Erich von Stroheim, and Mack Sennett. People went to see a picture because of a director. When they went to see a Griffith picture—or a DeMille picture, for that matter—they knew the quality they were getting.

"Now, DeMille was intuitive. He saw that producers like Irving Thalberg were taking power away from the director. DeMille was not about to let this happen. He instructed the Famous Players-Lasky publicists to play up his name, keep it in the advertising, make it prominent. He sought the limelight. He made himself into a brand. When he presented a new personality like Gloria Swanson, the public paid attention. She was anointed by Cecil B. DeMille. So Zukor let Pickford go. And Swanson became a star."

OPPOSITE, LEFT TO RIGHT: In this scene, the dour wife (Gloria Swanson) chides her husband (Thomas Meighan) for overspending on wine. "I never use a plot," said DeMille. "The 'plot' picture bores the audience of today. 'Oh,' they say when they finish the first reel, 'such-and-such a thing is going to happen.' And they sit back resignedly to await the finish."
• The seductive Sally Clark (Bebe Daniels) is ready to ensnare a hapless husband. "I am trying to do the 'theme' picture," said DeMille. "I love to take some vitally interesting theme and work it out according to life. That is what I am doing with *Why Change Your Wife?* These themes I am toiling on do a damn lot of good."

ABOVE, LEFT TO RIGHT: A waft of perfume transports Thomas Meighan from the disconsolate Swanson to the inviting Daniels. "The appeal of softly scented women, the rich textures of silken robes, and velvety rose petals—that is what I spend thousands of dollars to bring to the silver sheet," said DeMille. "I have my costumes designed to create an impression. I want to make my audience *feel* what I am telling." • Why change your wife, indeed, when she can change herself into a vision like this? *Why Change Your Wife?* was the first DeMille film released in the "Roaring Twenties," and it did contribute to the roaring. Portrait by Karl Struss.

CECILIA DE MILLE PRESLEY

"DeMille made the bathroom an ideal. He showed America how a room that had been overlooked could be transformed into something special, with beautiful mirrors, soaps, marble, and even perfumed water. He used the bathroom as a metaphor for the state of the marriage."

ABOVE, LEFT TO RIGHT: Polly Moran provides comic relief for Elliott Dexter and Gloria Swanson in *The Affairs of Anatol*, which was DeMille's first film with art director Paul Iribe, and his last with Dexter, Swanson, Daniels, and Wallace Reid. Adolph Zukor and Jesse Lasky did not like DeMille tying up so many stars in one film when each star could be bringing in box-office receipts in his or her own film. • "Wallace was a cause of constant anxiety to me," said Swanson. "His behavior never seemed quite right. He was forever offering me rides. I always found ways to refuse him politely, but he gave me the jitters."

OPPOSITE: Wallace Reid finished work on *The Affairs of Anatol* in late January 1921. He had been in chronic pain for a year, following a train accident, and was addicted to morphine. When DeMille tried to help him, it was too late. Reid died in January 1923.

INTO THE PAST

n 1920, Cecil B. DeMille formed a company within Paramount. It was called Cecil B. DeMille Productions. He felt that he was losing control of his work and he disliked having to ask Adolph Zukor for budget increases. By forming this partnership (and the subsequent corporation), he was able to negotiate profit percentages and his salary. "My friends drove a hard bargain," wrote DeMille. "They knew I would not leave the company I had helped found." His weekly stipend was raised to $2,300. He wanted more. Jesse Lasky tried to run interference for him but found it increasingly difficult. DeMille was spending more money on each film, and Zukor was not pleased, even though DeMille was raking it in. "Take every means in your power to cut the costs of your productions," said Zukor. "Without hurting their quality," he added, with a straight face. DeMille was not amused.

DeMille's friendship with Lasky continued, although slightly strained. "Jesse was more businesslike than brotherly," said DeMille. "The old affectionately bubbling Jess was submerged, not lost, and he rose to the surface when we met." William de Mille, meanwhile, had left the post of story editor to become a director. The films he made for Famous Players-Lasky were as different from Cecil's as a miniature was from a mural. The brothers worked in the same plant but things had changed. "At the beginning both men lived simply, walking to work in the morn-

ing and home in the afternoon," wrote Agnes de Mille. "They worked closely together. However, Cecil hankered for other ways of living, and their paths began to diverge. Cecil became almost fearsome in his growing power. Fortunately, his charm kept pace. Everyone recognized this. It was a charm full of energy, perception, and latent excitement. People adored him for it."

Conrad Nagel had acted in more than ten films when he came to FPL. "I loved working with Cecil B. DeMille and with William de Mille," recalled Nagel. "It was a special pleasure. William de Mille's approach was entirely psychological. He picked everything to pieces. You knew exactly why you were doing what you did. Cecil DeMille was more of a showman, one of those truly great figures of show business. A lot of people claim that he was a phony, a show-off. He was not. He was a superb showman."

The showmanship was not limited to films. DeMille sold himself as vigorously as his latest production. He sold both with photography. He was proud of the stills created to publicize his films. Most directors regarded the "unit stills man" as a

OPPOSITE: This costume design for Cecil B. DeMille's *Forbidden Fruit* (1921) was made by Natacha Rambova. Born Winifred Shaughnessy, she became Winifred Hudnut when her mother married the cosmetics magnate Richard Hudnut. Winifred took a Russian name to dance in Theodore Kosloff's Imperial Russian Ballet Company. She was married to Rudolph Valentino while working for DeMille.

department to devote more space to him, ensuring that his face and distinctive costume were known to filmgoers. "The announcement of a Cecil B. DeMille production to the public is a guarantee of pleasing entertainment," claimed one copywriter in 1918. "No one knows better than Cecil B. DeMille how to tell a story dramatically," wrote another. "The public has come to expect greatness from Cecil B. DeMille," promised a third. DeMille's name appeared above the title and in larger print, and journalists took up where publicists left off. DeMille became the proverbial household word. "Cecil B. DeMille is the one photoplay director who really looks the part," wrote the *Photoplay* columnist Cal York, without acknowledging that DeMille had originated the look.

Self-publicizing served more than one purpose in the early 1920s. A number of DeMille's colleagues at FPL were involved in scandals. He needed to distance himself from the rape trial of Fatty Arbuckle, the murder of William Desmond Taylor, and the drug-related death of Wallace Reid. DeMille chose to emphasize the positive. "I am an absolute advocate of beauty," said DeMille. "People are hungry for it. Everyone longs for it, gropes for it. The woman in the mining town may cut a color picture out of a Sunday supplement and paste it on her wall. That is her desire for beauty and the only means she has to gratify it. If I can give beauty to that woman, I am successful." While some reviewers found this attitude disingenuous, it was hard to argue with the trappings of a DeMille film. "I believe in beautifying the simplest commodities, even telephones," he said. "Everything possible, whenever possible. And it is always quite possible." DeMille was known for beautiful bathroom scenes and exquisitely designed

nuisance, hurrying him to capture the scene after the last take had been filmed. "Hold for stills" was an irritant to most directors, who were impatient to create the next setup with the cameraman. This was not the case with DeMille. He allowed the still photographer both time and artistic license, so a scene could be posed differently from the way in which the movie camera had just taken it. There was a painterly quality to these photographs. Occasionally DeMille would step in and direct a still photo himself. At the end of a production, the studio would have a huge "key set" of stills from the film, several hundred images. Large, gallery-quality prints were handmade as exclusives for important fan magazines. "I make far more stills than any other company," he told Lasky. "There is greater attention given to gowns, detail, story and direction than in any picture made today."

Creating handsome, dynamic images was not enough. Every DeMille film had the same star. He ordered the publicity

CECILIA DE MILLE PRESLEY

"Grandfather described Zukor as a visionary. Brave, indomitable, ruthless. He had no peer in the history of motion pictures. Zukor called him 'Cecil.' Grandfather never called Zukor anything but 'Mr. Zukor.' There was respect but no warmth."

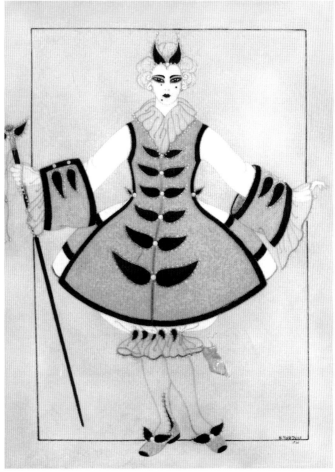

costumes. These helped tell his stories, but they were not the stories. For a new era, he needed a new kind of story. To do this, he would straddle epochs.

DeMille could no longer make small, personal films like *Kindling* or *The Golden Chance*. This was not the time for introspection or subtlety. Leaving those to his brother, DeMille made films for the Lost Generation. In the early 1920s, America was in the throes of change. There was a terrible letdown after the Great War. "The country felt that life was futile," wrote historian Frederick Lewis Allen. "Nothing mattered. An American might just as well take up the new toys that were amusing the crowd, and savor the scandals and trivialities featured in the tabloid press. By 1921 these toys and fads and scandals were forthcoming, and the country seized upon them feverishly." The toys included automobiles, radios, and bootleg liquor. Fads included flagpole sitting, marathon dances, and Mah-Jongg. Form-fitting, revealing fashions

that would have been considered immodest in the Edwardian era were not only accepted but also applauded. College students were reading Krafft-Ebing, drinking on the sly, and kissing in cars. If this younger generation—DeMille's target audience—was staying away from church, DeMille was only too happy to lure them into theaters that looked like cathedrals, the cavernous, lavishly appointed cinemas built by Samuel ("Roxy") Rothapfel and Sid Grauman. While Paramount tended its fallen stars, DeMille commented on the Roaring Twenties and helped amplify the noise.

OPPOSITE: A publicity still of Jesse L. Lasky consulting with Cecil B. DeMille on the set of *Triumph* (1924). "My youthful zeal," wrote Lasky, "to become a composer, opera star, novelist, and adventurer found expression in modified channels years later."

ABOVE: Rambova designed these costumes for the Cinderella Ball dream sequence in *Forbidden Fruit*.

ABOVE: Costumes for the Cinderella Ball settings in *Forbidden Fruit* were designed by both Rambova and Mitchell Leisen. Left to right: Bebe Daniels, Forrest Stanley, Agnes Ayres, and Julia Faye.

LEATRICE JOY

"Mr. DeMille loved to make movies that took you out of your seat and placed you in another time, another world. He was a great showman."

THIS PAGE: In *Manslaughter* (1922), DeMille shows what happens when a playgirl tries to cheat the law. Lydia Thorne (Leatrice Joy) stands to lose her liberty when she accidentally kills a policeman whom she had bribed to overlook her speeding. District Attorney O'Bannon (Thomas Meighan) convicts her to "save" her.

The accident scene was shot in full view of spectators and press. A stuntman named Leo Nomis was consulting with DeMille before the shot. "It's going to be an easy one," said Nomis, "unless I get tangled. I won't, of course. But if—Mr. DeMille, would you sort of keep an eye on the wife and kids?"

"I'll take care of them as long as they live," said DeMille. "So don't worry about that."

"There were ambulances there," recalled Joy. "Hundreds of people came to watch. You wouldn't think they'd want to."

"The giant motorcycle hummed," wrote Adela Rogers St. Johns. "The quiet of the countryside was shattered by the shock of tearing metal and crashing steel. A body vaulted into the air, flung as a child flings a rag doll."

"It was horrible," said Joy. "Although they'd put mats on the other side, Nomis broke six ribs and his pelvis. Now they shouldn't have risked a man's life for that shot. When you see it on the screen, it looks exactly like a dummy."

"The 1920s were the era of, among other phenomena, the flapper," wrote DeMille. "With her bobbed hair, her short skirts and her preference for the athletic Charleston over the sedate waltz, she became as much an obsession to the pointers-with-alarm as Hollywood itself. I decided to come to the defense of the flapper." DeMille was over forty, and Jeanie Macpherson was approaching it, yet they were making films about young people. Their premise was that every generation comes in conflict with the previous one; in the course of history, human behavior has not changed. "Youth always revolts," said DeMille. "It would not be worth its salt if it didn't." To demonstrate this, he adapted his "visions" into parables called "flashbacks." Jeanie Macpherson incorporated this device in an original story called *Adam's Rib*. "The flashback to prehistoric times," said DeMille, "enabled her to show that bare legs, short skirts, and feminine resourcefulness were nothing new."

Four of the six films DeMille made in the first two years of the new decade featured a flashback. This became as much a trademark as his bathtub scenes or the exquisite gowns worn by his actresses. And, like those elements, it became a target. When DeMille was interviewing Leatrice Joy for a film, her then-boyfriend John Gilbert asked her, "How can you work for that silly son of a bitch? He treats people like cattle and acts like he's doing them a favor by paying them anything at all for the privilege of working with him. You think he'll make you a star, but no one is going to notice you in those epics of his unless he has you riding around naked on the back of a Bengal tiger." Opinions in print were more restrained but no less nasty. "Mr. DeMille tends towards spectacular, lavish settings," said *Film Daily*, "but he seldom succeeds in making his story convincing." *The Filmplay Journal* wrote: "We really do not understand why Mr. DeMille wastes his talents as a motion-picture director when a bathroom fixtures company could engage him as an Extraordinary Advisor."

The three most hostile critics were Robert E. Sherwood Jr. at the original *Life* magazine, Frederick James Smith at *Photoplay*, and an anonymous writer at *Variety*. Sherwood was snide. "*Adam's Rib* is somewhat above the DeMille standard—which may be added to the Dictionary of Faint Praise." Smith was acidulous: "*Adam's Rib* is a mass of utter absurdities. And this is the man who could once intrigue audiences with his daring boudoir revelations." *Variety* was out for blood: "A silly, piffling screenplay executed in a particularly crude and obvious style."

DeMille took these attacks personally, and defended his parables. "All that I picture is true," he said defensively. "I am trying to teach the women of America things that they have never—well, believed. I am a man, not an angel. There is nothing, I venture to say, that I have not experienced. I have been no Sunday-school boy." Apparently women were happy to be instructed by the picaresque director; none of these films grossed less than three times its cost. "I make my pictures for people," said DeMille, "not for critics." People paid to see them, and DeMille grew rich enough to start a commercial aviation company and own a yacht. Still, he never forgot how far he had come. In his wallet he carried a memento of his lean years on the road, a twenty-year-old cardboard disc. It read: "Good for 1 Quart of Milk."

ADOLPH ZUKOR

"DeMille didn't make pictures for himself, or for critics. He made them for the public. He chose stories if he thought the public might like them. He was a showman to his smallest finger. He never started shooting until he had completed every detail of the script, and he followed through as he had prepared. With other directors, the management had to sign the stars and make the decisions. But Cecil did it all himself."

OPPOSITE AND OVERLEAF: The Roman orgy scene in *Manslaughter* set new standards. "Every director now and then conceives an idea of what an orgy should be," wrote *Film Daily*. "Most of them are distressingly weak and get nowhere. But Cecil B. DeMille decided that his orgy was to be a real one, and it is."

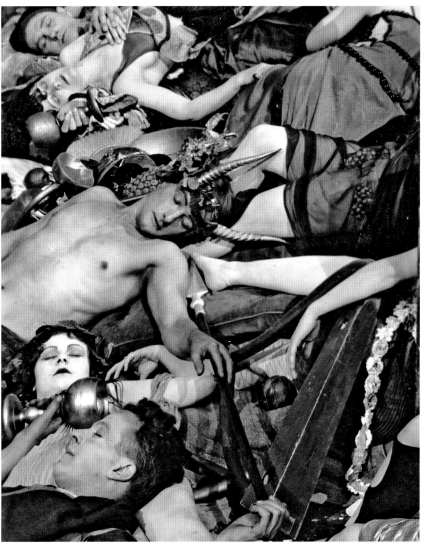

THIS PAGE: The Vandals, led by Thomas Meighan, crash the Roman party.

OPPOSITE, TOP TO BOTTOM: *The Golden Bed* standout set piece was a "Candy Ball." The musicians are dressed as candy canes. • The Candy Ball is enlivened by mouth-watering vignettes.

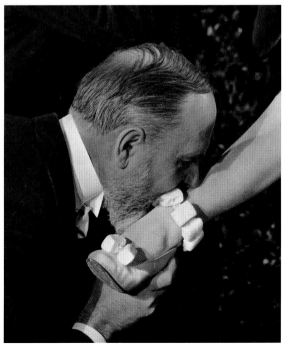

CHAPTER 3

THE RELIGIOUS EPIC

THE TEN COMMANDMENTS (1923)

By 1922, Cecil B. DeMille had made forty-four films. He had overtaken D. W. Griffith as the most renowned director in the world. This was an achievement, since Griffith had been making films five years before DeMille ever touched a camera. By 1919, DeMille had made Famous Players-Lasky the dominant film company. He was no longer the director general. He was the star director, a multimillionaire, as powerful as a motion-picture executive could be, influential in banking, oil, real estate, and aviation. Yet his heart was in filmmaking. From the days when he was thrilled by his first spotlight to the recent staging of a barbarian invasion, he was pushing the boundaries of both form and content. "I consider Cecil B. DeMille a master mind of the screen," said Gloria Swanson. "He is among the foremost technicians in the picture industry. He knows the screen value of every look and gesture, the effectiveness of every shadow and angle. He has developed more talent than any other man in pictures. I learned the technique of moving-picture acting from him."

Rod La Rocque had paid his dues in vaudeville and at Chicago's Essanay Pictures before working in Hollywood for a number of studios, none of which had advanced him beyond the level of leading man. He was twenty-four, living with his mother in a bungalow on Orchid Avenue. "We were always kid-ding," recalled La Rocque. "When I'd leave in the morning, I'd casually remark, 'Oh, by the way, Mother, if DeMille should call, tell him I'm busy,' or some inane comment like that." When he came home to find a message from DeMille's office, he assumed it was a joke, so he played along with it. Casting director Lou L. Goodstadt assured him it was not a joke. "Mr. DeMille is waiting to hear from you." La Rocque found it hard to believe that an executive would wait after hours for a call. "Can you come over to the studio?" asked Goodstadt.

"Do you mean now?"

"Mr. DeMille is in his office," said Goodstadt. DeMille usually worked late. La Rocque had been recommended by Paul Iribe, DeMille's new art director. (Wilfred Buckland had chosen to leave.) As was his practice, DeMille had viewed reels of La Rocque's work. "I freshened up and went over," said La Rocque. "Mr. DeMille was kind and sincere from the very beginning."

"We're going to make *The Ten Commandments*," said DeMille. This was not a secret. *The Los Angeles Times* had run a

OVERLEAF: Moses (Theodore Roberts) enters the court of Rameses II (Charles De Roche). Lighting design by Bert Glennon. Set photograph by Donald Biddle Keyes.

OPPOSITE: *The Ten Commandments* premiered in December 1923, and played through much of 1924, grossing more than $4 million.

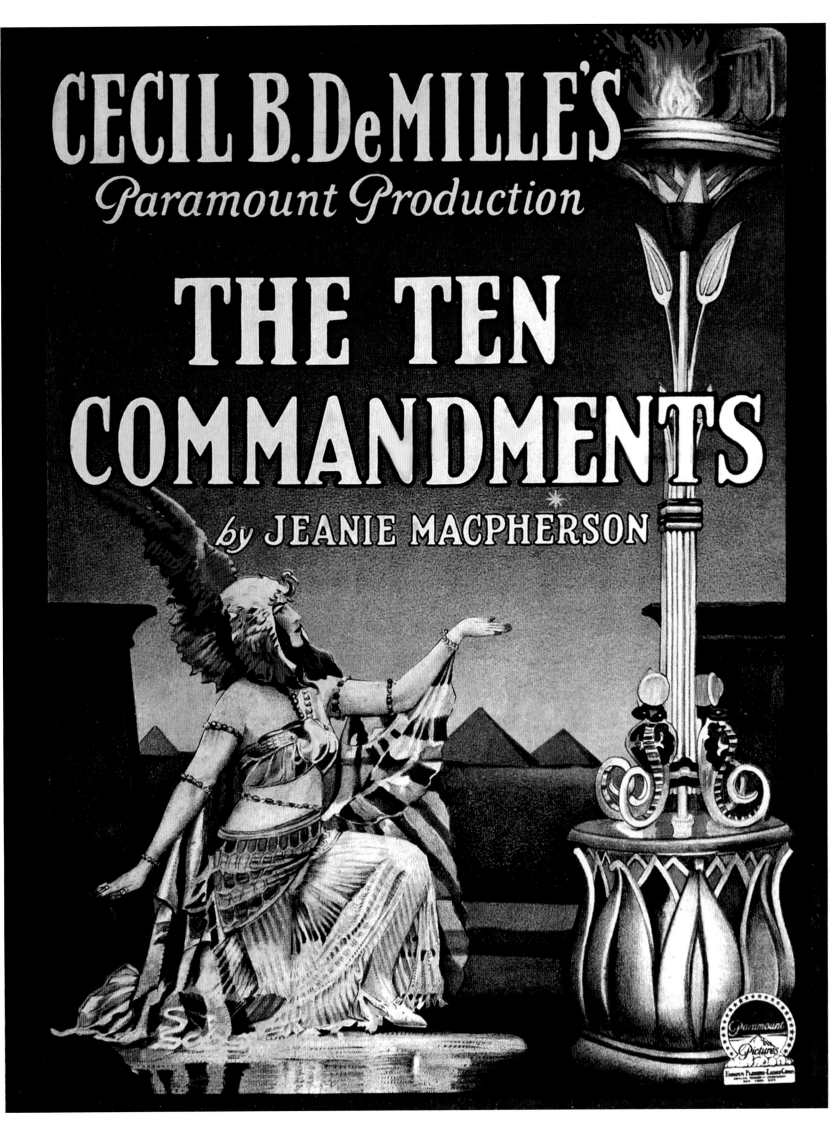

contest to find an idea for DeMille's next film. An F. C. Nelson of Lansing, Michigan, had suggested a premise: "You cannot break the Ten Commandments—they will break _you_!" The _Times_ and DeMille had paid Nelson the prize of $1,000. Seven other contestants had a similar idea; they were also paid, to prevent nuisance suits.

Jeanie Macpherson was unsure how to structure such a subject, but after a few dead ends, she was "inspired" and transcribed entire sequences as if by automatic writing. "We're going to do it in two parts," said DeMille. "In the first part, we have Pharaoh and the opening of the Red Sea and so forth. Then, in the second part, we do a modern story. Regretfully, we have to show that everything is the same today. The things Moses tried to tell us continue to be ignored. Truths are still violated. You'll like the script. There's a part in it for you. I hope you don't mind playing a heavy."

"I prefer it," said La Rocque. "I'll take a heavy any day."

Once DeMille felt that La Rocque was serious about the offer, he told him the plot, but solely from the point of view of his character. He would play in the modern story, acting the part of a selfish, heedless young man who steals his brother's girlfriend and gets rich off shady contracting deals. "Danny McTavish, whom I played, was the bad son, the contractor," said La Rocque. "Richard Dix was the upstanding brother, John. Leatrice Joy was Mary, the girl we rescued from the streets. I remember Edythe Chapman, as Mother McTavish, was overly religious, very arbitrary, and dictatorial. In one scene where the mother is remonstrating, I say, 'You're holding a Cross in your hand, Mom, but you're using it like a whip.' There were subtle things in the script." Subtlety and detail were elements more usually seen in the films of William de Mille, but Cecil was capable of using a fine brush—once he had done the broad strokes.

"I like spectacle," wrote DeMille. "I like to paint on a big canvas. But I spend much more time on dramatic construction than I do on spectacular effects. The story is the steel framework that holds up the building. Everything else—settings, effects, music—is just trimming." DeMille had not done a full-scale historical film in six years. The reason? Adolph Zukor was opposed to it.

The two were a study in contrasts. DeMille was tall, robust, and aggressive, a dynamic figure given to dramatic entrances. Zukor was barely five feet tall, slight, colorless, and solemn. He crept into a room, an ominous presence. What they had in common was a desire for power. It was no coincidence that the diminutive Zukor was the most powerful man in the film industry. His vertical monopoly invited comparisons with Napoleon. He was ruthless but also cunning. For the time being, he kept DeMille in check; in so doing, he denied the debt that Paramount owed the most successful director in the world. All that mattered to him was that DeMille maintained a veritable court: Jeanie Macpherson, Alvin Wyckoff, Paul Iribe, and a dozen more. None of DeMille's people felt loyalty to Zukor's organization. This rankled Zukor.

When DeMille finished the _Ten Commandments_ script, he asked Zukor for $750,000, which would cover both the scenes of ancient Egypt and those of modern San Francisco. "This is a big sum to put into a picture without being absolutely sure in advance that it will be a success," replied Zukor.

DeMille countered with two arguments. First, Paramount needed to rebuild its image after the scandals of Arbuckle, Taylor, and Reid. A religious epic could do that. The American movie-going public was primarily Protestant, so DeMille and Macpherson could draw on the King James Version of the Bible. Second, the world was in thrall to the recent discovery of Tut-

CECILIA DE MILLE PRESLEY

"Grandfather described Zukor as a visionary. Brave, indomitable, ruthless. DeMille thought he had no peer in the history of motion pictures. Zukor called him 'Cecil.' Grandfather never called him anything but 'Mr. Zukor.' There was respect but no warmth."

ankhamun's tomb. The fascination with ancient Egypt would ensure the success of *The Ten Commandments*. "The sensuous life of a great Eastern city has never, to my mind, been touched in pictures," said DeMille. "And the Bible has stood the test of eighteen hundred years. I believe this will be the biggest picture ever made, not only from the standpoint of spectacle but from the standpoint of humanness, dramatic power, and the great good it will do." Zukor was still not convinced. DeMille gritted his teeth. "I fully realize the responsibility of the enormous sum of money I am asking," he wrote Zukor. "As evidence of my faith in this picture, I hereby waive the guarantee under my contract on this picture, other than the regular weekly payments." Zukor was convinced.

As the unusual project got underway, massive Egyptian palace interiors were built in Hollywood and the city of Per-Rameses was built on the Guadalupe-Nipomo Dunes near Santa Maria, California. A construction crew of nearly a thousand completed the work in mid-May. Starting on May 21, DeMille shot a week of scenes in Hollywood and then moved his base of operations 160 miles north, to San Luis Obispo County. At this point his production assumed the character of a military campaign. On his five-acre location, he created a tent city to house 2,500 people and 4,000 animals. Trains and buses transported them from Los Angeles. Protocol modeled on martial law was established. DeMille could only be spoken to through a chain of command.

The night before shooting began, he assembled his company in a large mess hall. "Here on this sandhill," he said through a generator-powered sound system, "you have a chance to breathe into *The Ten Commandments* the vital, pulsing humanity that will bring home their fundamental laws, something that has never been done before." The wind was picking up, pulling a chill from the nearby Pacific. "If we disregard a few weeks of discomfort and even hardship, we will have a chance to leave to posterity a landmark in motion-picture history. You will endure an unpleasant location. You will miss the comforts of home.

Your skin will be cooked raw. In recompense, you will become an integral part of an enterprise which contemplates a forward step for motion pictures."

The crowds shivering in the twilight might have chatted that night about the project. Why was the master of the boudoir drama making a morality play based on the Old Testament? In the years since his father had read to him nightly from the Bible, DeMille had shown no inclination to attend services of any organized religion. He had, however, continued to study scripture. He had also developed the habit of visiting churches when they were empty in order to meditate in silence. In a cynical city and a jaded century, DeMille was a man of faith. His father had taught him that the laws of God are not mere laws, but are the Law. He had a sermon to preach.

"All through history," said DeMille, "there have been times when humanity has asked for guidance, for help, for someone to pull it out of the morass into which human nature has plunged it. And then some great soul comes along, lifts it out, sets it on its knees, and then gets it on its feet. And it crawls along until everything is well. Then it gets successful. And then, out come the gin, the jazz, the gasoline."

Working in the shadow of an Egyptian wall and sleeping in tents watched by monitors, the *Ten Commandments* company had no access to gin. An ensemble played classical music, not jazz. And gasoline was irrelevant. Sleds had to be used on the sand dunes. The only automobiles were those of the relay team charged with transportation of the day's exposed film to Hollywood. There was a lot of it. DeMille was using seven cameras, including Herbert Kalmus's two-color Technicolor camera; if the color footage turned out well, it would be incorporated in the finished film.

Alvin Wyckoff had left DeMille's company, so the camera crew was headed by Bert Glennon, who had become a cameraman after graduating from Stanford. *The Ten Commandments* benefited greatly from his lighting effects. Shooting alongside Glennon was J. Peverell ("Pev") Marley, a DeMille pupil par

excellence. "Pev came to me out of high school," recalled DeMille later. "He loaded film for Wyckoff. I saw his interest and I invited him to my home to read the great volumes that show the masters of engraving and painting, the images so magnificently lighted. In this way he could see the kind of lighting that we use to suggest different emotions. He studied those by the hour. I would come in and see him on his stomach on the floor of my library, learning the methods of lighting used by different artists."

Sequences to be shot at the Guadalupe location included the cruelty of the Egyptian taskmasters to the Egyptian slaves; the Exodus; and the Egyptian chariot pursuit. Red Sea scenes would be shot partly at the nearby ocean and at Southern California beaches, such as Balboa and Anaheim Landing. Other angles of the chariot pursuit would be shot at Muroc Dry Lake in the Mojave Desert.

Staging the Exodus was a huge endeavor, one in which DeMille simultaneously created a panorama and details. Interspersed among the thousands of extras and animals were visiting journalists. Hallett Abend of the *Los Angeles Times* had worked with DeMille on the original idea contest, and was consequently welcomed to the location to watch the Exodus. "Mr. DeMille's handling of this mass of humanity is extraordinary," wrote Abend. "Not always gentle, but invariably just. Really fine work always wins words of praise." Abend saw a touching vignette. "When the whole Jewish nation was on the march, Mr. DeMille spied one wistful little girl with dark red hair who was dragging along a wooden doll of Egyptian design. Her feet and legs were bare, her pink dress dirty, her hair disheveled by the ocean wind. He talked with the child a few moments and then ordered the cameras moved in for a closeup of the waif. Then the Exodus was resumed."

DeMille had cast his longtime character player Theodore Roberts as the prophet. "Moses strode across the sands," wrote Abend, "a truly patriarchal Moses. It was Theodore Roberts, garbed and made up after the John Singer Sargent painting. Among the players following in his wake were 224 Orthodox Jews. Many of them speak no English, they having recently come from Palestine and Turkey and Russia. To these Jews the making of the film was not business and not work. It was a transmigration to Biblical times." A Jewish extra spoke to a crew member. "We know this script," he said. "Our fathers studied it long before there were movies. This is the tale of our beginnings." A woman agreed. "It's just like living in dem times when we got the Torah," she said. "An' now we're going to get it all over again in a picture by Mr. DeMille."

The Exodus shots continued, and unexpected things happened. "Jews streamed out of the great gold gates of Rameses with tears running down their cheeks. One woman dropped to her knees in the sand, raised her fist to Pharaoh's city, and wailed. Without prompting or rehearsal, a group of Jews began singing in Hebrew the chants which have been sung in synagogues for centuries." Leatrice Joy was at this location, even though her role was only in the modern second half of the film. "God almighty, you never heard anything so sad as the dirge of

OPPOSITE AND ABOVE, LEFT TO RIGHT: A truck begins a five-hour drive from Hollywood to Guadalupe with two of the twenty statues for the Avenue of Sphinxes. The heads were sawed off because of the low clearance of an overpass on the highway. • Workers assemble the sphinx in Guadalupe. • A sphinx in place as the walls of Per-Rameses await completion. The walls of Per-Rameses were 109 feet tall, surpassing the Babylonian ramparts of D. W. Griffith's *Intolerance* (1916). • A view from inside the gates.

the Jewish people," she recalled. "They gave the impression that this was it, that it had never happened before. They were living the time, these people. They weren't acting." When the scene moved to the ocean and the musicians played the "Largo" from Antonín Dvořák's *New World Symphony*, journalist Rita Kissin wrote: "Tears trembled on wrinkled cheeks, sobs came from husky throats. For many, the world had moved back 3,000 years, and they stood once more on the shores of the Red Sea, viewing the good omen of deliverance."

DeMille returned to Hollywood in mid-June and got the news that he had already exceeded his budget and was running a bill of close to one million dollars. He pressed on, shooting the last of the Old Testament scenes. There were fireworks created by special effects technician Roy Pomeroy for the giving of the Law. There were more fireworks when Lasky told DeMille over dinner that Zukor wanted him to cut the production back. "What do they want me to do?" snarled DeMille. "Stop now and release it as *The Five Commandments*?" He stood up, threw

down his napkin, and stomped out of the restaurant. Still, it was true that DeMille was being drawn by the same siren song that would destroy Erich von Stroheim. He was in love with his film and could not stop shooting, even though he was working from a completed script and had every aspect of the production fastidiously planned. There were simply too many variables to consider.

A few days later, on July 5, DeMille and his attorney Neil McCarthy strode into Lasky's office at FPL. Sitting with Lasky were Frank Garbutt, a millionaire financier, and Elek Ludvigh, a Zukor associate who was outraged that DeMille had spent $2,500 on two coal-black horses for the Pharaoh's chariot.

OVERLEAF: A scene from *The Ten Commandments*. Photograph by Edward S. Curtis.

ABOVE: DeMille and his eight camera operators; Bert Glennon is above him and J. Peverell Marley is at his immediate left.

OPPOSITE: Heralds announce the coming of Pharaoh in this setting by Paul Iribe. Photograph by Edward S. Curtis.

"We've raised some money," said McCarthy. "You can notify your New York crowd. We're prepared to buy the negative Cecil has shot thus far for a million dollars." Lasky was shocked. He had no choice but to place a transcontinental call to Zukor. Garbutt got on the extension. "Have you seen the picture, Adolph? No? Don't sell what you haven't seen!" Once again, Zukor was convinced. DeMille was able to finish his film. The final tab was a jaw-dropping $1.475 million.

DeMille's editing sessions were interrupted by a family crisis. Beatrice was terminally ill with cancer. DeMille spent as much time with her as his project would allow, and she was always eager to hear about it. In the course of his life, her opinion was the most important. She died at home on October 8, 1923.

The Ten Commandments premiered at Sid Grauman's Egyptian Theatre in Hollywood on December 4, and at the George M. Cohan Theatre in New York on December 21. DeMille was at the overwhelming New York event. "It was

shortly after 8:30 when the huge tablets which formed the scenic background for the presentation slowly opened outward and the introductory title was revealed on the screen," reported *Motion Picture News*. "From that moment until the end, three hours later, there was not one second's abatement of interest. The applause and cheering were at times deafening. Waves of handclapping swept over the theatre in crescendo with the pursuit of the Children of Israel by the Egyptian charioteers, the opening and closing of the sea, the pronouncement of the Commandments and with the climax of the modern story."

Beyond the unforgettable premiere there was a touching reminder of the family that had started DeMille on this path. A telegram arrived on Christmas Eve, 1923. "I congratulate you, dear Cecil, on your wonderful achievement in *The Ten Commandments*. I'm proud of the little boy I used to bring candy to at Echo Lake, whose father was one of the most brilliant men that ever lived and the sweetness of whose mother I shall never forget. The DeMille family are all tucked away in my heart. David Belasco."

OPPOSITE AND ABOVE: The Bronze Man (Noble Johnson) carries the inert son of Pharaoh through the palace.

"AND MOSES STRETCHED OUT HIS HAND OVER THE SEA; AND THE LORD CAUSED THE SEA TO GO BACK, AND MADE THE SEA DRY LAND, AND THE WATERS WERE DIVIDED."

(Exodus 14:21)

OPPOSITE: The epic Exodus.

TOP: The Israelites pray for deliverance at the Red Sea.

BOTTOM RIGHT: Roy Pomeroy's effects stunned 1923 audiences.

OPPOSITE, CLOCKWISE FROM TOP LEFT: The prologue of *The Ten Commandments* climaxed at Mount Sinai. Miriam (Estelle Taylor) worships the Golden Calf. • The Giving of the Law. • The debauchery at the foot of Mount Sinai.

ABOVE, CLOCKWISE FROM TOP LEFT: The modern story in the second part of *The Ten Commandments*: Sally Lung (Nita Naldi) escapes from a leper colony and enters San Francisco undetected. • Mary (Leatrice Joy) looks away at the construction site as John (Richard Dix) confronts Dan (Rod La Rocque) while Robert Edeson and Eugene Pallette watch. • Mother McTavish (Edythe Chapman) is killed because of Dan's greed. • When Dan learns he has been exposed to leprosy, he slays the wicked Sally Lung. Photograph by Edward S. Curtis.

SECULAR EPICS

The triumph of *The Ten Commandments* should have calmed the tension between the partners of Famous Players-Lasky. After all, Cecil B. DeMille had made good on his promise, even if he had been extravagant. As the film played across the country in 1924, DeMille made two more films, *Feet of Clay* and *The Golden Bed*. They were not inexpensive. Apparently he had not been chastened. Adolph Zukor was resentful of DeMille, of his production cost advances, his sliding scale percentage of gross receipts, of his little empire. Zukor was determined to rein in DeMille, even to the extent of shutting down his company between films. Never mind that it was impossible to develop properties under such conditions. Zukor mistrusted DeMille's self-sufficient world. Besides being expensive, it was a threat to Zukor's power.

In early December Zukor notified Jesse Lasky and Paramount sales manager Sidney Kent that DeMille would have to sacrifice $150,000 a year in salary and profits, as well as his between-film staff. DeMille refused. He would not contemplate such restrictions. He met with United Artists and then looked at the Culver City studios of the recently deceased Thomas Ince. Zukor showed his hand. "We've got to get rid of Cecil," he told Lasky.

"All right," replied Lasky. "I'll do what you say. But you're making a mistake." On December 18, Kent issued an ultimatum

to DeMille. "It is not your advance we object to," wrote Kent, "as much as the added expense caused by your separate unit, from which we feel we get no return commensurate with the expense it costs us. Mr. Zukor feels that this must be taken off our backs."

DeMille had booked passage to Europe, scheduled to sail January 10 on the SS *George Washington*. On December 29, 1924, he took a train to New York with Constance, Jeanie Macpherson and her mother, Julia Faye and her mother, Mitchell Leisen, and Peverell Marley. It was the eleventh anniversary of *The Squaw Man*'s first shooting day.

On arriving in New York, DeMille went to the FPL offices for a lunch meeting with Lasky, Kent, and Zukor. DeMille told Zukor that he was not willing to give up his sliding percentage for a miserable 50 percent. Zukor stared at DeMille for a few moments.

"He looked at me," recalled DeMille in 1957. "His eyes were sharp as steel. I can still remember what he said. 'Cecil, you have never been one of us. If you do this, I will break you.' And his two fists came apart sharply, like a man breaking a stick."

On January 9, 1925, Cecil B. DeMille was ousted from the company that he had cofounded, this after making millions for

OPPOSITE: The celebrated photographer James Abbe made this portrait of Cecil B. DeMille.

it, and after delivering its highest-grossing film. Lasky and Kent made no effort to stop Zukor. His power play was cruel and direct.

"He did one of the most terrible things one man ever did to another," recalled DeMille thirty years later. "He said 'You're not one of us and you never have been one of us.' To the guy who had built the whole damned structure of pictures for him!" Being right—and having a contract—meant nothing. "They threw me out," recalled DeMille.

DeMille had just made a film about enslavement, escape, and redemption. Not surprisingly, he took the high road with Zukor and Lasky, perhaps consoling himself with the thought that some higher power would deal with them. He sat through

CECILIA DE MILLE PRESLEY

"Grandfather spoke to me several times about being thrown out of Paramount. He was an embellisher on the screen, but he was not an embellisher of facts, or his life. When he told me something, that was the way it had happened. For Adolph Zukor to throw him out after eight years of success showed that Zukor was concerned about the encroachment of his power.

"I find it incredible that Grandfather put this awful episode behind him. He did it in honesty. He did not hold a grudge. He rose above it. He chose to see the good in Zukor, the great ability, the incredible mind. Later, when Zukor was having a bad time, Grandfather went to him and helped him. At the end of his life, Grandfather revered Zukor. He never missed an opportunity to laud this genius who had created the business model for the American movie industry."

the negotiations of his severance, canceled his trip to Europe, and took his extended family back to Hollywood. "It was a wrench," wrote DeMille, "moving from the corner of Vine and Selma. The Lasky lot had grown up around Jacob Stern's old barn. It turned an orange grove into the capital of an industrial empire. But Jesse lived up to what he referred to in one of his letters to me at the time as 'the friendly spirit which you splendidly set forth, and which you may be sure I will do everything possible to maintain.'"

On March 2, most of Culver City joined DeMille in celebrating his new studio, which was the former Ince facility on Washington Boulevard. Ince had constructed a white colonial façade for his production *Barbara Frietchie*. DeMille turned the structure into a suite of offices, including one that was a virtual duplicate of George Washington's. DeMille had gotten his financing from an East Coast investor named Jeremiah Milbank. DeMille was confident that he could run a studio by making two big films a year, while his brother and several other directors cranked out program pictures. It looked good on paper, and, with DeMille's track record, it promised to work well. He moved his studio family into the Mount Vernon look-alike and began working.

DeMille's actual family had grown since the days in the Cahuenga Pass. Now sixteen, Cecilia had an adopted sister, Katherine, who was thirteen; an adopted brother named John, who was ten; and another adopted brother, Richard, who was two. Most of them waited up to greet their father when he came home. "That was an occasion, when he came in that front door," recalled Katherine de Mille. "He brought a surge of excitement

OPPOSITE, CLOCKWISE FROM TOP LEFT: Jeanie Macpherson followed Cecil DeMille from Famous Players-Lasky to his new company, Cecil B. DeMille Pictures, Inc., which was headquartered in Culver City. • Anton Grot made this concept sketch for DeMille's first independent film, *The Road to Yesterday* (1925). • "We had a train wreck in *The Road to Yesterday* that was terribly difficult to set up," recalled Mitchell Leisen. "I had all the bits and pieces wired so that when I pushed a button, it would all fall apart. Jetta Goudal was supposed to jump across the wreck and every time we tried to shoot it, she'd chicken out and not do it and we'd have to spend the rest of the day piecing it back together. This went on—for I don't know how long—until she finally did it."

into the house. We'd sit on the sofas and ask him questions. 'What did you shoot today? What does so-and-so—one of his stars—look like?' Mother would say, 'Don't ask too many questions. Father is tired. Let's let him eat in peace.'"

As DeMille settled into his new studio, he felt the need to expand his staff. He hired a costume designer named Gilbert Adrian. DeMille had seen Adrian's designs at the premiere of Charles Chaplin's *The Gold Rush* on June 26, 1925. Adrian's costumes were the high point of Sid Grauman's spectacular stage prologue at his Egyptian Theatre. When DeMille sent Adrian a job offer, it was one of five that Adrian received. DeMille's stature sealed the deal.

DeMille hired a new art director, the Polish-born Anton Grot, who had worked on the lavish *Thief of Bagdad* with William Cameron Menzies. DeMille also engaged a painter named Dan Sayre Groesbeck to prepare paintings of both scenes and characters, interpreted from each in-progress scenario. This practice was something new in Hollywood. It was neither a wardrobe sketch nor a set rendering. This "concept art" included elements of costume design, art direction, and lighting. Concept art helped DeMille communicate to all the departments in his studio how he wanted a scene to look.

OPPOSITE: Anton Grot made these concept sketches for *The Road to Yesterday*.

ABOVE, CLOCKWISE FROM TOP: A concept sketch by Anton Grot for *The Road to Yesterday*. • *The Road to Yesterday* had parallel stories, so Jetta Goudal played both a 1920s wife and a seventeenth-century gypsy. DeMille had thought to make her a star but changed his mind when she turned out to be the most temperamental actress in town. When he

canceled her contract, she successfully sued him. "Grandfather didn't like to hold a grudge," says Cecilia de Mille Presley. "He used to have Jetta Goudal and her husband, Harold Grieve, over for dinner. They were prominent interior decorators, and Grandfather thought she was amusing." • DeMille's studio serves as a backdrop for this group portrait, which was made in 1925, judging from the presence of Jetta Goudal, who is sitting between Jeanie Macpherson and DeMille, wearing a dark hat.

DeMille interviewed a scenarist named Lenore Coffee. She had worked for the "Boy Wonder," producer Irving Thalberg, both before and after his Metro-Goldwyn-Mayer merger. "I was ushered into one of those smoke-filled rooms," wrote Coffee. "There were six or seven people there, including Paul Iribe, the art director, and Jeanie Macpherson. Everyone had made suggestions, all of which had fallen flat. They were bored with the subject, bored with each other, and bored with themselves. The first thing I did was change the climate of the room with a positive move. I asked Mr. DeMille to give me a précis of the scenario." By the end of the day, Coffee had led the group to a story line, and DeMille had offered her a contract.

DeMille's first film at the studio had a personal resonance. Its pivotal scene depicted a train wreck like the one he had experienced with Constance in 1903. "It was near Parkersburg, West Virginia," recalled DeMille. "Mrs. de Mille was sitting next to me in the coach, admiring the wildflowers along the river bank through the window. Suddenly the train stopped. And this thing came on us from the back. Crash! A locomotive engine plowed right through the car! Right to where we were sitting! A little woman who was near us turned to look behind her. And here was this engine. She let out a shriek: 'Whhhaaa!'"

The train wreck in *The Road to Yesterday* transports four confused characters to an earlier time so they can unravel their problems. Macpherson believed in reincarnation. She had treated it briefly in *Male and Female*; here she treated it fully, and

as a fact. Perhaps because Jetta Goudal and Joseph Schildkraut were not star material, *The Road to Yesterday* was not the success that DeMille's new studio hoped for.

The multitalented Mitchell Leisen—costume designer, set dresser, draftsman, art director, assistant director—was brought back to the fold. "DeMille was hesitant to make me his art director right off the bat," said Leisen, "but he agreed to let me be art director on the program pictures the studio made, while continuing as set dresser on the DeMille spectaculars." The second "spectacular" at the new studio had a Lenore Coffee script based on a novel about the Russian Revolution. DeMille was close to the choreographer Theodore Kosloff, an émigré. Hardly a film was made without Kosloff either in front of the camera or behind it. He urged DeMille to tell the story of the revolution. DeMille was not convinced until he saw a diorama in a store window that showed a group of people with their heads bowed in shadow. Only one young man had his face lifted to the light. "It reminded me of mankind's long struggle for freedom," wrote DeMille, "led by the few who dared lift their heads from the shadows of oppression."

On May 18, 1926, *The Volga Boatman* opened the new Carthay Circle Theatre in Los Angeles. It was a hit. The film ran nineteen weeks there and eventually grossed three times its cost. "It was nothing of a spectacle," wrote Coffee, "yet it had what they call 'size.' What is more, it had heart." DeMille had regained his momentum, in time to approach a daunting project.

OPPOSITE, CLOCKWISE: Dan Sayre Groesbeck made these renderings of Russian characters to help DeMille cast *The Volga Boatman*. "Groesbeck was a genius," says Cecilia de Mille Presley. "He didn't use live models. He just stood at the easel with a cigar in his mouth and a glass of whisky next to him, painting away. The ashes and whisky got mixed in with the paint!" • Mitchell Leisen helped DeMille stage this scene of White Russians in peril. • William Boyd had been playing bit parts in DeMille films for six years before getting his big chance in *The Volga Boatman* (1926). Elinor Fair did not become a star but she did become Mrs. William Boyd.

THE KING OF KINGS

n June 1926, the corner of Selma and Vine was alive with the sound of rending steel. A studio was being scrapped. After thirteen years, Famous Players-Lasky was moving to Melrose Avenue, to the former United Studios, where a newly built Spanish Renaissance structure awaited. The only survivor of the Vine Street studio was the barn where Cecil B. DeMille and his troupe had made *The Squaw Man*. "Every man has his superstition," wrote Grace Kingsley in the *Los Angeles Times*. "Jesse L. Lasky is no exception. He is moving the old barn, in which his company began as a lusty infant, to the new studios of Paramount, and the very window frame from which he used to gaze onto Vine Street is to be removed and placed in his new office."

Six miles away, at the Cecil B. DeMille studios, there was no time for nostalgia, even though DeMille saved every possible memento of his career. Half a dozen films were in progress. Their directors included two D.W. Griffith alumni, Donald Crisp and Joseph Henabery. DeMille idolized Griffith, but the great man's alumni had caught little of his brilliance. Cecil's brother William was far more accomplished. To sustain momentum, the studio joined with the *Los Angeles Times* in another idea contest. DeMille had announced that he would only do one film a year, a million-dollar production. A story of Noah's Ark won the contest, but it transpired that Warner Bros. was building its own ark, so the money and ballyhoo were wasted.

DeMille was not caught off balance. He had something in prospect. In May a contract writer named Denison Clift earned his salary with a short proposal. "Why skirt around the one great single subject of all time and all ages?" asked Clift. "The most sublime thing that any man can ever put upon the screen: the Life, Trial, Crucifixion, Resurrection and Ascension of Christ. The title would be 'The King of Kings.'"

Before Jeanie Macpherson could change her typewriter ribbon, DeMille was handing her the Bible from which Henry de Mille had read to him in 1892. This was to be her sole reference book. While she devised a way to blend the four Gospels of the New Testament into one narrative, DeMille attended to what President Calvin Coolidge called the "business of the American people." DeMille was industrious. "As Uncle Cecil's power mounted, he made monstrous sums," recalled Agnes de Mille. "And he invested them well, thanks to Aunt Constance, to his attorney Neil McCarthy, and to his assistant Gladys Rosson." Constance had managed Cecil's income so well that they were worth $1.92 million. What DeMille had not managed was a profitable studio. By the summer of 1926, he needed an infusion of cash. Jeremiah Milbank agreed to provide it if DeMille filmed

OPPOSITE: H. B. Warner portrayed Jesus Christ in Cecil B. DeMille's 1927 film, *The King of Kings*, and Dorothy Cumming portrayed his mother, Mary. William Mortensen created this unique portfolio print in his Hollywood Boulevard studio.

his dream project, the life of Christ. For reasons known mostly to DeMille's family, he was happy to do the project. It would be many decades before anyone knew how Milbank provided the cash to save the studio. He padded the religious film's budget—by a million dollars—and siphoned that off to pay overdue bills.

Macpherson was still wrestling with the scenario when DeMille sounded out Lenore Coffee. "I wasn't keen about it," wrote Coffee. "Jeanie was his special writer, and this sort of thing she did particularly well." Coffee was apprehensive when she approached DeMille on a set to tell him that she and her husband, director William Cowen, were expecting their first child. "Not really, Lenore!" exclaimed DeMille, taking both her hands in his. "Not really! Oh, I am so pleased." He took her aside and spent a few minutes with her. "Now you're going to learn the real meaning of the word 'unselfishness.' You're going to learn what it means to care more for someone else than you do for yourself—than you do even for your own life. But you've been working all this time and you haven't been feeling ill? Well, now, don't overdo it. You can work at home whenever you like. Take good care of yourself." Coffee, after some years in matter-of-fact Hollywood, was moved. "I've never forgotten the little homily he gave me. I've never been spoken to so kindly, so warmly, in all my life."

According to DeMille's family members, his relationship with his mother had been a defining one. "At the praise or condemnation of his mother," wrote Agnes de Mille, "Cecil's heart jumped. She remained critical, hard to please, and enormously proud of her extraordinary son." For years after her death, it was Beatrice de Mille's opinion that mattered, and it was her spirit that guided him.

"Father had a lot of women technicians," said Katherine de Mille Quinn. "He believed in women's abilities. Not many other producers were hiring women for jobs behind the camera at that time." Of course there was gossip, especially about the women who worked with him most closely; Gladys Rosson, Julia Faye, and especially Jeanie.

There was more talk about the new project, which was both a departure and a risk. "Whenever I wanted to do a subject that was different," said DeMille, "no one was in sympathy with it. 'What the public wants is melodrama,' the sales department insisted. The screen was overcrowded with melodrama. I felt that the world was ready for the life of Christ. When I suggested it, we almost had to resuscitate the sales department." Equally controversial was his casting. "When I found that he was casting H. B. Warner," wrote Coffee, "I couldn't understand it. Jesus, at the beginning of his mission, was only thirty and had been a carpenter. Warner was fifty years old. I said to Mr. DeMille, 'If Harry Warner picked up a hammer, he'd drop it on his toe!'" In fact, Warner was in prime condition, with a well-toned torso. He looked reserved and distinguished, but he was a "skirt chaser." This was more of a problem than his appearance. As DeMille cast his film, he made his actors sign contracts with a clause requiring them to "behave in a chaste and becoming manner" for the duration of filming.

As the script neared completion, DeMille's motives were a mystery to many. Others thought they understood. "Uncle Cecil had a fervid attachment to mysticism," wrote Agnes de Mille. "He believed—with sincerity—that he was spreading the word of God and fostering the brotherhood of man. He considered himself a dedicated person and that his pictures were, at least partially, instruments of religious faith." After two years, Coffee felt she knew her boss. "I never saw Mr. DeMille so thoroughly steeped in what he was doing," she wrote. "Contrary to general opinion, he was, au fond, a deeply religious man; not in the sense

OPPOSITE: *The King of Kings* script shows the many emendations that DeMille made in the process of shooting his film; he was truly the author of his work.

Scene 760 "IN"

Int. Upper Room - VERY CLOSE UP of Christ's head and shoulders ONLY

He turns and looks straight out and into the lens (as if He

were speaking to the public when He says title, "FEED MY SHEEP!")

Scene 761.

Int. Upper Room - LONG SHOT of entire room

Christ now turns from Peter and calls all of the other disciples

around Him for the FAREWELL. (As the disciples gather and place

themselves to hear Christ's FAREWELL, (make this look like some

wonderful painting.) It should be as beautifully lighted as the

"Last Supper". (NOTE: Mark is with Mary Magdalene.). As Christ

stands in the center of the group, he turns and gives them His

final message:

469. Spoken Title:
JOHN 20:21
MATT. 28:19
MARK 16:15

"As my Father hath sent me, even so send I you.
"Go ye therefore and teach all nations, and preach the gospel to every creature!"

(CUT TO:)

Scene 762.

Int. Upper Room - SEMI CLOSE UP Mary, the "mother," Mary Magdalene & Mark

Mark anxiously pantomimes to Mary Magdalene that Christ means him as well as the others. He pulls himself up importantly and indicates that he must take his place with the OTHER disciples. Mary smiles and lets him go toward inner circle.

of holding to dogma or conventional beliefs, but nonetheless deeply religious." His daughter Katherine had no doubt. "He made *The King of Kings* because he loved the Lord," she said.

"A recent examination of over nine thousand college students brought forth this result concerning their understanding of the Bible and the life and ideals of Jesus Christ," DeMille told his staff. "Sixteen percent did not know where Christ was born. Sixty percent did not know what Christ meant by, 'Love thy neighbor as thyself.' Nine percent thought that 'sin' meant debt. Some thought that the Elders were a sort of bush from which you get berries to make wine." After the laughter died down, DeMille continued. "We must interest this class and hold them, as well as the class that was born with a Bible in their hand, who will criticize and hurl curses if we change an 'if' or fail to dot an 'i.' The purpose of the story is to treat all classes fairly, particularly the Jew. It was not really a matter of the Jew having persecuted Jesus, it was Rome, Rome with her politics and graft."

Since DeMille was venturing into uncharted territory, he deemed it wise to secure the endorsement of religious leaders. Agreeing to act as consultants were the Reverend George Reid Andrews, a leader of the Federal Council of Churches; Rabbi J. M. Alkow of San Bernardino, California; and Father Daniel Lord, a Jesuit who was a drama teacher at St. Louis University. DeMille took to the erudite young Lord, and included him in numerous production activities, including rehearsals, which included spoken dialogue, even though the film was silent. "H. B. Warner said the word fish as 'fish' with an English accent. Ernest Torrence repeated the word as 'fuuush' with a strong Scottish burr. Joseph Schildkraut in a Yiddish accent said, 'Oy, feeeesh?'"

To seclude his cast, DeMille built a village on Catalina Island. "The idea," said DeMille, "is for us all to live and eat and sleep here, to stay in the mood of the setting which we took so much time and care to create, and to let this atmosphere soak

OPPOSITE: Alan Brooks as Satan tempts Jesus. Portrait by Mortensen.

into us." Filming commenced on August 24, 1926. DeMille was more than pleased with the world he was evoking. "This has been the happiest day of my life," he said that evening.

Sunday services were held on the island. "Mass was spoken by Father Lord," wrote Grace Kingsley of the *Los Angeles Times*. "He stood at an improvised altar on the veranda of the carpenter shop, under a sunny blue sky, before a congregation of players all clad in colorful biblical robes, with the sea glinting in the distance."

When the company returned to Culver City, it was to huge Jerusalem sets. DeMille strove to maintain the transporting atmosphere, but he was hard pressed. In addition to guiding a huge production, he was dealing with financial pressure. His company was failing, and he was prevented by his private busi-

KATHERINE DeMILLE

"I was at the Santa Barbara School for Girls when Father made *The King of Kings*. I used to go down and sit on the set. I was there on Christmas Eve. They had just finished shooting the Crucifixion. There were the three crosses on the hill and—I don't know—hundreds, maybe a thousand extras. Everyone had worked about twelve hours. It was about nine o'clock when Father said, 'Okay, cut. Finished. Done.' And the people began to scurry to get home.

"All of a sudden, his voice boomed across the set. 'Ladies and gentlemen, if you'd stop for just a moment.' And you could hear them saying, 'Son of a gun! What now?'

"'I would like you all to take five minutes—just five minutes—to think about what you have seen tonight—something that truly happened. I want you to think what it has meant to you. I'd like you to take a few minutes of quiet.'

"He had an organ on the set. At first only it could be heard. Then the orchestra joined in, I think with J. S. Bach's *Christmas Oratorio*. It was amazing. There were many who wept. Some got on their knees facing the cross. There was just the sound of that music.
"In a few minutes, he said, 'Thank you, ladies and gentlemen. Let's go home to our families—have a wonderful Christmas,' and they walked off in total silence."

definitely assured?" While he waited for an answer, he worked. And spent more money.

"This was the battle of time with art, and time means money," said DeMille. "*The King of Kings* cost $19,000 a day, or $2,225 an hour. You can see what a moment's indecision involved—a little absent-mindedness on the part of a director or the forgetfulness of a property man who leaves a certain prop at home." As DeMille saw it, only discipline could prevent these expensive snafus. He enforced discipline with the method he had learned from David Belasco. "This was to build," said Agnes de Mille, "from a simple statement of displeasure, through long developments of sarcasm to a fulminating climax of operatic splendor. Uncle Ce held the belief that he got the best work from people when he had stripped their nerves raw, when they could no longer think, when they acted through an instinct of rage and desperation."

DeMille was frustrated with Paul Iribe's failure to come up with adequate set designs. Mitchell Leisen found the French art director both lofty and lazy. The Crucifixion scene was not ready on schedule, so DeMille turned to the prison. Iribe went through several drafts. When DeMille looked at the latest one, it

ness partners from using that money to aid the film company. He had to get capital somewhere. The stress was unspeakable. He bore it and kept on, pausing occasionally to seek remedy. "I have been working eighteen to twenty hours a day on *King of Kings*," he wrote McCarthy. "Do not take my not answering your wires as lack of interest. Do you consider future financing of company

DANIEL A. LORD, S.J.

"De Mille was a strange and fascinating blend of absolute monarch and charming gentleman, of excellent host and exacting taskmaster, of ruthless drive on the set and a complete letdown the moment that the day's shooting came to an end; a Renaissance prince who had the instincts of a Barnum and a magnified Belasco; an excellent listener and a voice that spoke with the most compelling possible command; an Episcopalian whose deeply beloved mother was a Jewish convert to Christianity."

ABOVE LEFT: Dorothy Cumming as Mary. Photograph by William Thomas.

OPPOSITE, TOP: To the consternation of his religious consultants, DeMille interpreted Mary Magdalene as a high-priced prostitute enamored of Judas. When DeMille asked Jacqueline Logan to nuzzle a leopard, she paused, and then said, "If Gloria Swanson can do a lion, I suppose I can do a leopard." *The King of Kings* was alive with animals, all of whom served a symbolic function, as Whitney Williams noted in the *Los Angeles Times*. "Mary's leopard expresses her passionate, untamed nature. Her zebras say that she is a woman of a certain stripe. When she repents, she is shown with a donkey. Likewise, the townspeople are shown with oxen, to underscore the yoke of Roman rule. And the Virgin Mary is introduced with white doves."

OPPOSITE, BOTTOM: Art director Paul Iribe and cameraman Pev Marley created this tableau for *The King of Kings*.

" Harness my zebras — gift of the Nubian King! This Carpenter shall learn that He cannot hold a man from Mary Magdalene!"

was no better than the previous. "Is this your final design?" he asked Iribe.

"Yes," replied Iribe.

DeMille pushed it off the drafting table and onto the floor. "You're goddamned right it's your final design!" DeMille shouted. "Now get the hell out of here and don't let me ever see you again." The art director walked out of the room. DeMille turned to Leisen, who was watching, and said, "Take over the picture."

MITCHELL LEISEN

"There were spectators all over the place, but I never allowed anybody to see Christ get up on the cross or get off it. I dropped a curtain in front of it, and when he was in place, we'd raise the curtain. Harry Warner was never allowed to smoke on the stage, nor was anybody else in the cast. They also had to sign agreements that they would behave themselves for the next year and not get divorced or cut up in a nightclub."

"Oh no," said Leisen. "I'll let you know tomorrow—after I see where we stand." The next day he looked DeMille in the eye and said, "I will take over this picture, Mr. DeMille, but if you ever mention Paul Iribe's name again, I'll walk out." Leisen finished the film.

Leisen found a way to defuse his boss. "Whenever DeMille started to get apoplectic about something," said Leisen, "I would say very quietly, 'There's a bishop right behind you.' That was my revenge for all the hell I got from him." Eventually not even that ploy worked. Father Lord was complaining

ABOVE, LEFT TO RIGHT: Josephine Norman as Mary of Bethany. Portrait by Mortensen. • Jacqueline Logan as Mary of Magdala, the Courtesan. Portrait by Mortensen.

OPPOSITE: DeMille had Rudolph Schildkraut play Caiaphas to his son's Judas. "DeMille engaged both Father and me under a five-year contract," wrote Joseph Schildkraut. "I love DeMille for one reason above all: he regarded Father as the greatest actor he had ever seen." Photograph by William Thomas.

about so many elements of the production that DeMille lost his temper. "Oh, go to hell," the exhausted director told the punctilious priest.

"I'm afraid that won't be possible," said Father Lord. "I have a reservation elsewhere."

The stress finally lessened. DeMille got some money. He had to. The project was too important and too promising not to be bailed out. But what about the film itself? What was he getting? What was the point of three thousand props, two-color Technicolor, one-hundred-foot columns?

"On a veranda," wrote Grace Kingsley, "stood a man who startlingly resembled the Christ. The sight was breathtaking. He

CECIL B. DeMILLE

"In Mexico, when the churches were closed by government edict, people went to see *The King of Kings* and knelt in the theater to offer the prayers they could not say in church. From Egypt came reports of a mother walking twenty miles with her children to see the film, and of people, Christian and Moslem alike, going up to the screen to kiss the place where Jesus' feet had walked. During World War II, a doctor whom I knew, then with the American Army in the Far East, wrote me about screening *The King of Kings* for boys who watched it, sitting on the ground or on empty oil drums, in the rain. Then the next day they went out to die."

"When Cecil B. DeMille sat down with Jeremiah Milbank to look at the finished *King of Kings*, they decided to do something very unusual. They decided to take no profits from their share of the film. Milbank used his profits to make and distribute new prints of the film that would go to churches and monasteries. DeMille's profits went to charity. After Grandfather died, I wrote hundreds of checks, all to his favorite charities. *The King of Kings* has made a lot of money. And it's done a lot of good."

LEFT: William Thomas made this scene still of the apostles Bartholomew (Clayton Packard) and James the Lesser (Charles Requa).

OPPOSITE: The chalice in the Last Supper scene was one of the props made by studio artisans. When planning the scene, DeMille told his staff to "get Leonardo da Vinci out of your mind. This is a group of men facing tragedy."

wore a long, white mantle and in his face were lines of character, and of sadness, too. But it was his eyes that impressed you the most. This was our first glimpse of H. B. Warner in the sacred central role of the King of Kings."

The public's first glimpse of this entity took place as DeMille opened yet another movie palace with a much-awaited road show. *The King of Kings* premiered at the grand opening of Sid Grauman's Chinese Cinema Temple on May 19, 1927. Fifty thousand spectators lined Hollywood Boulevard as celebrities arrived. Grauman's typically overproduced prologue, interspersed with fulsome speeches, ran until nearly 11 p.m.,

at which time the film finally began. When it ended, there was stunned silence. Audience members, even in jaded Hollywood, were unsure whether applause would be irreverent. They rose to their feet and walked out in silence. Naturally DeMille took this as a sign of displeasure, but it was repeated at every performance, even at the New York road show engagement. People were awestruck by *The King of Kings*. And moved. And inspired. *Life* magazine, *Vanity Fair*, and *Photoplay* praised the film. The gamble had paid off. DeMille had brought his concept of Jesus Christ to millions of people.

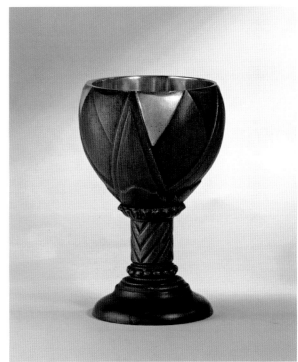

ABOVE: Marley's study of engravings in DeMille's library came to full fruition in *The King of Kings*. "What better source could there be than Gustave Doré?" asked DeMille. "The photographic quality of this master's drawing seems to me peculiarly akin to the needs of the movies. When I work, I compose a scene by looking through the lens of the camera. This gives me a top, bottom and side, just as there would be to a canvas. I originally think of this in black and white, just as anyone who paints begins by drawing his composition before he puts on color. When the people have been placed, I turn to the cameraman and tell him what kind of lighting is wanted. We paint with lights as a painter uses his brush."

OPPOSITE: A scene of remorse on the Way of the Cross. Photograph by William Mortensen.

ABOVE: The Calvary set was one of the largest yet built on a silent-film stage. Mitchell Leisen devised a system of revolving arc lights projected through cutout metal scrims to give the effect of lowering skies. For the cataclysm following Christ's death, Marley had to create a dust storm that was visible to the camera.

"How could you photograph it?" he asked. "Light reflects from dust. You never see a ray of light unless there's something in the atmosphere. But here we had to give the impression of swirling dust without light streaks, the illusion of a storm—dank, gloomy light—and still have enough light to expose the film."

ABOVE: A William Mortensen photograph of Jacqueline Logan and H. B. Warner. "The two great civilizing influences that exist in the world today," said DeMille, "are a little round lens, the eye of the movie, and a round disc, the microphone of the radio. Neither has been with civilization very long, and yet they possess the greatest educational power society has known. They can bring peoples with different creeds and of different races together. Whether we believe that Jesus was a divine being who descended to humanity or a human being who rose to divinity, His ideals apply to all of us."

THE GODLESS GIRL

Cecil B. DeMille had done the apparently impossible with *The King of Kings*. He had made a popular success of a religious film. It ran at Grauman's Chinese Theatre from May until November of 1927. If this was not a record-breaking engagement (*Ben-Hur* and *The Big Parade* had run longer), it was certainly a vindication. DeMille even survived a series of attacks in the Jewish American press. What he could not escape was financial reality. The program pictures were pulling his company down, and his big films did not help. His only salvation lay in a merger, however distasteful. On April 25, 1927, DeMille's company and the Producers' Distributing Corporation were joined to the theater chain Keith-Albee-Orpheum and the undistinguished film company Pathé.

DeMille continued production, sometimes stepping in to direct films credited to others. *Chicago* was based on Maurine Watkins's play and a true story. A married woman shoots her boyfriend and then becomes a tabloid celebrity. DeMille directed most of *Chicago* but gave Frank Urson credit; perhaps the film was too racy to follow *The King of Kings*. DeMille's next project was also topical, a dramatic look at "modern youth," both in high school and in reform school. "Crime among youth has grown out of all proportion to the population," DeMille told *Picture-Play Magazine*. "Youths of fourteen are committing crimes that were formerly committed by twenty-year-olds."

DeMille had his researcher Elizabeth ("Bessie") McGaffey send a team of undercover agents to infiltrate schools and penal institutions. Reports from McGaffey's agents were scary: unsanitary conditions, beatings, and torture. Agents got affidavits from victims.

America was rich. Why were young people committing crimes? Was it a loss of ideals? "The great god business was supreme in the land," wrote Frederick Lewis Allen. "Added to a general apathy toward church is the propaganda of atheism," said DeMille. "In one high school in Los Angeles, we found two hundred students paying dues to an atheist society." DeMille's project was called *Atheist*, then *The Fiery Furnace*, and finally *The Godless Girl*.

On October 6, 1927, a movie milestone occurred at the Warners' Theatre in New York. Warner Bros. premiered Alan Crosland's *The Jazz Singer*, the first feature film with talking sequences. Paramount producer Walter Wanger was there. When the audience heard Al Jolson speak dialogue, there was a gasp, then cries of disbelief, and then cheers. Wanger rushed into the lobby and phoned Jesse Lasky. "Jess," he yelled into the receiver, "this is a revolution!" Response to the film was violently enthusiastic. There was an immediate call for an all-talking film. On

OPPOSITE: Lina Basquette played the title role in Cecil B. DeMille's 1928 film *The Godless Girl*. With her here is the scene-stealing monkey, Josephine.

his yacht, the *Seaward*, DeMille discussed the phenomenon with Peverell Marley, Lenore Coffee, and Jeanie Macpherson. Hollywood could not convert to talking pictures, they agreed. To upset an entire industry for the sake of a fad was absurd. The technical challenges were insuperable. "How can you keep the whir of the camera from being heard by the microphone?" speculated Marley.

"You'll probably end up in some kind of a soundproof box with your camera," said DeMille. "With only a little window to shoot through." This was such an outlandish idea that everyone laughed.

The Godless Girl went into production on January 3, 1928. DeMille cast an unknown as the eponymous high-schooler. Lina Basquette was more mature than her twenty years would suggest. At sixteen she had been a *Ziegfeld Follies* dancer. At eighteen she had wed Sam Warner, one of the founders of Warner Bros. They had a child, Lita. One day before *The Jazz Singer* premiere, Warner had died of a brain abscess. Basquette was still in the throes of grief when she reported for work on *The Godless Girl*. The film would require all her powers of concentration.

"We had a big fire scene," recalled Mitchell Leisen. "I had to burn the whole school building down but protect the people. I fireproofed everything—the set, the furniture, the actors' clothes. I even flame-proofed their hair and makeup. I worked out every movement and every flame until I was satisfied there was no danger." This was not how it looked to *Screenland* writer Clarence Slifer. "The actors were in constant danger," wrote Slifer. "Some of the fire came from jets and some was from guns, like liquid flame. The smoke came from powder and burning oil

MITCHELL LEISEN

"Cecil used to say, 'The camera has no ears. If you want to say it, get it on the screen.' That is the advice I've taken throughout my career, in talking pictures as well as silent. No matter what, get it on the screen. The visual image carries more impact than dialogue."

rags. Fire trucks were standing by, with eight hose lines connected for immediate use." The climactic scene called for Basquette and leading man George Duryea to rescue Noah Beery, the sadistic guard. "The flames got too close and too hot," recalled Basquette. "George got scared. He took off. DeMille was yelling, 'Stay there! Stay there!' The cameras were grinding. I was screaming. My eyelashes and eyebrows were singed. DeMille was impressed with that kind of guts. But my eyebrows never grew back."

In March 1928, DeMille faced a crisis. "I did not have enough 'picture money,'" he wrote, "to be completely independent, to make only the pictures I wanted to make. Nor did the holders of the purse strings have a sufficient understanding of picture-making to show confidence in me. My directing was suffering, both from restrictive outside control and from my being head of a studio. News reached me that Joseph P. Kennedy was interested in taking hold of the Pathé and Keith-Albee-Orpheum companies. I decided that it would be better for DeMille Productions to sell its Pathé stock, at a very handsome profit, and for me

CECILIA DE MILLE PRESLEY

"Pev Marley and DeMille were very close. They thought alike. They revered the Old Masters. Some people thought they could communicate without speaking. I remember Pev coming to my grandparents' golden wedding anniversary. I can see them greeting each other. It was a warm, respectful relationship."

OPPOSITE, CLOCKWISE FROM TOP LEFT: George Duryea leads a pack of teenage Fundamentalists in an attack on an atheist meeting. • DeMille was as concerned with camera mobility as any German Expressionist director. There was no such thing as a camera crane in 1928. F. W. Murnau, Paul Leni, and E. A. Dupont used overhead tracks. To show a dynamic cross section of a student riot in *The Godless Girl*, DeMille worked with Peverell Marley, Mitchell Leisen, and studio manager Roy Burns to build a camera elevator. • For a subjective-camera shot of a girl's fall down a stairwell, the team used a double exposure of the downward shot and a tracking shot into the face of the girl (Mary Jane Irving). • The fall was shot with a modified chairlift.

'It's breaking — the rail's breaking!'

ABOVE: Inmates panic during the fire.

OPPOSITE, LEFT TO RIGHT: "See and hear Cecil B. DeMille's *The Godless Girl.*" This display is from the film's second release; talking sequences made DeMille's last silent film a "goat-gland talkie." • DeMille took Lina Basquette and George Duryea to Las Turas Lake (now Lake Sherwood) to film this romantic scene. The real romance was between Lina Basquette and Pev Marley. They were married a year later.

to form a connection that was free from the uncongenial burden of studio administration." A sidelight to this chain of events was the invitation that DeMille extended to Lasky several years earlier. "I offered Jesse Lasky the presidency of Cecil B. DeMille

—— CECILIA DE MILLE PRESLEY ——

"Grandfather believed that whatever we are, although we die, the mind never dies. Perhaps we change forms. Perhaps we are no longer individuals. But no matter what, we continue to exist. The mind continues."

CECIL B. DeMILLE

"When I visited the Soviet Union in 1931, I found *The Godless Girl* a popular feature and myself something like a national hero. I could not understand this. The story, after all, is of redemption by faith. This did not seem quite the thing that the Communist masters would welcome. It was not until the end of my trip that someone enlightened me. The Soviets did not screen the last redeeming reel. They simply played the picture as a document of American police brutality and the glorious spread of atheism among American youth."

Productions," recalled DeMille. "He preferred to stay where he was." How different would Hollywood history have been if Lasky had said yes? Or if the public had said no to talking pictures?

The Godless Girl suffered a strange fate. It was released in August 1928, just as the first all-talking pictures hit the market. The stampede to the noisy new attraction left the film sitting in silence. A few months later, DeMille's new superiors gave it a second chance. Pathé executive Benjamin Glazer asked DeMille to direct two new sound sequences. *The Godless Girl* could be re-released as a part-talkie and recoup its losses. DeMille politely declined, and the actor-director Fritz Feld performed the chore. *The Godless Girl* had its second release in March 1929. Delinquency, atheism, and flames were no match for "All-Talking, All-Singing, All-Dancing." M-G-M's first talkie, *The Broadway Melody*, wiped out the competition. DeMille had a full-fledged flop.

The Champion Driver reined in his steeds. He couldn't beat M-G-M. Why not join them? He headed his steeds down Washington Boulevard. "On August 2, 1928," wrote DeMille, "I signed a contract to make three pictures for Metro-Goldwyn-Mayer. By September, the DeMille Studio was no more."

CHAPTER 4

TALKIES AT M-G-M

DYNAMITE

When Cecil B. DeMille left Famous Players-Lasky in early 1925, the company was already known as Paramount. Whatever its name, it was leading the pack, grossing more than William Fox, First National, or any of the other companies in Hollywood. One of those companies was Metro-Goldwyn-Mayer, which was created by a merger in 1924. This was the brainchild of theater magnate Marcus Loew, who believed that the combination of three modest companies would yield showy results. He was right. By 1928, M-G-M was overtaking Paramount. Managed by Louis B. Mayer and guided by Irving G. Thalberg, M-G-M was showing a profit of $8.6 million. Paramount was showing $8.7 million. M-G-M's stable of stars, its directors, writers, cameramen, art directors, and wardrobe designers set a standard that even Paramount had to acknowledge. M-G-M had become the Tiffany of Hollywood. It was to this exalted domain that DeMille reported on September 8, 1928, with his staff in tow; Jeanie Macpherson, Pev Marley, Bessie McGaffey, Mitch Leisen, and Roy Burns. DeMille Productions, Inc., would function as an independent unit within the walls of M-G-M. The DeMille company would receive a guarantee per film from $150,000 to $175,000 plus a percentage of gross profits. DeMille had complete authority as to story, production, and cast. This raised eyebrows. Thalberg exercised total control of M-G-M's films.

Mayer made an exception for DeMille because he was part of Mayer's early history, even though they had not met until the Twenties. "Louis B. Mayer told me that he bought the states' rights for *The Squaw Man*," recalled DeMille. "He had the Springfield, Massachusetts, territory, I think. He got two prints. 'I put those prints in a suitcase,' he told me. 'And I went around New England with them. That made my fortune. Anywhere you went with that picture, the exhibitor would grab it. That started me in the picture business.'"

Dynamite, DeMille's first M-G-M film, would be a talkie, but not all theaters in America were wired for sound, so he would also have to prepare a silent version. After some friendly meetings with Mayer and Thalberg, DeMille and Macpherson began work on the script, assisted by two M-G-M contract writers, playwright John Howard Lawson and silent-film scenarist Gladys Unger. (The term *scenario* would soon be as dead as silent films.) The studio supplied DeMille with an additional assistant, Florence Cole. As she recalled, a newspaper clipping had fired DeMille's imagination: "Man Marries Woman Two Hours Before He Is Hanged for Murder."

OVERLEAF: Reginald Denny dances with Kay Johnson high above New York in a scene from *Madam Satan*.

OPPOSITE: When Cecil B. DeMille began his term at Metro-Goldwyn-Mayer in September 1928, the publicity department had him visit Ruth Harriet Louise's portrait gallery.

To cast his first talking film, DeMille turned to the theater. He engaged the Broadway star Charles Bickford to play a miner. To play the rich girl, he hired a young Hollywood actress named Carole Lombard. Bickford's first meeting with DeMille took place on a balmy Christmas eve, in his office, during the studio's annual party. Lombard was there, along with the entire staff. When the tall red-headed actor entered, the room fell silent. "A sturdily built, sun-bronzed man came toward me with his hand extended," recalled Bickford. "Although I had never met De Mille, nor seen a picture of him, I knew that this must be he. The pongee sports shirt, well-tailored riding breeches, leather puttees and Napoleonic stride seemed to proclaim the fact that here was the director to end all directors."

After a handshake that almost turned into an arm-wrestling contest, Bickford sized up DeMille as a serious artist—and a contentious man. "Although he was smiling," said Bickford, "I detected the glint of antagonism in his eyes. This was interesting because of the mutual respect we held for each other. I considered his work extraordinary. He was in a class by himself. As there was only one P. T. Barnum, so there was only one C. B. DeMille. Beyond any argument, he was a great showman."

Because *Dynamite* was DeMille's first sound film, he was not doing individual readings. He was convening the entire group. When Bickford arrived, he was surprised to see that Lombard had been fired. "DeMille made a test of Carole and decided she wouldn't do," said Leisen. Lombard was replaced by the Broadway actress Kay Johnson, who was also a newcomer to Hollywood. DeMille ascended a dais and addressed his staff. "It was a masterly oration," said Bickford, "comprising the history of his film career from its inception in a Vine Street barn to the moment in which a panting world viewed his first masterpiece in the new medium of sound." DeMille, instead of handing out scripts, began reading from one. His training with the distinguished actor E. H. Sothern had left him with a mid-Atlantic accent and an orotund, stentorian tone. "DeMille had been an actor in his younger days," said Bickford. "If one was to

judge by his stilted speech and ponderous emphasis, his acting must have left plenty to be desired." Mitchell Leisen was in the room. "DeMille had no nuances," Leisen recalled. "Everything was in neon lights six feet tall. Lust. Revenge. Sex. You had to learn to think the way he thought, in capital letters. Roy Burns was his business manager, and whenever he and I went through a new script to figure the costs, he'd say, 'Here it is again, two squirrels in a tree, makin' love to each other.' Script after script had the same crap in it. It wasn't until Jeanie Macpherson left that he saw the light and stopped doing the same old shit over and over again."

Making a talkie was a new kind of ordeal. "The motion picture was being revolutionized," recalled Conrad Nagel, who played Johnson's married beau. "In silent pictures, you wanted as little talk and as much action as you could get. All of

ABOVE: M-G-M boss Louis B. Mayer reminisced about carrying DeMille films around Massachusetts fifteen years earlier.

OPPOSITE LEFT: DeMille's first film at M-G-M was also his first sound film. In this scene, the "Aero Wheel Race," DeMille used the moving camera to challenge the restrictive sound requirements of the early talkies.

OPPOSITE RIGHT: Jeanie Macpherson came to M-G-M with DeMille as his star writer.

a sudden, you wanted as much talk as you could get and as little action as possible. You couldn't move the microphone." Worse yet, the camera could not be moved. "The camera department at M-G-M had put the camera in a box," recalled DeMille. "All the companies had done that so the grinding sound of the camera mechanism wouldn't disturb the microphone. The camera and the operator were locked in a big box with padded walls and a little window. The camera lens was right up against that window. It couldn't pan. It couldn't tilt. It couldn't follow an actor. It couldn't do anything but shoot through that little window."

CECIL B. DeMILLE

"I think that was my first contribution of any value to sound pictures, retaining the silent techniques, and combining those techniques with sound. Such great, great value, that the moment you put the sound with it, you were back in the stage and all that the stage could give you, and the whole technique of the stage was at your disposal, plus being able to paint on the broad canvas of the silent screen."

Putting the camera (and the cameraman) in a soundproof booth that looked like a cross between a cold storage and a torture chamber had an effect on the art of the cinema. "Everything that the silent screen had done," said DeMille, "to bring entertainment and the beauty of action, was gone. You were

CLOCKWISE FROM TOP LEFT: Barton Hepburn and Leslie Fenton play a murder confession scene for DeMille, his script clerk, and Mitchell Leisen. Trapped inside the hot, airless, soundproof camera booth is Pev Marley. This is how talkies were made in January 1929, with an immovable camera. • DeMille instructs Charles Bickford and Muriel McCormac in the use of multiple microphones. Since sound mixing was not yet possible, movie sets had both hanging microphones (above) and microphones on stands (lower left). Within a few weeks, DeMille had rigged a camera boom; directors W. S. Van Dyke and Lionel Barrymore were also doing this. • After suffering two weeks of stationary

MITCHELL LEISEN

"DeMille directed actors well. He had a very positive idea of what he wanted, and he wasn't satisfied until he got it."

camera booths, DeMille took action that resulted in the first soundproof camera blimp (left). His original Pathé camera is at right.

back on the stage. The progress of that whole period was lost, about to be wiped out." DeMille was not going to allow this. On the newly named "soundstage," Bickford saw a uniformed guard open a door and announce, "He's coming."

"Who's coming?" Bickford asked a studio worker.

"God. Who else?"

"DeMille swept through the door," wrote Bickford. "Three paces behind him and in near-military formation were his assistant director, unit manager, film cutter, script clerk, megaphone bearer, chair bearer, and secretary. Every move he made found them moving with him like shadows, an arm's length behind him. If he wanted his megaphone, he had merely to extend his hand and it would be immediately placed in his grasp. If he were about to sit, he didn't look to see if the chair was there. He just sat."

DeMille was too agitated to sit. "They said there was a madman loose on Stage A," recalled DeMille. What he wanted was for the camera to follow an actor up a flight of stairs. The soundproof booth could not be moved there. He lost patience. He yelled at Marley, telling him to pull the camera out of the soundproof booth.

"But Mr. DeMille!" said the sound engineer. "The noise!" The engineer threw down his script and headed for the soundstage door.

"Just a moment!" said DeMille. The engineer kept going. DeMille turned to his crew. "Go to the property department.

CECILIA DE MILLE PRESLEY

"In the days of the early sound films, the noisy camera had to be boxed and stationary or the microphone would pick up the noise. Grandfather wanted his moving camera back. The technician told him he couldn't have it. Grandfather promptly pulled the camera out of the box. When he did that, the sound man walked off the film. But Grandfather saw what could be done. He ordered blankets and mattresses to wrap the camera. That's where the camera blimp came from."

Get some blankets. Wrap them around the camera. That will deaden the noise." Using heavy blankets and makeshift belts, the crew enveloped the Mitchell camera. A different engineer took over and did a level test. "Well, I can still hear it," he said, "but it isn't nearly as loud." The microphone was still picking up the whir of the camera gate. "Send for quilts," said DeMille. "Send for a mattress." In a few minutes, three technicians were flopping around with bedding and springs like college boys on moving day. As the fourth layer was secured, a visitor arrived. Douglas Shearer had been the head of M-G-M's sound department for less than a year. He listened intently as the next test was made. This time the microphone picked up nothing but room tone. The camera was a little unwieldy, though. "It looked like a hippopotamus with the mumps," said DeMille.

"I can see what you want," said Shearer. He promised to work on the problem with John Arnold, the head of the camera department. In three days, Arnold had designed and delivered a "camera blimp," so called because it was a large silver case, hugging the camera with padding. The entire assembly could be mounted on a wheeled tripod, which would allow camera movement. While every other M-G-M director was being dominated by engineers, DeMille was restoring freedom to the medium.

To create the film's spectacular finale, DeMille drew on more resources. As written, the scene showed a coal mine caving in and trapping the film's principals. "The cave-in was tremendously difficult to rig up," recalled Leisen. "Working with that crude sound equipment was murder. There was no way you could dub in any sounds later; all the sound effects had to be recorded during the take." Conrad Nagel was impressed by DeMille's ingenuity. "DeMille remembered from his old stage days that when you wanted a roar of great thunder, you built a big trough backstage and rolled cannonballs down it. So they built one, and it was perfect."

Dynamite was the success that DeMille needed to start his stint at M-G-M. Other than a few inappropriate laughs at New York screenings, it was received as the thrilling entertainment

that it was, not because it talked but because it both talked and moved. "Cecil B. DeMille has emerged as a pioneer in effects," wrote Edwin Schallert in the *Los Angeles Times*. "He has an amazing grasp of the medium. You may rave at certain phases of the hokum plot that he presents, but the audible screen gives him the opportunity to disclose an entirely new bag of tricks. In unexpectedness and interest, *Dynamite* is a peak."

ABOVE AND OPPOSITE: DeMille's first film at M-G-M brought him into the orbit of the formidable art director Cedric Gibbons, a devotee of Art Deco. M-G-M had a full complement of Deco furnishings, so all Mitchell Leisen had to do was design settings for them. These scenes from *Dynamite* show Charles Bickford surveying Kay Johnson's bedroom; and a mirror framing Johnson in an Art Deco setting. • A closer view of the bed and mural. • DeMille demonstrates to Johnson how to hit Bickford with a perfume bottle.

THESE PAGES: Conrad Nagel recalled: "In *Dynamite* I'm the rich young socialite, Kay Johnson is a very social dame with millions of dollars, and Charlie Bickford is the coal miner. The climactic scene is a mine cave-in. Charlie, Kay, and I are trapped. We've got air for just so many hours. There's a concrete bulkhead blocking our way. It's the only way to get out. And we've got to get out by a certain time or we'll die. We find some dynamite. The dynamite has no caps to set it off. We can use a big sledge hammer instead. Now which one of us is going to swing the sledge hammer?"

MADAM SATAN AND THE SQUAW MAN

The 1920s were coming to a close. The most colorful, memorable, inane decade in America's short history was ending on a high note. Everybody had money, and Hollywood had more. Weekly movie attendance was 90 million—in a country with a population of 122 million. More than 75 percent of America's entertainment spending went to Hollywood. Talking pictures were making Hollywood obscenely rich, and the stock market was booming. Cecil B. DeMille played the market. Everyone did. It was easy. You bought shares on margin by putting 10 percent down and then paid off the rest in installments. In the spring of 1929, the worth of shares traded in a day hit an unprecedented $5 million. "The prosperity band wagon rolled along," wrote Frederick Lewis Allen. "The throttle was wide open and the siren was blaring."

DeMille rarely drank and did not smoke. He observed the ritual of an icy swim at dawn, followed by a cold shower. He was self-disciplined and temperate. Though the gay night life was not for him, his next film would be a catalog of pleasure seeking. Louis B. Mayer had been urging him to do a musical film. *The Broadway Melody* had just grossed $4.8 million, and audiences wanted music. "Everybody said, 'You must do a musical,'" recalled Katherine de Mille. "Everyone's making musicals!'" DeMille had not dealt with songs since *California*, the operetta he wrote and staged with Jesse Lasky nearly twenty years earlier.

In 1913 he saw a primitive flicker with the title *Madam Satan*. It stayed with him. He assigned Jeanie Macpherson the task of writing a musical to match that title.

Madam Satan was the story of a young wife whose prim ways send her husband on drunken sprees with a saucy showgirl. To win him back, the wife goes to a masquerade ball disguised as the infernal émigré. DeMille cast Kay Johnson as the wife; she was one of the reasons for *Dynamite*'s success. To write the music for this opus, DeMille considered Cole Porter, Oscar Hammerstein II, and Albert Ketèlbey, but none was available. He settled for middling tunesmiths Jack King and Clifford Grey, who worked with M-G-M's in-house composer Herbert Stothart.

On Tuesday, October 29, DeMille was in his office, dictating letters on this subject, when there was a commotion outside. People were yelling at each other, trying to get to the nearest telephone. DeMille paid no attention to it. It was not an earthquake. There was no shaking or rumble. There should have been. "The gigantic edifice," wrote Allen, "honeycombed with speculative credit, was breaking under its own weight." The stock market was crashing. But there was no sound when $30 billion evaporated.

OPPOSITE: In the spring of 1930, Cecil B. DeMille sat for a portrait by George Hurrell.

DeMille was on the boards of several banks. He had been warned. A month earlier, he had told Gladys Rosson that if a rush occurred, that she should sell, but at a half point above the market. In the panic of October 29, prices never stabilized. They plummeted. Rosson froze. DeMille lost $1 million. He did not chide her. The script of *Madam Satan* included a party on a dirigible. The party ends when the craft is struck by lightning, as if God were sticking a pin in the inflated balloon of the Roaring Twenties.

Some people wanted to stick pins in Hollywood. One of them was Father Daniel Lord, DeMille's advisor on *The King of Kings*. He saw (and heard) that talking films were taking license with the new technology, using rough or suggestive language, secure in the knowledge that local censor boards could not cut the film. It had no sound track. The sound came from a sixteen-inch acetate disc. Vitaphone was uncensorable, yet many felt that cuts were needed. "Plots had narrowed down to seduction and murder and illegitimate children and immoral women and rapacious men," wrote Lord. "Silent smut had been bad. Vocal smut cried to the censors for vengeance."

Hollywood paid little attention to its critics until Will Hays, the head of the Motion Picture Producers and Distributors of America (MPPDA), warned that Congress could enact federal censorship. There was too much to lose in 1929. A committee was formed to draft a document that would regulate the content of films, starting with each script. The committee included Father Lord; Martin Quigley, a Catholic publisher of film magazines; Irving Thalberg; and Colonel Jason S. Joy, a former Red Cross executive. Since 1927, Joy had functioned as a de facto censor in the MPPDA's Hollywood office, the Studio Relations Committee (SRC). On February 17, 1930, the studios ratified a "Production Code," and they agreed to submit both scripts and films to Joy for approval. DeMille would have a long relationship with the Code.

On February 22, DeMille gave his daughter Cecilia in marriage to Frank Calvin, the son of a railroad president. For all the upheavals in his business life, DeMille remained devoted to Constance and his children. He invited Katherine to play a bit part in *Madam Satan*, one of the wives of "Henry VIII" at the airborne masquerade ball. On March 3, the film went into production. Mitchell Leisen was working for the second time as a credited assistant director. "That one was hell," recalled Leisen. "Metro didn't have enough soundstages for all the pictures they were shooting, so each stage had three companies who worked consecutive eight hour shifts in it. We had to dismantle the entire set every night before we left, and then reassemble it as quickly as possible the next day."

Leisen was an extremely valuable employee, one who could read a blueprint and adjust an actress's hemline with equal skill. DeMille piled the work on him: huge dirigible sets, frantic schedules, long hours. Leisen bore it, along with the occasional outburst. Not everyone did. One day, DeMille yelled at the other assistant director, Cullen ("Hezi") Tate, and at Harold Rosson, the cameraman (and Gladys's brother). Both technicians walked off the set. "DeMille might raise holy hell on the set," said Leisen, "but often that was to put fear into the actor by criticizing me or the prop man. The minute we walked off the stage, he couldn't have been more charming. He'd even apologize for blowing his stack: 'There was nothing personal in that.' And I'd say, 'I know. Don't worry. I've been with you long enough to know that.'" Knowing it was not enough. "The strain was so great," said Leisen, "that I had a nervous breakdown and had to quit entirely for a while."

"I'm not worried about Mitch," DeMille told Katherine and her friend Natalie Visart. "He's tougher than anything. He'll be back."

"They were still shooting when the doctors let me come back and work an hour a day," said Leisen.

No one knew if DeMille's anger was displaced. He had reason to be frustrated. The script was not cohesive. The publicity department had failed to get as many placements in the fan magazines as his own department had in years past. *Photo-*

play magazine was particularly hostile to him. When he moved into his new office, the magazine ran one photo, accompanied by a snide caption. "This is the Imperial Throne Room," it said. "In other words, King Cecil B. DeMille's new office. In the foreground is the bench, unpadded, where supplicants await an audience with the Master. In the middle distance is the sanctum where his secretary puts them through the ritual and takes their fingerprints before admitting them to the Holy of Holies."

ABOVE: A Wilfred Buckland concept painting for *Madam Satan*.

The *New York Times* called *Madam Satan* "a strange conglomeration of unreal incidents." The *Los Angeles Times* said that "there is staginess about the result that casts aside anything approaching conviction." Even DeMille's colleagues disliked it. "It contains no semblance of reality," said Thalberg. Critics rejected its baroque conceits. DeMille's films required a willing suspension, not only of disbelief, but also of *un*belief, of disrespect, of disdain. His effects comprised powerful images, throbbing music, and fevered dialogue. Orchestrated by him, this was persuasive and transporting. Analyzed in the light of day, it made no sense. It was not meant to be analyzed. Critics insisted on analyzing it. It was in its own category, and there was no

Slave Market in front of End Balcony of Hanging Gardens —

convenient noun to describe it, so they inevitably used the term *hokum*, an imprecise and ultimately inaccurate term. But it stuck. And it was repeated, over and over. DeMille rankled at this. He took every occasion to respond. "Hokum," said DeMille, "is anything that glorifies good. It is the opposite of the vices."

> It is the fashion now to deride hokum. But the true things, the good things, will always live. The style in drama has changed but audiences have not. Today we dress our hokum in silks and satins, and still we love it. There is a saying. "No matter how thin you slice something or other, it is still something or other." Baloney? I used to think that hokum meant trickery, like that practiced by the old shell-game sharks at carnivals when

> I was a boy. Perhaps, to those who have grown up on Nietzsche and Freud, it is. Oh, I know the tendency is to ridicule the virtues now. It is easier than not to grow crude and blasphemous. I can speak a naughty word, and you can reply with a naughtier word. Simple. My picture is hokum. Beautiful hokum. It is the same cycle, over and over again. From Thaïs to Rain. From Why Change Your Wife? to Madam Satan. Hokum endures.

Hokum would endure. The vogue for talking-singing-dancing films did not. Although DeMille completed *Madam*

ABOVE: A Wilfred Buckland concept painting for *Madam Satan*.

Satan ahead of time and under budget, he was too late. Audiences were already sick of musicals. Not that *Madam Satan* had catchy tunes. It did have eye-popping spectacle and fantastic gowns by Adrian, captured in excellent photographs, but few of them were seen in print; the blackout continued. And, although the film previewed well, its cast did not appeal, and word of mouth killed it. *Madam Satan* barely earned its million-dollar cost.

By the end of 1930, when the box office was being tallied, DeMille could see that the problem was not entirely in his peculiar film. The country was feeling the chill of depression. The crash had been followed by smaller crashes, and the market kept sliding. Money tightened. Spending decreased. Businesses panicked. "Each employee thrown out of work decreased the potential buying power of the country," wrote Allen. By late 1930, business was 20 percent below normal, and five hundred banks had closed. Factories were closing. Breadlines were beginning to form on city streets. In early 1931, the film industry saw receipts drop. Studios began laying off employees and closing for weeks at a time.

DeMille had one project left in his M-G-M contract. What would it be? "I cannot find any inspiration at all in the type of pictures the producers want me to make," DeMille wrote Father Lord in January 1931. "They are in a state of panic and chaos. They rush for the bedspring and the lingerie the moment the phantom of empty seats rises to clutch them. I cannot find a producer who is willing to do anything but follow the mad rush for destruction." Macpherson, Coffee, and Janis reviewed story ideas with DeMille and came up with nothing. "I wonder if a sense of quiet desperation had anything to do with my decision to make *The Squaw Man* for a third time," wrote DeMille. He admitted desperation to no one, putting a brave face on his odd choice. "You don't throw away a Renoir after you've seen it once. You want to see a masterpiece time and again."

At this announcement, the sound of razzes could be heard from coast to coast. "Willy-nilly, the studios report plans for re-filming stories of all kinds," wrote Philip Scheuer. "From

M-G-M will come *The Squaw Man*. With television, three dimensions, and the 'smellies' just ahead, the chances for re-revival are simply elegant." *Photoplay* was just plain mean. "DeMille says he's so devoted to his *Squaw Man* that he wants to re-film it every ten years. Heigh-ho! Lackaday! The only consolation is that we'll be too old to see it or hear it!" The play's author had kind words for DeMille. "The greatest kick I get," said Edwin Milton Royle, "is the thought that I was lucky enough to have written something that has given employment to so many artists and their assistants through the years."

For location scenes, DeMille went to Hot Springs Junction in Arizona, which was not far from where he and Oscar Apfel had considered shooting in December 1913. The English manor scenes were made on a large interior set at M-G-M. DeMille devised some tricky angles for the scene in which the embezzlement is discovered. He knew as much about screen direction as anyone, but even he got crossed up occasionally. "When C. B. started breaking down the scene for over-the-shoulder shots, he'd reverse the angle and there'd be no set behind Warner Baxter. C. B. would be stuck! I'd be summoned from wherever I was to bail him out. I'd been setting the cameras for him at Metro. I would stage the action, which left him free to concentrate on the performing."

M-G-M directors like Clarence Brown were getting more camera movement in their films, even if it meant building an

CECIL B. DeMILLE

"I used to feel insulted when people called me 'The King of Hokum.' It began to dawn on me that those who use the term hokum do so to diminish the tender virtues of life. A scene of parents worrying over a sick child. That's hokum. Scenes of self-sacrifice are hokum. Mother love is hokum. In the last ten minutes of your life, the thing that will count is the extent to which you have developed hokum in your soul, this hokum which unthinking critics profess to despise."

elevator on wheels. In 1929, Universal had constructed a huge crane to lift the camera in the air. It was built for a Paul Leni film called *Broadway*. The crane was used again in 1930, by Lewis Milestone in *All Quiet on the Western Front* and by Tod Browning and Karl Freund in *Dracula*, but it was unwieldy. DeMille did not endear himself to production manager J. J. Cohn when he demanded that M-G-M design and build a crane for use on *The Squaw Man*. He got it, and even took it to Agoura for the scenes of Jim's cabin. To his list of innovations DeMille could add the camera crane, for while he was not the first to use one, he was the first to streamline and popularize it.

Photographic excellence could not save *The Squaw Man* from becoming another victim of the Depression; it failed. Mayer had socialized with DeMille, even been a guest on his yacht. When it came time to deliver the bad news to DeMille, he let the Boy Wonder do the dirty work. "I'm sorry, C. B.," said Thalberg. "There is just nothing here for you." DeMille had seen this coming. "I do not know whether M-G-M or I was more glad to see my contract come to an end." With his guest tenure over, DeMille found himself in an unaccustomed stance. "I could not get a job in Hollywood." After founding the industry and bringing $28 million to it, he was persona non grata. "There is a saying in Hollywood," wrote DeMille, "that you are just as good as your last picture." His last two had flopped, and *The Godless Girl* had, too. Forget *Dynamite*. Forget *The King of Kings*. *You are just as good as your last picture*. Doors were closing.

DeMille met with Lasky, hoping that Paramount would be open to a religious film. Surely that could overcome the Depression handicap. Lasky presented the proposal at several meetings. "I am very sorry," he told his old friend. "I could not put this over. I know you will also be disappointed." DeMille was more than disappointed when an entire industry turned its back on him. "I do not enjoy failure," said DeMille. "When Hollywood executives manifested their profound lack of interest in the obviously washed-up Cecil B. DeMille, Mrs. de Mille and I decided to look at the situation of motion pictures in Europe."

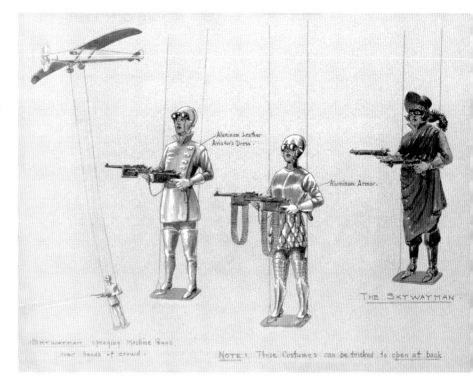

KAY JOHNSON

"Of course there is hokum in every picture. It is a necessary factor. Truth has to be doctored before it appears real through a camera. At the bottom of Mr. DeMille's hokum is an element of truth. That is why it becomes plausible to an audience."

CECILIA DE MILLE PRESLEY

"Some actors had trouble with DeMille because of the dialogue. Sometimes it was too flowery, too mannered. But it was part of his style. When you were in that theater, seeing it with all the color and pageantry, on that big canvas, it seemed to work."

ABOVE: A Wilfred Buckland design for *Madam Satan*. Only the uniform at left was used in the film.

OPPOSITE: The ball on the airship begins with "Ballet Mécanique," a futuristic montage choreographed by LeRoy Prinz. At center, dancing the role of "Electricity," is DeMille's colleague and friend Theodore Kosloff.

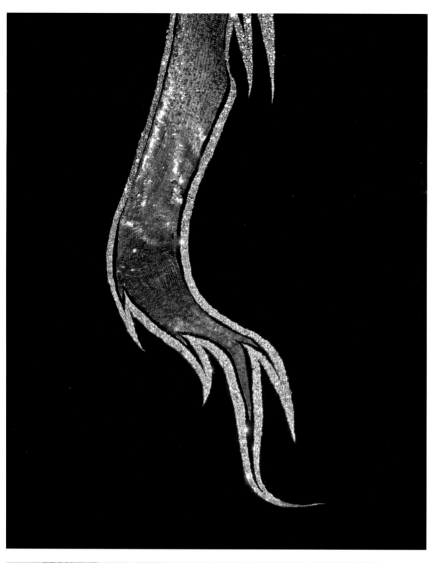

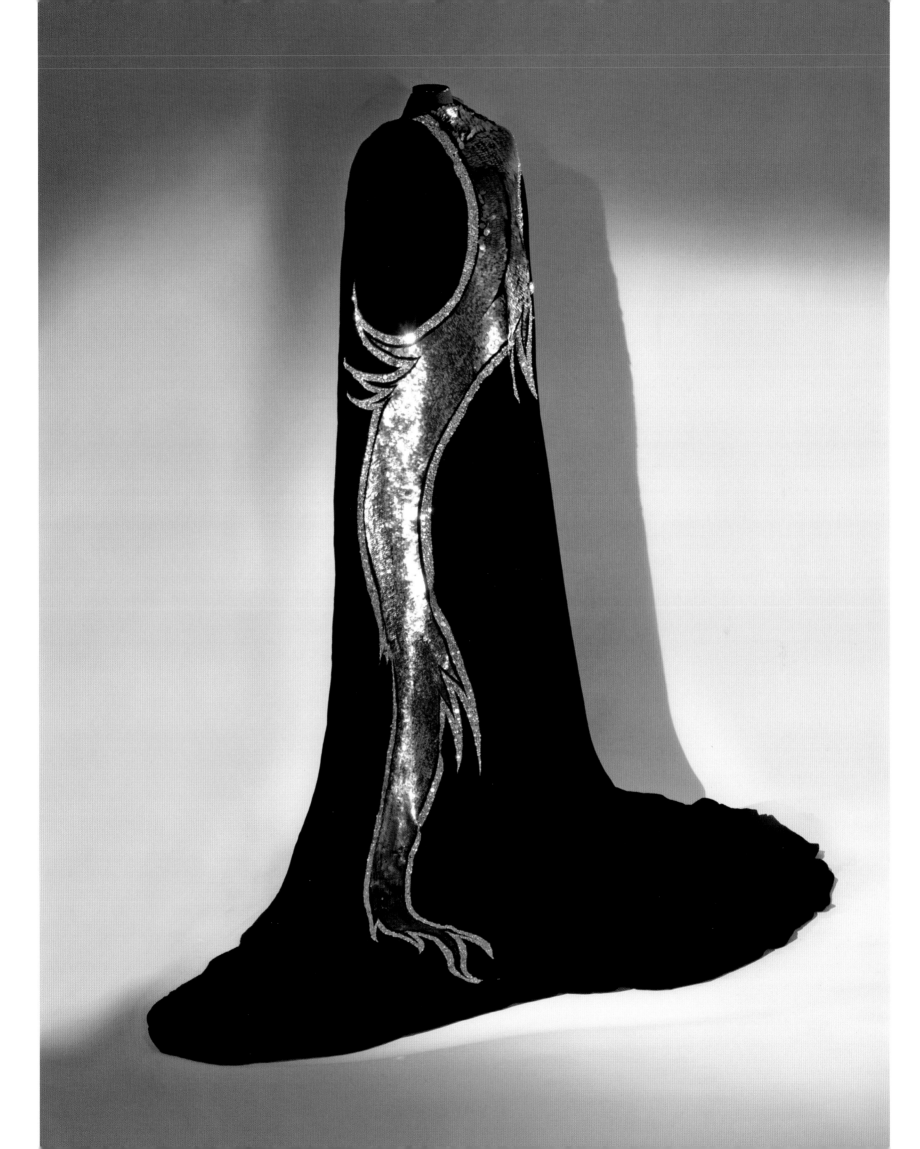

PAGE 170, CLOCKWISE FROM TOP LEFT: A detail of the restored garment. • The costume designed by Gilbert Adrian for *Madam Satan*. • The restored *Madam Satan* cape. Photograph by Mark A. Vieira. • The brilliance of Adrian's design can be seen in this photograph from *Madam Satan*.

OPPOSITE: Kay Johnson and Reginald Denny in *Madam Satan*.

ABOVE: In the 1931 M-G-M version of *The Squaw Man*, Lupe Velez played Naturich.

If DeMille was a great man, he surely had a woman standing behind him. "Mrs. de Mille was vice-president of Cecil B. DeMille Productions in more than name; she took an active part in all business affairs." In this time of introspection, DeMille turned to family. In August 1931, he and Constance embarked on a world tour. Before they sailed on the SS *Île de France*, DeMille spent a few days in New York. The Depression was impossible to ignore. "The gloom in New York is more better expressed by the bitter looks of the men on the park benches then in the 'speak easys,'" DeMille penciled in a small journal. "Though for once the upper class is as gloomy as the lower." The tour took in London, Belgium, and the Netherlands (to visit

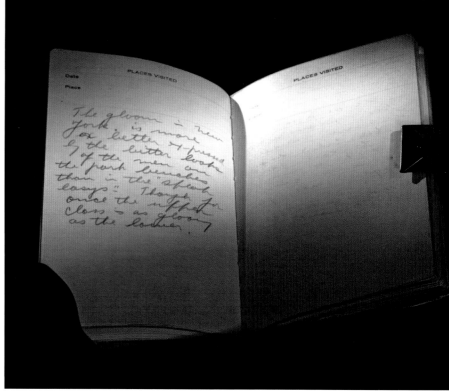

the church where his forbear Anthony de Mil had been married in 1653). Then Cecil and Constance, with Theodore Kosloff as guide, entered the Soviet Union. "I talked with the people," wrote DeMille. "I found drama and comedy and tragedy every foot of the way." He did not find a film deal, there or in Germany, France, or England. After passing through Egypt and the Holy Land, he returned to the States. He arrived in New York on November 24 and met with Lasky again. Paramount was in trouble, trying to pay mortgages on a huge theater chain. It was better off than RKO Radio and Universal; they were in receivership.

DeMille returned to Hollywood on December 6, contemplating his next move. When Paramount celebrated its eighteenth birthday on December 30, he was not in a jovial mood. His new *Squaw Man* was a miserable flop. The intelligent Edwin Schallert wrote an article about it in the *Los Angeles Times*. "Will Erstwhile Kings Reshine?" praised the film. "DeMille has always known what the public wanted, how to catch their fancy with glitter. He has been a superior actor's director." Schallert's opinion was not shared by the executives whom DeMille visited. Most of them had been helped by him; no one was willing to help him. "I couldn't get a job," recalled DeMille. "Nobody would even listen. I was just like one of the Egyptian mummies we'd seen, a curiosity, something rather boring. I was through. I was dead. I was just dead."

ABOVE, LEFT: DeMille introduces Eleanor Boardman, who plays Lady Diana in the 1931 *Squaw Man*, to Winifred Kingston, who played Lady Diana in the 1914 *Squaw Man*.

ABOVE, RIGHT: DeMille carried this journal with him on the world tour he took with Mrs. de Mille in 1931. Photograph by Mark A. Vieira.

OPPOSITE: Warner Baxter and Lupe Velez in *The Squaw Man*.

CHAPTER 5

THE BEST SHOW IN TOWN

THE SIGN OF THE CROSS

Paramount had a snappy slogan. "If it's a Paramount picture, it's the best show in town!" The slogan could have been: "If there's a show in town, it's probably Paramount." Adolph Zukor had gone on a buying spree. The company owned more than three thousand theaters, including the Balaban and Katz chain. After buying the Publix theater chain in 1930, Paramount changed its name to Paramount-Publix. "Zukor was obsessed with acquiring real estate," says Betty Lasky. "He was driven. It meant power." Zukor paid for these properties partly with stock. As the Depression worsened, the stock lost its value, but its original price had to be honored, and mortgages had to be paid. The theaters became millstones. Even so, Paramount showed a profit of $6 million in 1931.

Jesse Lasky and B. P. Schulberg ran Paramount's West Coast production. The company was rich with talent. It had directors like Josef von Sternberg, Ernst Lubitsch, and Rouben Mamoulian, and stars like Maurice Chevalier, Jeanette MacDonald, Gary Cooper, and Marlene Dietrich. The studio should have been turning out hits. It was not. By 1932, its films were too sophisticated for the Midwest and South, where most of its theaters sat, and it was feeling the depression. "The Great Depression was more than a matter of work and bread," wrote Cecil B. DeMille. "It was a national mood—gray, discouraged, sometimes sullen. People who are psychologically depressed

may be helped by going to the movies. People who are economically depressed cannot afford to buy tickets." In the first quarter of 1932, Paramount found itself in the red.

Sam Katz, the president of Publix, castigated Zukor and Schulberg for not supplying the films his theaters needed, and he accused Sid Kent, Paramount's sales manager, of underselling them. Katz took action. He called in shareholders Albert Lasker, the "father of American advertising," and John Hertz, the semiretired founder of the Yellow Cab Company. They secured $13 million in bailout money and forced Zukor, Lasky, and Schulberg to slash both film budgets and salaries. It was obvious that beyond the emergency measures, Katz, Hertz, and Lasker wanted control. "Our house is invaded by vermin," wailed Zukor's son, Eugene.

"I'm getting out of this mess before they shove me out," Kent told Lasky. "I've been offered the presidency of the Fox

OVERLEAF: Charles Laughton as Nero dominates this scene from Cecil B. DeMille's 1932 classic *The Sign of the Cross*. Ian Keith stands to his right. At his left is an actress doubling for Claudette Colbert, who had completed all her scenes and gone on to another film.

OPPOSITE: Paramount Pictures was on the verge of bankruptcy in 1932. To keep it solvent and restore DeMille's career, *The Sign of the Cross* had to succeed. Charles Laughton was one of its many attributes.

Film Corporation. You'd better come with me." Lasky was unwilling to leave the company he had helped found. Kent decamped to Fox. Lasky held on. "The pioneers get into trouble sooner or later," said DeMille. "Then come the harpies and the bankers to feed on them. They try to apply methods of financing to the creation of drama. Then comes a period of chaos, with neither money nor ideas. And they fall to earth in a bleeding wreck."

Because of his friendship with Lasky, DeMille was privy to this turmoil. He formulated a plan. In 1895, Beatrice de Mille had taken him to see a play called *The Sign of the Cross*. It starred Wilson Barrett, who had written it to answer the atheist Robert Ingersoll. Like the popular novel *Quo Vadis*, the play retold the fable of a Roman prefect who falls in love with a proscribed Christian girl, while Nero and Poppaea pull the strings from above. The play made a deep impression on young Cecil.

The Sign of the Cross had been filmed in 1914. "It starred William Farnum," said DeMille. "It was pretty terrible, even for a Famous Players picture." Ten years later, Zukor sold the rights to Mary Pickford. DeMille approached her about *The Sign of the Cross*. If he filmed it, he could complete a trilogy. "*The Ten Commandments* was the giving of the law," he explained. "*The King of Kings* was the interpretation of the law, the fulfillment of its promise. *The Sign of the Cross* will be the preservation of the law, the struggle of humanity to live up to it." Pickford wanted $50,000 for the old warhorse. DeMille countered with $30,000. Pickford held tight. DeMille offered $35,000. Then he waited. Pickford finally agreed to $38,000. DeMille got the property. He needed a producing partner—and was willing to put up half the money. Lasky pitched him to Paramount. No one was interested.

Then the sun rose behind the Paramount peak. At a meeting in March 1932, Schulberg repeated DeMille's offer, then yelled at his confreres. "You gentlemen are all crazy! You've got here one of the greatest minds in the industry. He built Paramount with Jess once before. Maybe he can do it again. Grab

him!" Zukor was hesitant. He authorized a deal for only one film. DeMille could return to the studio that he had cofounded, but the terms were stiff. He would have to make his million-dollar project for $650,000, and Paramount was willing to proffer only half of that. He would have to borrow the balance. Paramount would advance him $50,000 against future royalties that would not be charged to the negative cost. From that DeMille would be paid a modest $14,322 in cash with $9,678 deferred. For a director of his stature, this was a humiliating drop in salary. Zukor was still suspicious of DeMille's staff; he was not to bring Jeanie Macpherson or Anne Bauchens. Worst of all, Paramount required him to submit to a supervisor of a know-nothing newsreel producer named Emanuel Cohen. DeMille agreed to the terms. Working with Lasky was a happy prospect, and they could count on Schulberg's support. Neil McCarthy began formalizing the deal.

DeMille asked Mitchell Leisen to return as art director. "He had paid me $800 a week at M-G-M," recalled Leisen. "Now it was the Depression and I got a fast $100." Once the bank loans had been secured, DeMille instructed Leisen and production manager Roy Burns to keep him informed of the bank balance, right up to the minute. As he was moving to Paramount, there was a shakeup in the executive offices.

The tremors began in late April. At a stockholders' meeting in New York, contracts were renewed for Zukor, Hertz, Lasker, and Cohen, but not for Lasky or Schulberg. Admitting a deficit of $20 million, Zukor said, "My pride is broken. My heart is torn. I want to rebuild the company to which I have given my life." In a few weeks, his colleagues would learn what he meant by rebuilding.

On May 5, Schulberg was the keynote speaker at a Paramount sales convention in Chicago. He engaged his audience,

OPPOSITE: DeMille filmed Nero (Charles Laughton) burning Rome at the Paramount Ranch. This was DeMille's second film with a camera crane. He accomplished breathtaking shots with it—and looked impressive riding it.

confirming the company's strength. Then DeMille spoke, enthusing about *The Sign of the Cross*. When Cohen praised Schulberg's leadership, DeMille knew something was up. In New York a few days later, he asked Lasky to hire Charles Laughton. "I had just seen Laughton in *Payment Deferred* at the St. James's Theatre in London," wrote DeMille. "I knew that he was the only man to play Nero." Lasky wired Zukor in Chicago, asking for approval. When he received a reply, he showed it to DeMille. "Laughton is nothing like Nero," it said. "Not acceptable in any way. We do not wish Laughton for Nero." DeMille knew what this meant: "They were going to question me but hit at Jesse. They could say to the board of directors, 'Look what Lasky does. We must get rid of him.'"

DeMille refused to accept this. "I'm going to engage Laughton," he told Lasky. "If Paramount doesn't want anything to do with him, all right. But they have to distribute the picture, so they have to advertise him. After that, they can throw him out and they can throw me out again, but I don't care. That's what I'm going to do." DeMille knew that Laughton was not the issue. Lasky was.

On May 17, a board meeting removed both Lasky and Schulberg from their positions. "I was forbidden to set foot inside the very walls I had ordered built," wrote Lasky. "At long last I knew how Sam Goldwyn and Cecil DeMille must have felt when they had been eased out of the company the three of us had launched." Schulberg tried to put a brave face on his firing. "Father joked that he'd been the victim of a palace revolution," wrote his son Budd. "He said he was lucky to be out from under. And now he'd be like DeMille, an independent producer, with his own bungalow and staff." Without Schulberg and Lasky to watch out for him, DeMille was on shaky ground. And who should take Schulberg's job but the eminently unqualified Cohen. *The Sign of the Cross* was a crucial project for DeMille, one of the four most important projects he had done—or would do. Faced with these challenges, he called up the courage of the Champion Driver. And he cracked the whip.

To adapt *The Sign of the Cross*, DeMille engaged two Paramount writers, playwright Sidney Buchman and veteran screenwriter Waldemar Young. He then hired an artist named Harold Miles to do what Dan Sayre Groesbeck had done earlier. "I have to deal with a dozen departments," said DeMille. "If I tell them I want a red barn, they'll come up with twelve shades of red." Once DeMille approved the concept sketch, Leisen and the draftsmen could start on the sets. There were fifteen, many more than in DeMille's last film, and a big story to tell. He needed to show the secret world of the hunted Christians, the decadence of the imperial palace, and the brutality of the amphitheater. How could he do this on a limited budget?

"Boy, the pennies were pinched!" recalled Leisen. "DeMille had seen some spectacular German picture in Europe and he just couldn't understand how they got so much production for so little money. I said, 'We can do it too, if you just shoot what I give you and don't try to do anything more.'" Working with cameraman Karl Struss, Leisen devised ways to get epic effects without epic costs. "I used every trick I could think of," said Leisen. The fire scene could be accomplished by building a palace balcony on the Paramount ranch and using forced perspective for a row of burning buildings behind it. The arena establishing shot could be a combination of full set, miniatures, prismatic lens effects, and matte shots.

MITCHELL LEISEN

"I owe Mr. DeMille everything I ever learned about making pictures. The most important thing of all is the power of concentration, of never deviating from your objective. Once he started on a project, he concentrated on that and thought of nothing else. Through him, I learned how to be the same way."

OPPOSITE, CLOCKWISE FROM TOP LEFT: DeMille posed with a concept painting made by Harold Miles. • DeMille cast Charles Laughton over Paramount's objections. Photograph by Otto Dyar. • How DeMille recreated the burning of Rome.

"DeMille asked me if I would do the costumes, too," recalled Leisen. "I said, 'Yes, for an additional financial consideration.' He gave me twenty-five more a week." DeMille was taking a cut; so could everyone else. This did not apply to stars. If DeMille had learned a lesson at M-G-M, it was that stars sold tickets. Fredric March was riding high on Mamoulian's *Dr. Jekyll and Mr. Hyde*. DeMille agreed to pay him $2,100 a week to play Marcus Superbus, the Roman prefect. Charles Laughton would receive $1,250 a week for Nero. After testing Miriam Hopkins, Ann Harding, and Loretta Young for the Christian girl Mercia, DeMille borrowed Elissa Landi from Fox Film, possibly because she was of noble Italian extraction. He interviewed the fading silent stars Norma Talmadge and Pola Negri for the plum role of Poppaea. Neither one filled the bill.

"On my way out of the executive offices at Paramount one day," said DeMille, "I met a young actress named Claudette Colbert. She'd not done much, just playing pansy roles." Colbert's most recent was as George M. Cohan's daughter in *The Phantom President*. "I was bored with these roles," recalled Colbert. "Because I happened to look like a lady, that's all they wanted me to play."

"I think they've got you wrong," DeMille told her. "You should not be playing these little girls. To me you look like the wickedest woman in the world. Would you like to play her?"

"I'd love to!" replied Colbert.

"Claudette's test was the shortest on record," said DeMille. He brought her and Fredric March to a soundstage. "You harlot!" said March.

"I love you," said Colbert with a half smile and a shrug.

"That's enough," said DeMille from the camera. "You have the part."

Poppaea may have been the wickedest woman in first-century Rome, but Barrett's play soft-pedaled her sins. DeMille's script made her pointedly lustful. "We modern women can learn a lot from Poppaea," Colbert told an interviewer. "We go about, demanding our rights, arguing with a man for what we want.

But Poppaea let down her hair, perfumed her body, and arrayed herself in her most daring costumes for his pleasure. Then she did whatever she pleased." Colbert's description only hinted at the wickedness DeMille intended.

At the SRC, Jason Joy and his staff were reeling from an onslaught of sin. "There seems to be a real and distressing tendency at Paramount to go for the sex stuff on a heavy scale," SRC censor Lamar Trotti wrote Will Hays. "Talk about pictures having to have 'guts' and about having to do this or that to make a little money to pay salaries is too frequently heard." As if to calm the censors, Emanuel Cohen spoke to the *Los Angeles Times*. "We have gone as far with sex as we are likely to go," he said. "The public likes a touch of the spiritual in times like these. *The Sign of the Cross* should be the answer."

Because of DeMille's prominence, Joy would review *The Sign of the Cross* himself. Joy had helped DeMille get *Madam Satan* past a Midwest censor board, prompting a thank-you note. "Hurrah for you and the Ohio censors!" wrote DeMille. "Let Joy be unconfined!" Joy was a reasonable man, trying to find a middle ground between the requirements of the Code and the artistic license of America's sixth-largest industry. It was not an easy job. DeMille's script could have been a shock to his system. The film was to start shooting on July 11, and Joy received the script on July 3. He approved it on July 5. His only advice to DeMille was not to shoot the scene of a gorilla

OPPOSITE, CLOCKWISE FROM TOP LEFT: A Roman mob attacks two men suspected of being Christians. DeMille allowed still photographer William Thomas time to compose this image. • On August 10, 1932, Fredric March rushed from Paramount to M-G-M in full Roman costume to attend Norma Shearer's birthday party on the set of *Smilin' Through*. Also present were (from left) cameraman Lee Garmes, actor Leslie Howard (in elderly makeup), and producer Irving Thalberg, Shearer's husband. • This angle shows DeMille directing a scene. Cameraman Karl Struss is at his left. The red gauze filters that Struss used to soften the shot are visible on the camera. • In the scene, Marcus Superbus (Fredric March) is attracted to Mercia (Elissa Landi), even though he thinks she is a Christian.

approaching a naked girl tied to a post. Joy said that the film's message of religious tolerance warranted the depiction of various sins, but such depiction might cause problems with regional censor boards. (The Code had been written not only to keep innocent minds from being corrupted, but also to keep release prints from being butchered.)

DeMille got in touch with Father Daniel Lord and asked him to read *The Sign of the Cross*. "I had loved that old melodrama in my boyhood in Chicago," wrote Lord. "When Mr. DeMille decided to film it, I congratulated him." Lord was not as liberal as Joy. "You must not make your Christians into plaster saints who are dull, plodding, and uninspiring," Lord wrote DeMille. "When your pagans are attractive, warm-blooded, alive human beings and are modern and almost night-clubbish, they make sin look as fascinating as it often seems to be."

The start date of *The Sign of the Cross* was pushed to July 18 because Fredric March was finishing *Smilin' Through* with Norma Shearer at M-G-M. The film ran over another week, so Irving Thalberg paid DeMille $7,459.00 for lost time. On July 25, ancient Rome came to life. After five months of preparation, DeMille was ready. He was eager, fit, and focused. He had to be. A great deal was riding on this project, not only a debt of $325,000 but also his future in Hollywood. The first scenes were shot on a Roman street. DeMille had gotten poor publicity at M-G-M; at Paramount he was constantly visited by journalists. "A DeMille set is recognizable almost before one comes to it," wrote Edwin Schallert in the *Los Angeles Times*. "There were throngs of extras, a veritable pageant of many-colored costumes. Donkeys, vegetables, a bread shop, and a wine shop. All these

CECIL B. DeMILLE

"I will always resist, as far as I am able, the claim of any individual or group to the right of censorship. When opposition to *The Sign of the Cross* began to swell, I determined to resist it."

were part of a Roman street where soldiers cast lots, bartering the lives of early Christians to turn over to Nero.

Since announcing the new production, DeMille had received hundreds of letters from unemployed players. Extra work paid $10 a day [$300 in 2014]. DeMille rode hard on the casting department to be sure that players whom he had promised work were indeed called. "Or else I will not shoot," he said. He also put his foot down with middle management. The secretary assigned to him was so eager to leave for the day that she locked him out of his new office. He replaced her with his preferred Florence Cole. Then he had trouble with another department. "The head cutter George Arthur had a bitter dislike for me," said DeMille. "I didn't know him but he hated me. He said he wouldn't let Annie Bauchens come in with me to cut *The Sign of the Cross*. He said I had to take a cutter named Alexander Hall. After the second day of shooting, Hall rushed to Cohen."

"For God's sake," said Hall, "let me go anywhere. Let me die. Just get me away from this guy." Cohen let Hall go, and he soon became a director. "So Annie Bauchens came in," recalled DeMille. "I put it in my contract that she should cut every one of my pictures."

After the first week, DeMille had a problem with upper management. Cohen sent for him. "Cecil," he said from behind his desk, "I hear that everything you've done has to be retaken."

"Manny, I never have to do retakes."

"Well, George Arthur told me that some of the men who have seen your stuff say that it's so bad it's funny."

"I don't think they're quite right on that, Manny. You'd better let Annie Bauchens put a few scenes together and then we'll have somebody from outside the studio come in and see it. Get Adolph's brother-in-law Al Kaufman to come and look."

"All right, Cecil. We'll do that. But remember. You're on trial with this picture."

OPPOSITE: In another DeMille bathtub scene, Poppaea (Claudette Colbert) bathes in asses' milk.

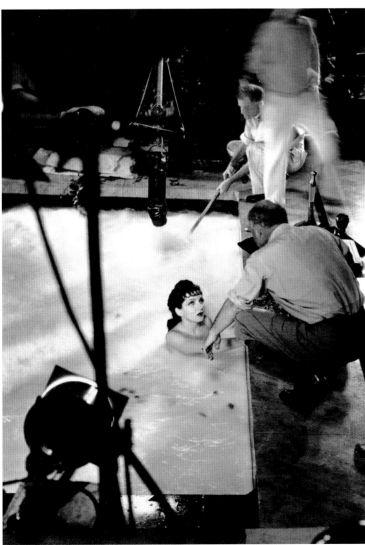

The review of the first-week footage took place shortly thereafter. The scenes showed March breaking up a riot with a whip. After the lights came up, Kaufman turned to Cohen. "What the hell's the matter with you, Manny? This is some of the greatest stuff ever made."

"Oh, well," said Cohen. "I suppose it's all right then."

"Manny was my greatest trial," DeMille said later. "Perhaps Manny found me something of a trial, too. But I had a picture to make. And I wanted it right."

Getting it right with a daunting schedule and a restricted budget meant that DeMille had to delegate more authority than usual. Burns, Struss, and Leisen each did a masterly job. DeMille was lucky to have Struss again. No other cameraman in Hollywood could have given *The Sign of the Cross* its unique look.

"I shot the whole black-and-white picture through bright red gauze," recalled Struss. "Gauze wasn't much used then, as it had been in the silent period. We'd gone over to diffusion disks. I used gauze throughout, to give a feeling of a world remembered."

DeMille was very lucky to have Leisen at his side. If Leisen had been only a superb art director, or a skilled costume

ABOVE: DeMille used a moving camera, dialectical montage, and contrapuntal sound to create a scene of a Christian child being tortured.

OPPOSITE, LEFT TO RIGHT: Arthur Hohl portrayed Titus, a fictional Christian leader. Photograph by William Thomas. • Elissa Landi was loaned by the Fox Film Corporation. Photograph by Otto Dyar.

designer, or a gifted assistant director, he would have been a precious asset. To have all three in one person was nothing short of miraculous, and a miracle was what DeMille needed. While he was shooting scenes in the Christian home, Leisen went off to look at the arena. On another day while DeMille was at the Paramount ranch, Leisen blocked the scene in which Marcus follows Mercia to a well of pure water and flirts with her as she tries to go up a stone stairway. Leisen designed the scene so that when Marcus gains an advantage over Mercia, he is above her on the stairs, but when she regains control, she is above him. When DeMille returned to the set, he shot the scene as Leisen had choreographed it.

DeMille made sure that the Christian girl was always shown with symbolically pure water. Poppaea was introduced with milk, but not in a glass. Reverting to type, DeMille showed her bathing in a marble pool filled with the milk of braying asses. "Poppaea bathing in asses' milk is a historic incident," said DeMille. "She bathed in asses' milk every day."

"That milk bath was really quite funny," recalled Colbert. "But you didn't make jokes with C. B. To him it was important that everything be absolutely correct. He was very serious about that, and about giving the public what it wanted." The milk bath was funny in principle; getting it on film was not. It was scheduled for August 3, but completion of *The Phantom President* held up Colbert, and the bathtub set was mistakenly struck. It had to be reconstructed, and the scene moved to August 16. "It was real powdered milk," said Leisen. "DeMille wanted the milk to just barely cover Claudette's nipples. I had her stand in the empty pool the day before and I measured her to get the level just right. When we shot it, we had compressed air blowing up from the bottom to make it foamy, and she said, 'Ooh, it tickles!'"

On September 8, DeMille began shooting the amphitheater sequence. That he was able to mount a set piece of this magnitude for less than $60,000 was a tribute to his imagination, technical skill, and shrewd management. Once more, Leisen did

the apparently impossible, turning slices of sets into enveloping vistas. "The arena was a miniature," recalled Leisen. "We built several flights of stairs with ramps at each level so the people walked in and that was all. As the crowd entered the arena, we craned straight down the side of the set. There was nothing on either side of the arches." Likewise, the burning of Rome was accomplished with the proverbial movie magic. The *Los Angeles Times* reported:

> *Thirty miles from Hollywood, at Paramount's ranch in the foothills of the Santa Monica Mountains, history's most famous conflagration was repeated when a man turned on a gas valve. Gas pipes running through small replicas of Roman structures gave the blaze a quick start. Before the fascinated eyes of hundreds of workmen, flames burst out among the buildings, great billows of smoke rolled skyward, and Nero played. Charles Laughton, armed with a lyre, or "fidicula," sang an ancient Roman ditty while the flames illumined a face that shone with maniacal ecstasy.*

After this, DeMille returned to the Paramount lot to shoot sequences that would lead him into new territory.

Although *Manslaughter* included an orgy scene with a brief shot of two women kissing, that was as far as DeMille had gone with "sex perversion." *The Sign of the Cross* would go further. It would be a festival of excess in a pagan province, with Leisen as its all-too-willing guide. Leisen lived an unconventional lifestyle; he was married to Sandra Gale, an opera singer, but was living with Eddie Anderson, a pilot. He no doubt knew about the

recent scandal involving the bisexual director Edmund Goulding. An orgy in September had gotten out of control and injured two women. Drawing on Hollywood's private life, Leisen enhanced the film with picaresque details. Shots of couples fondling and osculating during the orgy scene were far more provocative than anything previously shown in a major studio

OPPOSITE: Mitchell Leisen designed both this set and Claudette Colbert's costume. "Making the costumes for Claudette was a real pleasure," said Leisen. "She has just about the most beautiful figure I've ever seen. I slit her skirts right up to the hip to show her marvelous legs. She didn't have a stitch on underneath." Leisen also set up the scene for DeMille, so that every cut showed a fresh angle.

ABOVE, LEFT TO RIGHT: An Otto Dyar portrait of Fredric March. • An Otto Dyar portrait of Claudette Colbert.

film. There was "The Naked Moon," performed by an exotic named Joyzelle Joyner, in an exhibition of Sapphic seduction that promised to go the limit. And there was Charles Laughton as Nero, who flew in the face of DeMille's interpretation.

"DeMille visualized Nero as the menace in the film," said Elsa Lanchester, Laughton's wife. "Charles thought him merely funny. DeMille was shocked by the idea. He had old-fashioned ideas of villains and heroes."

"Nero was one of the wickedest men who ever lived," DeMille insisted. "Look how he treated the Christians."

"After a long argument with DeMille," said Lanchester, "Charles was allowed to give Nero a preciousness which he felt would make the orgies more evil." Laughton typically tortured himself into becoming a character for each film, but this one was different. It subsumed him. "Nero was nuts," Laughton told a reporter. "I play him straight." He also played him as a triple-jointed voluptuary, a thumb-sucking psychopath.

Back at the arena, DeMille was shooting the last of the grisly scenes in the sand. He was still checking with Burns. "Let me know when we run out of money," said DeMille. "I won't spend one penny more."

DeMille wanted to contrast the shot of Christians climbing the steps to the arena with a shot of lions running up their own steps, eager to attack. Instead of charging, the lions lay down and groomed themselves. "Listen!" said DeMille to Melvin Koontz, the trainer. "This is costing a frightful lot of money. When are those lions going up?"

"Lions don't know anything about that," said Koontz, "They don't go up stairs."

"Well," said DeMille, "these lions are going up these stairs!" With that he seized a chair and a whip and began swearing and yelling at the recumbent beasts. Startled, they rose and backed away. He continued his advance. They began climbing the stairs, turning to roar at him. Other than the odd offscreen look, the scene worked.

Out on the sand, Leisen had prepared dummies of Christians made of lamb carcasses. The lions would not eat them. "We couldn't get the lions to do anything," said Leisen. "They just walked around as if they were saying, 'What have you been doing since our last picture together?'" Koontz and his staff did more goading. They finally had to don Christian costumes and wrestle with the lions. The extras who were dressed as

ELSA LANCHESTER

"Charles [Laughton] and I ate in the Paramount commissary while he was in *The Sign of the Cross*. If we saw a bunch of clean-shaven, brutal men with hair on their chests, we knew they were Romans. If we saw a lot of weak, kindly old gentlemen with staffs and long white beards, we were safe in saying those were Christians. DeMille made the difference very marked, perhaps so the lions wouldn't eat the wrong people."

Christians were terrified, and not only of teeth. "This is an outrage!" DeMille shouted at Koontz. "Your goddamned lions are urinating on my martyrs!"

Time was running out. "We were in the arena," said Leisen, "with pygmies being slaughtered, when Roy came up to us and said, 'We've just used up the budget. You haven't got a dime.' DeMille yelled, 'Cut,' and we stopped right then and there. We didn't even finish that day." That was September 25. Unfortunately for the legend, DeMille did shoot a few more days, running the budget up to $694,000. Even so, he had made a film that looked like a million.

The Sign of the Cross had to be approved by the SRC before it could be released. Jason Joy reviewed it on November 15. James Wingate, the former New York censor, was there, too, learning the ropes. Joy had accepted the job of story editor at Fox Film. "The Code was not working," recalled SRC staffer Geoffrey Shurlock. "It had no teeth, and Jason was not about to spend his life fighting a losing battle."

The Code prohibited "dances which suggest sexual actions, whether performed solo or with two or more, and which are intended to excite." Joyzelle's dance fit that description, yet Joy chose not to censor it. "Ordinarily we would have been concerned about those portions of the dance sequence in which the Roman dancer executes the 'Kootch' Movement," wrote Joy and Wingate. "But since the director obviously used the dance to show the conflict between paganism and Christianity, we are agreed that there is justification for its use under the Code." Joy was known to excuse infractions if a film was the work of a serious director, not a middling effort with sexy elements tacked on to make it marketable. He was sufficiently impressed with *The Sign of the Cross* to see its sensational scenes in context. DeMille was fortunate.

The next screening was an industry preview. This did not go as well, at least in DeMille's estimation. The film began with the scene of Nero lolling and writhing as he burns Rome. No one was prepared for Laughton's outrageous interpretation.

It made the camp performers at the Ship Café in Venice look restrained. "The audience howled with laughter," reported *Photoplay*. "Rolled right out into the aisles. Wailed hysterically on one another's shoulders. Blasé Hollywood simply went wild." DeMille was furious. "Well, you sure spoiled everything," he said to Laughton. "They were all laughing at you."

"But I wanted them to laugh at me."

"What can you play after this? What do you *want* to play?"

"I would love to play *you*, Mr. DeMille."

DeMille threw back his head and laughed.

The next screening was the New York premiere on November 30. DeMille was there. It was a triumph, even though audience members screamed during the arena scenes. The reviews were excellent. "The old master returns to form with a sure-fire hit of magnificent proportions," wrote Norbert Lusk, the New York correspondent for the *Los Angeles Times*. "Surely DeMille has never staged a spectacle more stately or powerful than his arena sequence nor touched such spiritual splendor as when his hero and heroine walk hand in hand to their death." *Variety* was more pragmatic. "This picture is going to stir up some two-sided sentiment wherever it is shown, much of it being the boldest censor bait ever attempted in a picture." As the film began an audacious road show—reserved-seat tickets at $2.00 when people could not afford ten cents—there came a firestorm of controversy that rivaled the torching of Rome. *The Sign of the Cross* was a hot topic.

Christian Reisner, a Methodist Episcopal minister and the author of *God's Power for Me*, attacked the film. "It is repellant and nauseating to every thinking Christian," he wrote. "It endeavors to get a lot of lewd scenes and sex-appeal exhibitions on the screen and then dresses the whole with a cheap and unhistorical hodge-podge of incidents from sacred Christian martyrdom. This picture will cheapen and dishonor the sacred emblem, the cross."

There were angry comments from other Protestant writers, but most of the condemnation was Catholic. "This film, with

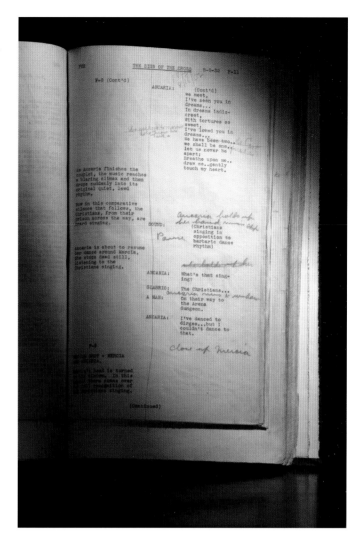

CLAUDETTE COLBERT

"To us, even then, a lot of DeMille's ideas were corny. But I certainly don't think you can call him a phony. He truly believed in what he was doing. When we did the scene with the Christians being eaten by the lions, he really suffered."

ABOVE: The revised script dated August 8, 1932, includes the lyrics to "The Naked Moon," the song used in a controversial dance scene. Photograph by Mark A. Vieira.

OVERLEAF: The wicked Ancaria (Joyzelle Joyner) performs "The Naked Moon." "It was an alluring dance," wrote DeMille. "Dramatically, it had to be, to bring out by contrast the greater strength and purity of Mercia's faith. But some thought it too alluring."

its sadistic cruelty, its playing up of Roman lust and debauchery and crime, is intolerable," wrote DeMille's adviser, Father Lord. Cleveland Bishop Joseph Schrembs called the film a "damnable hypocrisy." *Jesuit America* magazine called Joyzelle's dance "the most unpleasant bit of footage ever passed by the Hollywood censors." Catholic publisher Martin Quigley wrote: "This scene becomes an incident liable to an evil audience effect."

DeMille had taken a chance in making the film. Would the censor boards slash it to ribbons? After a few anxious weeks, reports came in to the SRC. Not one board had cut the so-called "lesbian dance." The few who did cut the film concentrated on alligators, apes, and asses' milk.

OPPOSITE, CLOCKWISE FROM TOP LEFT: Colbert as Poppaea. Photograph by William Thomas. • Laughton as Nero. Photograph by William Thomas. • A Harold Miles rendering of Nero's court.

ABOVE: Nero's court, as designed by Leisen.

OVERLEAF: In the Roman amphitheater, a gladiator (John Carradine) speaks: "Hail Caesar! We who are about to die salute thee!"

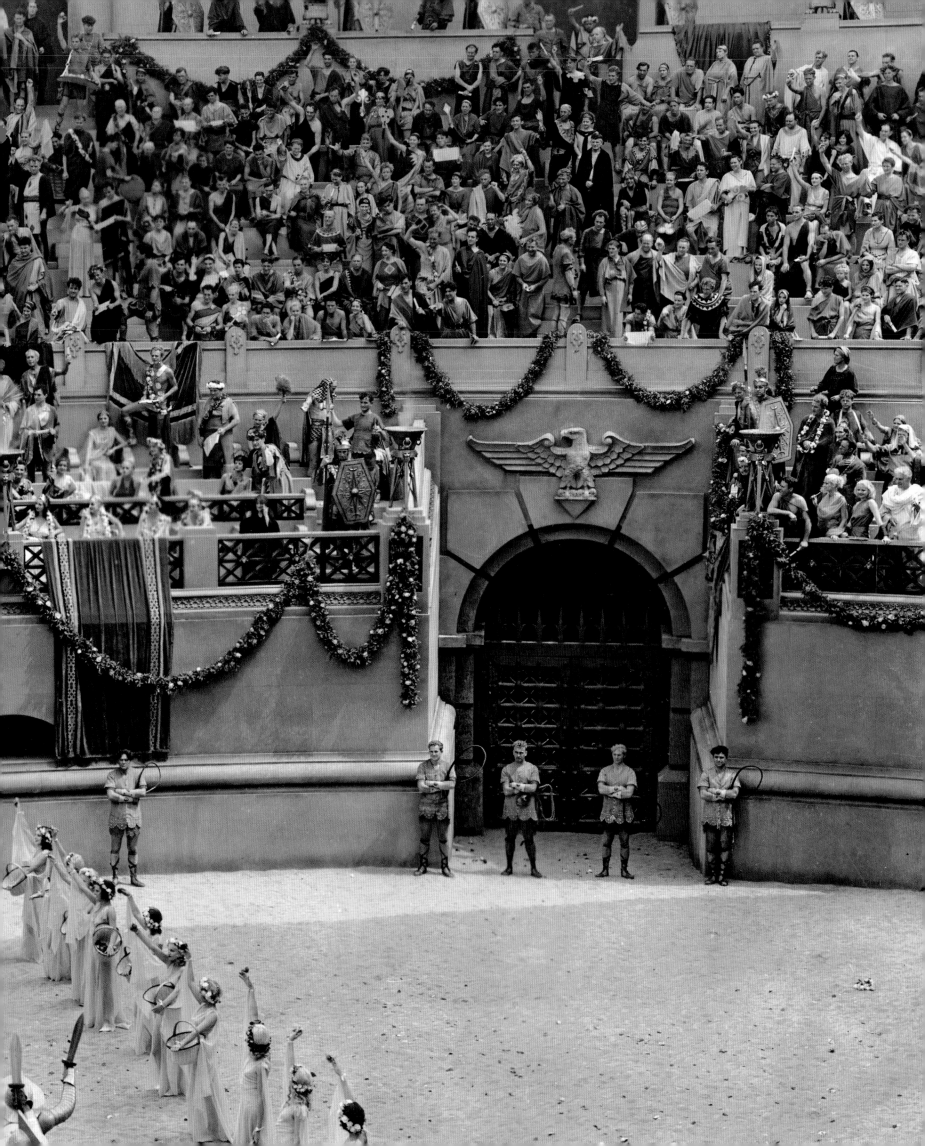

The Sign of the Cross went into general release just as the Depression sank to its nadir. Newly inaugurated President Franklin Delano Roosevelt learned that banks were shipping gold out of the country. A total economic collapse was imminent. To prevent this, he declared a bank holiday. This, in turn, prevented citizens from getting the cash they needed to see DeMille's new film. "Without cash," wrote DeMille, "people offered unsecured IOUs to theater managers. These were scribbled on little pieces of paper, as admission to *The Sign of the Cross*. When cash began to flow again, nearly every one of them was redeemed."

CECILIA DE MILLE PRESLEY

"Grandfather waited until I was old enough to understand *The Sign of the Cross* before he ran it for me. He told me about Will Hays asking him what he was going to do about the "Lesbian Dance." Demille said, 'Listen to me Will. You might want to repeat this. Not a damn thing.' It was released uncut.

"Years later I was concerned to discover that the print of *The Sign of the Cross* we had in his vault was the only complete print in existence, the only one that showed the full extent of what he'd done in those difficult days. The poor film had been cut, I think, in 1935, in 1938, and then again in 1944, for various reissues, so by the time it got to TV, you weren't seeing his movie at all.

"I was lucky to be able to do something about that. In the early 1990s I joined with Universal and UCLA and the Packard Foundation to preserve Grandfather's print and make the full-length version available. It premiered in the Festival of Preservation on American Movie Classics in 1993. That was a satisfying moment for all of us."

Meanwhile, there were reports of a backlash. Catholic dioceses and parishes in New Orleans, New York, and Oregon were endorsing the film. A Michigan priest shepherded a group of altar boys to see it. A group of fifty Louisiana priests made a field trip to a screening and were edified.

Those who attacked the film bore witness to an artistic feat. DeMille had told so transporting a story that even isolated elements could be affecting. In 1932 Hollywood mastered the art of the sound film. Even so, *Shanghai Express*, *Scarface*, *Grand Hotel*, *Love Me Tonight*, *A Farewell to Arms*, *Trouble in Paradise*, and *The Sign of the Cross* could not be fully appreciated for the achievements they were. The critical vocabulary was insufficient. Only in retrospect could these works of art be properly appraised.

With *The Sign of the Cross*, DeMille made the first fully integrated sound film. It was bold, polished, and powerful. Every shot counted. Every transition was assured. His use of symbolism, crowds, crane shots, dialectical montage, contrapuntal sound, music cues, sound effects, and even silence was masterly. He could no longer be accused of making static tableaux. This was truly a moving picture. He had caught up with the talkie trailblazers—Sternberg, Hawks, Goulding, Mamoulian, Borzage, and Lubitsch. He had surpassed them. No one else could have made *The Sign of the Cross*. It was a mesmerizing fusion of image and sound, of the sacred and the profane. It was a masterpiece.

OPPOSITE: DeMille flew across the Roman amphitheater, populating his montage with vignettes that were both touching and repulsive. His attention to detail made *The Sign of the Cross* a monumental achievement.

THIS PAGE: "Among the more outré casting demands issued recently," said the *Los Angeles Times*, "was a call for thirty Amazon wrestlers and thirty fighting dwarfs, to do battle in Nero's arena, dressed only in an abbreviated tiger or leopard skins." This scene caused some audience members to faint.

OPPOSITE: "DeMille's attempts to horrify for theatrical effect are unprecedented," wrote *Variety*. "Most of it will be nauseating to those with sensitive stomachs. The first thought may be to turn away, but all of it is holding, and it makes the heart beat faster for a solid hour. There is something in this brutal slaughter that nails fascinated attention." The only scene to be cut before the premiere was the alligator wrestling; it slowed the arena sequence.

ABOVE: A Harold Miles rendering of the Christians climbing the dungeon steps to the arena

OPPOSITE: The scene as executed by Leisen, Struss, and DeMille.

OVERLEAF, LEFT: As lions climb another flight of steps, the cold-blooded Poppaea presides over the bloodbath. *The Sign of the Cross* was written with a prologue that was cut to save screen time, but it was quoted by DeMille in his autobiography. "The sacrifice of those martyrs who gave their lives on blood-red sands of Roman arenas preserves for us an eternal Truth. The faith born then is still available."

OVERLEAF, RIGHT: *The Sign of the Cross* ends with its hero and heroine going to their deaths. This was a downbeat ending for a film that was released in the worst months of the Depression, yet it was a huge hit. DeMille had created another world, a tantalizing meld of the sacred and profane. Although *The Sign of the Cross* was censored in 1935, it remained in circulation for decades, and became a TV staple. When the De Mille Estate and Universal restored it to its road-show length in 1993, *The Sign of the Cross* was recognized for the work of art that it is. If DeMille had done no other film, his reputation would be secure. *The Sign of the Cross* is a glistening masterpiece.

THIS DAY AND AGE
AND FOUR FRIGHTENED PEOPLE

On January 13, 1933, the Fox Film Corporation hosted a party to celebrate Jesse L. Lasky's twentieth anniversary in Hollywood. Cecil B. DeMille was present, showing support for his friend. The event was slightly suspect. Nineteen years had elapsed since the miracle on Vine Street, not twenty. The real purpose of the party was to publicize *Zoo in Budapest*, Lasky's first film for Fox. Sidney Kent had not been able to get him the post of production chief, but he had gotten him an independent producing contract and his own new building. "I feel today," said Lasky, "as I did when Mr. DeMille and I started *The Squaw Man*. I start anew." His sentiments were apt, since his Fox salary would be a modest $3,000 a week. As the economy hit bottom, he was lucky to have a job. Hollywood was in a panic. RKO Radio had gone into receivership. So had Fox's theater chain. Paramount was selling its theaters. Yet DeMille sat in the eye of the storm. He had a new contract.

DeMille's contract called for three films and gave him 50 percent of net profits. His first project was an echo of *The Godless Girl* but did not decry juvenile delinquency. It reproached America's leaders. "The pall of depression was at its darkest," recalled DeMille. "Government seemed paralyzed. Prohibition, however noble in purpose, had brought evils into American life. To call attention to the evil of racketeering, and to point up the uncontaminated idealism of American youth, I made *This Day and Age*."

The film was based on an original story, "Boys in Office." The youth-story specialist Sam Mintz wrote it at the kitchen table in his ten-room Beverly Hills home. The gangster-story specialist Bartlett Cormack adapted it. His teenage dialogue sounded too mature; DeMille consulted kids. "High-school boys don't talk that way," said teen critiques. "It isn't adolescent enough. You have them talking like grown-ups." DeMille was fifty-one, and his children were adults, as were the actors portraying the teens in the film. "I had to spend weeks attending student-body meetings," he said. "Student government didn't exist when I was in school."

DeMille wanted to show that the social chaos of 1933 was harming young people and that they had the right to correct it,

OPPOSITE: Cecil B. DeMille posed for an on-the-set portrait in May 1933 while making *This Day and Age*.

even if it meant usurping authority. "Some critics thought *This Day and Age* fascist," wrote DeMille. "It was not my intention that high school students all over America should kidnap racketeers and let rats nibble their toes. This was a case, like the dance in *The Sign of the Cross*, of painting in heightened colors for dramatic effect."

DeMille's vision of the teen world, if not entirely accurate, was tolerant, populated by races that were usually demeaned in Hollywood films. A gentle Jewish tailor defies the racketeers and is killed. To sequester the murderer, the teens ask help from a brainy African American student. He impersonates a shoeshine boy so they can surprise and subdue the gangster. "The critics made no mention of the sympathetic representation of minority groups—Jews and Negroes—in *This Day and Age*," wrote DeMille. In an era of unrestrained racism, DeMille was known to be color blind. Perhaps his years on the road with Constance, and their contact with every level of society, had freed him from the prejudices that affected much of society. Perhaps it was the example of his parents. For whatever reason,

DeMille was never known to disparage a person because of race or sexual orientation.

DeMille had spent his years on the road as an actor, not as a director. From all accounts, he never lost the need to perform. With the success of *The Sign of the Cross*, he asserted himself as the biggest star of every DeMille production. The performance was what mattered. *Photoplay* sent Sara Hamilton to the set of *This Day and Age* in expectation of a "scene." One had occurred near the end of *The Sign of the Cross*. There was sure to be another. *Photoplay* still had it in for DeMille.

Hamilton watched and waited. DeMille was warming up, which meant that the teenage actors were not. He blew a whistle and stretched out his hand. The megaphone flew through the air. DeMille grabbed it. "Before you children were born," he thundered, "I was a supernumerary in the repertory of the great Richard Mansfield." The teens looked at each other. Who was that? DeMille continued, "When I was with Mansfield, we *acted*. *Really acted!* If Mansfield said, 'The mob muttereth,' we immediately muttered, 'Rumba, rumba, rumba, rumba.'"

"Yes, Mr. DeMille," said one cheeky boy, "but I've never learned to do the Rumba."

"Get off my set," shouted DeMille. "Get off this lot! Never let me see your face again!"

ABOVE: When Cecil and Constance DeMille sailed for Hawaii on August 19, 1933, three of their four children came to see them off. Left to right: John, Katherine, and Richard. While Cecil was away, Katherine took a stage name and looked for work as an actress. She fooled no one, so she had to use her name. Cecil made a point of not interfering, and she won roles on her own.

OPPOSITE, CLOCKWISE FROM TOP LEFT: Boris Leven made this concept rendering of a mob-rule scene for art director Milo Anderson in the production of *This Day and Age*. • This is the scene as it was filmed by DeMille and Peverell Marley. • A concept painting by Boris Leven of the teenagers' march through town.

Anyone who had been with DeMille longer than a week was familiar with this routine, but no one ever got used to it. His acting was convincing, his rages too towering to be ignored. His training with Belasco had been complete. This was his model. Belasco was famed, not only for his stained-glassed, bear-carpeted office, but also for the operatic fits that he threw when some minion was unlucky enough to fail him. Hamilton dutifully recorded this exchange, but nothing she saw surpassed what had happened on *The Sign of the Cross*.

That was a doozy. . . .

On that day, DeMille was high above the arena, sitting on the camera crane, microphone in hand, issuing orders to Christians, pagans, and lions. From out of the corner of his eye, he saw some movement. He looked. Up in the stands, one extra girl was whispering to another extra girl. While he was issuing orders! With his free hand, he pointed at her. "So! Our little movie is unimportant, is it?" The girl cringed. "Well, we'll just discontinue our little movie while you finish your talk." The girl hung her head. "Or, no. Better yet, we'd all like to hear what you just said. Come here." He waved grandly. "Here. To the center of the arena. And tell us the very interesting things you were saying." The girl was petrified. "Either come forward or get off this lot," he bellowed. "And stay off it!"

The girl crept down the steps of the arena stands, descended the modern stairs behind it, and fearfully walked across the sand. Lions, trainers, and crew members watched her walk by. The crane lowered to the sand. One of the four assistants took the microphone from DeMille. He reverted to his megaphone. "All right, now. Here's the microphone. Tell us all what you were saying. We're all interested, I'm sure."

An assistant held the microphone in front of the girl. "It's too embarrassing," she whispered.

"Speak up," snapped DeMille.

"I can't," said the girl, lowering her face.

"Speak the truth. Or leave."

The girl slowly raised her face to the microphone. "I just said—"

ABOVE, LEFT TO RIGHT: Filming *Four Frightened People* in the jungles of Hawaii required ingenuity. • *Four Frightened People*'s opening showed a desperate wireless operator and the burial of a cholera victim.

OPPOSITE, LEFT TO RIGHT: On October 3, 1933, this mechanical cobra provoked more exasperation than fear. Left to right: Mary Boland, Herbert Marshall, William Gargan, and Claudette Colbert. • DeMille's jaunty style endured the encroachments of the jungle.

"What?"

"I just said, 'When is that bald-headed old bastard going to let us go to lunch?'"

There was a shocked silence. Young girls did not use such words.

Suddenly DeMille threw back his head and roared. Ha! He loved it! "This bald-headed old bastard is going to let you go to lunch this minute!" He turned to his assistants. "Lunch!"

As the extra girl—and many others—learned, DeMille respected courage, and he respected honesty. Jeanie Macpherson once said that you would end a working relationship with DeMille if you made excuses, lied, or blamed someone else. As long as you did none of these things, you would keep working—even after he had fired you.

This Day and Age was a modest four-week production, and, while it had one spectacular sequence, it was hardly an epic. It did have controversial elements and suspense, but a film without stars could only do so well. President Roosevelt's recovery programs were barely in force. Money was tight. "Good old melodrama reigns," wrote Edwin Schallert in the *Los Angeles Times*. "It is all fairy-tale stuff but enough to put an audience into that sort of frenzy when it bursts into applause over any exciting scene." The frenzy did have a postscript. A few months af-

ter the film's release, in a grim paraphrase of its plot, a mob in San Jose broke into a jail, carried off two alleged kidnappers, and lynched them.

On July 7, Cecil and Constance DeMille entered Jacob Stern's barn for the first time in more than ten years. It had been moved from Selma and Vine to the front area of the Paramount lot, near the popular Oblath's Café, and was serving as a gymnasium. The occasion was a celebration of DeMille's twentieth anniversary in films. For some reason they were observing the date of the mid-August meeting at Claridge Grill, when he, Lasky, and Sam Goldfish had agreed to form a film company, rather than their advent to Hollywood. On August 16, there was another anniversary event, a banquet at the Alexandria Hotel. There was a sad undertone to this event. Lasky had just declared bankruptcy, surrendering to receivers a part interest in his Fox Film projects.

It was at this time that DeMille chose to leave Hollywood, but not permanently. His next film would be shot 2,500 miles away, on the so-called "Big Island" of Hawaii. *Four Frightened People* was a variation on *The Admirable Crichton*, a comedy of manners played against a jungle fraught with poisonous snakes and poisoned darts.

DeMille had not been able to keep Mitchell Leisen on salary after *The Sign of the Cross*. The multitalented Leisen had

been snapped up by Emanuel Cohen. Just as Leisen was about to direct his first film, DeMille wanted him back. Cohen told DeMille no. Leisen was needed on *Cradle Song*, a story of nuns and an orphan. "DeMille was furious," said Leisen. "He thought it was my fault, and he didn't speak to me for a long time. Then he saw *Cradle Song* and he thought it was the greatest thing he'd ever seen. It was the kind of thing he couldn't do, a little picture, told with nuances." DeMille was forced to use the art director from *This Day and Age*, Roland Anderson. He was a fine art director, but he was not Mitchell Leisen; he could not do sets *and* costumes *and* assistant direction.

On August 19, DeMille sailed for Honolulu on the Matson liner *Malolo*. Constance accompanied him, but the trip was devoted to production meetings with Anderson, Cormack, Karl Struss, and Roy Burns. Shooting on location was going to be rough, even for the hardy DeMille. After checking into the Royal Hawaiian Hotel, DeMille took a plane to scout locations. Then the crew began moving generators and lights to the Big Island.

The cast members were scheduled to leave Los Angeles on August 25 on the *Lurline*—Claudette Colbert, Herbert Marshall, Mary Boland, William Gargan, and Leo Carrillo. Not all of them sailed. Boland's mother fell ill, which necessitated the actress's flying to New York, then back again, and then taking an August 30 boat. She racked up 8,225 miles in nine days. She was only allowed to do this because of a bigger crisis. Colbert had been hospitalized on August 24 with appendicitis. (Gossip said that she had complications from an abortion.) Remembering the cast of *Male and Female*, DeMille cabled Gloria Swanson, but she was unavailable. Colbert began to recover, and her doctor approved her going back to work. Just in case, he sent a nurse with her.

On September 1, DeMille approved Cormack's rewrites, and the company moved to the Big Island. DeMille and his stars stayed in the colonial home of Leslie Wishard, manager of the Union Mill Sugar Plantation. Shooting began five days later, but

only lasted a week. When DeMille insisted that Colbert immerse herself in a swamp in one scene, she fell ill. DeMille decided to shoot Boland's scenes.

Boland did not speed the process. She was a Broadway star and was known to drink on the job. "September 28," reported script clerk Emily Barrye. "Shooting Mardick Village. 8:30 call. Miss Boland half hour late. Miss Boland watched rehearsal with her double, and then went to location dressing room to have her eyelashes put on. She refused to have anyone but Monte Westmore, who was getting the natives made up, put them on her. The crank turned at 11:12. Camera noise too great to shoot. It was the same camera that was repaired yesterday." On October 3, a prop cobra developed mechanical difficulties.

Marshall had lost his left leg in the World War and was having a tough time walking on banyan roots with his prosthesis. Boland tried to cheer him up. "Tell me, Bart," she said. "Do you think the old-fashioned waltz is coming back?" Marshall was good-natured about it, but DeMille was cranky. Boland would have none of it. "I wonder when that—that *Gila monster*—will let us finish the scene!" *Four Frightened People* was starting to feel like a jinxed project.

"I knew they were in trouble over there," said Leisen. "I got a telegram from Roy Burns and he signed it, 'One of the four frightened people.'" The trouble was in the setting. DeMille was unable to bend it to his will. "He went there so he could shoot a real bamboo forest," said Leisen. "Then it was murder because it was all standing in lava. They had to lay tons of sawdust to even walk through it."

The bigger issue was that much of the jungle was simply not photogenic. It defied DeMille's sense of spectacle, Struss's skill with lighting, and Anderson's designs. Paramount

OPPOSITE, TOP TO BOTTOM: Lighting Claudette Colbert and Leo Carrillo in a banyan grove at night posed special problems for cameraman Karl Struss. • A Pekingese-toting matron (Mary Boland) confronts a Malay chieftain (Tetsu Komai) over conjugal rights in *Four Frightened People*.

complained that the footage looked muddy. DeMille backed up Struss, but it was not his fault. Nothing separated; there was no contrast in the tangled brush. The only recourse was to use cross lighting and shoot tight. "DeMille shot the picture with a two-inch lens," said Leisen. "The background was blurry, just nothing. He'd gone all the way to Hawaii and none of the expense showed on the screen."

There was one scene where too much showed. James Wingate of the Studio Relations Committee (SRC) was an embattled bureaucrat in late 1933. Producers wanted him to approve adult themes, and Will Hays wanted him to censor them. Unlike Jason Joy, he had no feeling for story. "Wingate couldn't explain what needed to be done to make a given script acceptable to the Code," said Geoffrey Shurlock. "He didn't get on very well with these emotional Jewish producers. He was not an unpleasant man, just simple-minded and logical, really quite square. They had wild ideas, but he'd say, 'No, no! Cut it out!' What they wanted was not to cut it out but to do it differently."

The scene in question was one of DeMille's trademark bathing scenes, this time set under a waterfall. Colbert's double had worn an "Annette Kellerman," a body stocking

RIGHT: In *Four Frightened People*, the DeMille "bathtub" was out of doors. Colbert's stand-in is watched by Gargan and Marshall. The scene caused censorship problems. When the film was released to TV, the 16mm prints included the topless shots in this scene, so it was up to MCA-TV to cut the shots from hundreds of prints.

marketed by the famed swimmer of an earlier era. But Colbert's medium close-ups revealed that she was topless. To pacify the powerful New York censor board, Wingate wanted to cut them. "There are no nude shots in the bathing scenes," DeMille wrote Wingate. "The girl wears a Kellerman suit. The scenes are staged in good taste. All who have seen the picture class these scenes as ones of artistry. I have never made a personal request to any censor board, but in this case I beseech you to reconsider, as it took us a great sum of money to take the company to Hawaii." Wingate was too tired to argue that Colbert's close-ups had been done on a set in Hollywood and were indeed nude. He passed the scene.

Four Frightened People needed more than titillation. On December 15, Leisen attended its sneak preview in Huntington Park. DeMille was in Washington, DC, with Constance for a tax hearing. Irving Thalberg frequently used Huntington Park for previews. He called it "the cross section of America" because of its heterogeneous population. America was not ready for a survival comedy. "The audience reaction was terrible," recalled Leisen. "I didn't know how I could ever tell DeMille the truth politely. Fortunately I bumped into Manny Cohen in the lobby. 'Forget it,' he told me. 'I'll send Cecil the bad news.'" DeMille took his film to a preview in Stamford, Connecticut. "I was the fifth frightened person," he recalled. The reception was flat. He returned to Hollywood and trimmed twenty minutes. At the film's premiere, the *New York Times* reported that "the terror in some scenes stirred up almost as much mirth from the audience yesterday as did the levity in others." *Four Frightened People* lost $260,000.

While DeMille was on the East Coast, he went to visit Zukor. Paramount had gone into receivership in early 1933. John Hertz resigned, and fingers pointed at Zukor. It was his turn. "Mr. Zukor was forced out of the presidency," wrote DeMille. "Fortunately the stockholders had power enough to keep him on the board, and he was left in general charge of production. I went to see Mr. Zukor on some business. He was showing the strain in ways that saddened me. Right in front of me, he took out a bottle and started drinking. This was in the afternoon, in his office. I told him he shouldn't." DeMille looked at the man who had treated him so heartlessly nine years before. He chose not to take revenge. "I told him what he had meant to the motion picture industry, how much it owed him and how it still needed him. If he accepted defeat, not only he but also Paramount—and the whole industry—would be irreparably the losers."

The only thing that would bring Zukor back and keep DeMille at Paramount was a series of hits. Zukor thought for a while and then came back with a suggestion. DeMille had only lost his audience when he had tried projects that were not his style, like *Madam Satan* or *Four Frightened People*. "A man does best what he enjoys doing," wrote DeMille, "and leaves whimsical stories to directors like Preston Sturges." Zukor suggested that DeMille do a historical film, like *The Sign of the Cross*, but with more emphasis on "romance." An epic with sex. Wingate was mismanaging the SRC, so pushing sex scenes through that office would be easy. DeMille had been preparing a project called *Antony and Cleopatra*, but had let it lapse. He revived it, and changed its name to *Cleopatra*.

CECIL B. DeMILLE

"If I make a light comedy like *Four Frightened People*, someone immediately starts referring to it as an epic, and the public is disappointed if it doesn't maintain that character. I didn't want *Four Frightened People* to be taken that seriously."

OPPOSITE: Roland Anderson built this jungle idol for a romantic interlude in *Four Frightened People*.

CLEOPATRA

The spring of 1934 was an auspicious time for an epic. Thanks to Franklin D. Roosevelt's New Deal, the economy was improving, and the film industry was rebounding. The Depression was far from over, but by the end of the year, the gross national income would increase by $10 billion. Weekly film attendance would rise from 60 million to 70 million. Hope was in the air. Fox's *Stand Up and Cheer* featured a rousing song "We're Out of the Red!" It was not true. Fox, RKO, and Paramount were in receivership. Still, the keynote was optimism. Paramount could afford a Cecil B. DeMille spectacular. M-G-M had Greta Garbo in *Queen Christina*, Paramount had Marlene Dietrich in *The Scarlet Empress*, and Norma Shearer was planning *Marie Antoinette*. As one magazine quipped, "Hollywood is queening it!"

There were certain quarters in which the "doin's" of Hollywood did not elicit laughs. One was the Hollywood office of the SRC, where Joseph I. Breen looked at the mess that James Wingate had made. The so-called "Hays Office" was littered with the detritus of failed censorship. "Producers have reduced the Code to sieve-like proportions," cracked *Variety*. "They are outsmarting themselves. No longer is the industry up against bluenose factions. Responsible people—lawyers, doctors, and other professionals—are resenting the screen and lettering by the bushel

about it." A typical letter came from a Mrs. W. Noble of Auburn, New York. "It is only fair to ask motion pictures to maintain the highest standards and not turn our movie houses into burlesque shows." Not everyone agreed. "As a small-town theater owner," wrote Ralph Menefee of Hoxie, Kansas, "I know that we can scarcely take in film rental costs on the so-called 'good, clean' pictures like *Little Women*. We pack our house with a Mae West film." As West kept Paramount afloat, she also caused controversy. "Mae rubbed people the wrong way," recalled censor Geoffrey Shurlock. "They weren't used to having sex kidded."

In slow-motion desperation, the unctuous Will Hays asked Breen to administer the SRC. Hays knew that Breen was a militant Catholic. What Hays did not know was that Breen was a double agent, reporting the SRC's failures to Roman Catholic clergy in Chicago. There were twenty million Catholics in America, and the "Midwest bishops" wielded tremendous influence over them. These working-class people lived in urban centers where film companies had picture palaces, the huge theaters that could make (or break) a film in a week. Breen looked

OPPOSITE: "You'll find, to your sorrow, I'm still queen of Egypt," says Cleopatra (Claudette Colbert) to the men who have abducted her from her palace and left her in the desert. Cecil B. DeMille filmed the scene in El Segundo, California. Photograph by Ray Jones.

at the list of "immoral" films that had slid past Wingate and was furious: *The Story of Temple Drake*, *Hoop-La*, *Convention City*. "Joe Breen nurtured not the slightest seed of self-doubt regarding his mission or his rectitude," wrote censor Jack Vizzard. "He was right, the moviemakers were wrong, and that was that." Still, without an enforceable Code, his hands were tied.

Father Daniel Lord sat in his St. Louis office, lamenting "the thousands of boys and girls before whom motion pictures were parading undressed women, lustful scenes, vice, crime, seduction and rape." He had helped to write the Production Code in 1930. Four years later, all he could see was a double-cross. The films of 1933 had been marred by immoral scenes; the films of 1934 were entirely immoral. There was no way to cut one or two scenes and make *Nana* or *Of Human Bondage* decent. They were bad through and through, and Father Lord was "mad through and through." Mae West was later credited with pushing the Code too far. She did her share to offend the heartland, but the real offender was *The Sign of the Cross*. Catholics felt that DeMille had appropriated Catholic mythology. Their rage ignited a holy war.

On November 15, 1933, Bishop John Cantwell of Los Angeles spoke at Catholic University in Washington, DC, saying that something had to be done about immoral films. He called *The Sign of the Cross* "vile and disgusting." Lord was sitting in the audience—on the hot seat. He turned to fellow Jesuit FitzGeorge Dinneen, who was with the Chicago archdiocese. "Father Dinneen and I talked over a nationwide boycott," wrote Lord, "something to make the industry pay attention." But how? "We needed to throw the power of Chicago's Catholicity behind a movement. 'The Legion of Decency' was thought of as a title. I do not know by whom." This was not Hollywood. No one was fighting for title credit. They were fighting for decency. A Legion of Decency could make grass-roots resentment a political weapon. As formulated by Cantwell, Lord, publisher Martin Quigley, and the Midwest bishops, the legion would boycott films named from the pulpit and militate for a new Code. The

plan was ambitious. If it came to pass, it would collide with DeMille's sex epic.

DeMille started work on *Cleopatra* in late 1933. There was no question that Claudette Colbert would portray the Egyptian queen. After a year of hits, her star was shining brightly. The *Cleopatra* script included Julius Caesar and Marc Antony. DeMille considered John Gilbert for Caesar, then heard that audiences were laughing at Gilbert in *Queen Christina*. DeMille decided on Warren William, whose claim to fame was a series of Warner Bros. films in which he played a chuckling roué. His rich voice and brazen confidence would translate to Ancient Rome. Casting Antony was more difficult. Fredric March had been slated but was doing expensive films back to back and could not be spared. DeMille had to look elsewhere. A battery of tests ensued.

"The actor I choose must be like a St. Bernard dog," DeMille announced in January 1934, "with a chest on which he can camp an army. He must be a persuasive talker of the type that can sway a nation's policy with a twenty-minute oration. He must be virile enough to drink his soldiers under the table, yet romantic enough to complete the conquest of the world's most desired woman." Philip Scheuer of the *Los Angeles Times* doubted that DeMille could find "huskies who can get into tights without looking like the last act of a varsity show." DeMille took the bait, averring that there were not enough "actors" in Hollywood. "We have a tremendous holdover of gangster types," complained DeMille. "They are unsuitable for the Roman era or for Biblical times." This caused no end of comment. One columnist suggested that DeMille cast King Kong. Even Irving Thalberg had to weigh in. "I can't subscribe to a deficiency of talent here," said the M-G-M producer. "There has never been a place so full of people of exceptional ability. Five years ago I could not have said that. The talkies were too new,

OPPOSITE, TOP TO BOTTOM: Harold Miles made this concept painting of Julius Caesar holding court in Egypt. • The palace designed by Hans Dreier and Roland Anderson owed a great deal to the 1925 Exposition of Decorative Arts.

too undeveloped. We couldn't draw the best actors. Then came the Depression. It was a stroke of fate. Today it is possible to get the right actor for any type of role."

DeMille was crafty, manipulating the press as deftly as his extras. He already had his Marc Antony. He had found him while screening tests. One day in early December, DeMille had been carrying reels of chariot horses to his favorite screening room, Number Five, and found it occupied. Instead of leaving, he stayed to watch tests of an actor whom producer Benjamin ("Barney") Glazer was bringing from England. Harry Wilcoxon was twenty-eight, with experience in the Birmingham Repertory and starring roles in London's West End, not to mention six British films. He was handsome, virile, and convincing. DeMille saw what he had seen in Gloria Swanson years earlier: authority. He persuaded Manny Cohen to let him have Wilcoxon.

"Everything you see in a spectacle has to be made," said DeMille. "You can't run around the corner and pick up an Egyptian helmet." In January 1934, the Paramount studio jewelry shop was ferociously busy, making models of rings, circlets, and bracelets. From these models metal implements were then cast and plated. This work was executed in concert with Jeanie Macpherson and her research staff. "What about Cleopatra's palace at Alexandria?" DeMille asked her. "Julius Caesar is seated in an Egyptian chair. What sort of room was it? How was it furnished? How was his hair cut? I want to see it all."

At the end of the month, Harry Wilcoxon arrived at DeMille's office, all six feet, four inches of him. "At last," said DeMille. "I meet Marc Antony!" DeMille sized up the actor. "I trust the fittings for your armor went well?"

"Oh, yes, but couldn't I have worn something from the costume department?"

"And have it not look right? All armor was custom made in those days, and, as for Antony, he was a ruler as well as a commander. These things must be correct in every detail." DeMille

OPPOSITE: When DeMille chose Warren William to play Julius Caesar, the actor was known for the charming cads he played at Warner Bros. in the period now known as "pre-Code." *Cleopatra* was filmed at the end of this era and it was released just as the Code was reconstituted.

ABOVE: An on-set portrait of Claudette Colbert by Ray Jones.

RIGHT, TOP AND CENTER: This is how Harold Miles envisioned Cleopatra's entrance into Rome.

RIGHT, BOTTOM: This is how DeMille filmed it.

looked at Wilcoxon's torso and legs. He thought that he would need shaving. Other alterations would be needed. "How are you with animals?"

"I love them! I know how to ride and—"

"I've decided Antony would keep dogs. I'm sending you out to Pasadena to a kennel that has a pair of Great Danes I like. They'll live with you while we prepare. I want them to follow you wherever you go on the set." DeMille paused and looked at his new employee. "I like you, Harry. I think I've chosen well. We should get along just fine. What do you know of me?"

"Well," said Wilcoxon, "I know we might be sitting in Arizona, except it was raining in 1913."

"That's just publicity. Makes a good story. Actually, to tell the truth, the terrain was uninteresting and I didn't like the light." DeMille moved from his story to Cleopatra's. "I want to make ancient history accessible, Harry. People are the same

down through the ages. They may dress differently, live in different houses, but human emotions, desires, failings, needs are the same the world over. People laugh, people cry, people die for love and honor." After a brief review of Wilcoxon's résumé, DeMille had a question for him. "What's the hardest thing you had to learn to do onstage?"

"Laugh."

"I believe in humor in the most tragic of plays," said DeMille. "It's essential. I want people to laugh with our characters so they

ABOVE AND OPPOSITE: DeMille's depiction of the Ides of March was as studied as it was violent. "The child DeMille saw the great Gustave Doré exhibition in New York," wrote art critic Arthur Millier in the *Times*. "It made an indelible impression on him. He will tell you that Doré is his favorite artist. Perhaps DeMille is the reincarnation of his idol, come back to a second and even greater earthly success."

will cry with them later." Then came some unpleasant news about Paramount. They wanted to change Wilcoxon's name. "They think Harry isn't dignified enough; in this country it's a diminutive of Henry, more of a nickname." Seeing that Wilcoxon was incensed, DeMille reached over and put his hand on Wilcoxon's shoulder. "Henry was my father's name," said DeMille, smiling. "I couldn't give you a greater compliment. But whatever your name is—Henry or Harry—you're my Marc Antony."

Hollywood had another auspicious visitor in January. Sol Rosenblatt, an administrator of President Roosevelt's New Deal, met with Jason Joy, James Wingate, and Joseph Breen. Rosenblatt told the censors that the threat of federal censorship was real. The Studio Relations Committee needed to exert control of film content at the script level. This was not news; coming from Washington, it carried weight. On February 5, Will Hays installed Breen as head of the SRC. Joy returned to Fox, and Wing-

ate returned to upstate New York. The Midwest Catholics were pleased. If anyone could clean up the movies, it was Joe Breen.

DeMille was interested in cleaning up at the box office. He intended to make *Cleopatra* a sex fable, and that was that. His niece Agnes was in London, basking in the glory of a hit play. She had just choreographed C. B. Cochran's production of Cole Porter's *Nymph Errant*. Three years earlier, DeMille had seen Agnes perform as an Ouled Naïl dancer. Her interpretation of a belly-dancing, betel-chewing Algerian prostitute was slightly scandalous, and it sparked DeMille's Oriental fantasies. He invited Agnes to choreograph *Cleopatra*. "You are the most interesting dancer I know," he wrote her on March 6. "Your dances are different and have drama in them." Drama was not all that he needed.

Antony comes to Cleopatra's barge to arrest her, but the hunter becomes the prey. She seduces him with music—and

ABOVE: Boris Leven made these concept paintings of Cleopatra's barge.

OPPOSITE: Hans Dreier and Roland Anderson gave the barge a wall of ostrich plumes. The fan bearer at right is Oscar Rudolph, who began with DeMille as a child actor, did a few adult roles for him, became his assistant director, and later directed series television. DeMille mentored many artists.

dancers. "Cleopatra is putting on a show deliberately," DeMille wrote Agnes, "with the intention of so astonishing the tough, hard soldier Antony that he will have to remain long enough for her to get in her deadly work. Antony has seen all the regular dancers in the world, so they cannot interest him. Cleopatra would not make the mistake of staging just a dance. When Antony tries to free himself from the spell being cast over him, I see a bull led before him, on the back of which lies a beautiful dancer, whose costume suggests the mate of the bull. Perhaps her headgear is horns, and her shoes are hoofs, like Edmund Dulac's *Europa and the Bull*. This entire barge sequence should be the most seductive, erotic, beautiful, rhythmic, sensuous series of scenes ever shown."

DeMille made it clear that although the dances would be choreographed in full, the playing out of the sequence would not allow them to be shown in full. "No numbers will be seen from beginning to end," he explained. "The effects must be quickly seen and passed. We will only see portions of each number." In later years, Agnes de Mille would remember being horrified by DeMille's ideas upon reading the script when she arrived in New York in mid-March. In fact, the *Los Angeles Times* had printed an item on February 19 saying that DeMille wanted her to perform a "very exotic dance on a black bull." There was a reason for Agnes's tangled memories. There was tension in the family. Her father, William, had been lost in a shuffle of early-talkie flops. He was reduced to borrowing money from Cecil. Agnes had been struggling in London, but after the success of *Nymph Errant*, she became disenchanted with Cochran, Porter, and the rest of the company. She felt that they had snubbed her at a cast party. In truth, she was a bit difficult, and she was heading for Hollywood with quixotic notions. "Uncle Ce thinks the dances should only be flashes," she wrote Anna George de Mille, her mother. "I'm sure that when he sees how effective they are, he will include more."

While DeMille and Colbert were still in Hawaii, he had discussed *Cleopatra* with her. Colbert had claimed that she was

getting $50,000 as her standard fee. DeMille knew she would be getting far less for her next film, *Night Bus*, which was being made at modest Columbia Pictures. Instead of laughing in her face, DeMille explained the benefits she would derive from starring in *Cleopatra*. But Colbert knew her worth. Who else could he get? Garbo? Colbert stuck to her price. They compromised at $47,000. There was another sticking point. The Hawaiian wildlife had unnerved Colbert, particularly its reptiles. "You remember how Cleopatra died," said DeMille. "She committed suicide by putting an asp, a venomous snake, to her bare breast and letting it kill her."

"Oh, Mr. DeMille," gasped Colbert, "I couldn't do that! A snake? I couldn't possibly—"

"Wait, Claudette. Don't say positively that you can't, or I cannot give you the part. You want to play it, don't you?"

"Yes, but—"

"Now wait, please. I want you to play it. I don't want anyone but you for *Cleopatra*. Will we just not say any more about the snake until we come to it? Will you trust me if I tell you that you can play the scene?" Colbert agreed. While Colbert was in fittings, *Night Bus* was retitled *It Happened One Night* and released. It became an immediate hit. Colbert could not have been happy about her Paramount fee. She was distinctly unhappy about her costumes.

DeMille had hoped to get Mitchell Leisen back, but Leisen had found directing the best way to utilize his talents. He was scheduled to direct *Death Takes a Holiday*, another reason why Fredric March was unavailable for Antony. DeMille settled for a designer named Victoria Williams. She would coordinate the work of in-house designer Travis Banton with that of Ralph Jester, but it was still a massive task. Williams complained that the costume department was unorganized. On March 9, three days before shooting was to begin, she quit.

"The studio made it clear that DeMille was not going to have Mitchell for *Cleopatra*," recalled Natalie Visart, who was a close friend of Katherine de Mille. "Mitchell agreed to help

DeMille find somebody. Mitchell had been teaching me. He persuaded C. B. to take me on as sort of an apprentice." DeMille had seen this girl around the house for years. "C. B. thought Mitchell was really doing the work and letting me take credit," said Visart, "but Mitchell straightened him out about that. Mitchell did do a couple of sketches for *Cleopatra*, just to keep his hand in."

Banton did most of Colbert's gowns but was not happy to have Visart in his way. (She was also Leisen's girlfriend.) Banton had his hands full. Knowing that the SRC was in turmoil, Colbert had told him to make her gowns as low cut as possible; this was to draw attention from her short neck. She approved the sketches, but when she put on the costumes, she changed her mind. Banton had to work twenty-four hours to remake them. "Costumes not ready," said the production report on March 12, 1934, but at least Colbert's were. Filming commenced.

DeMille's intuition about Wilcoxon paid off. He was superb as Antony. Warren William was splendid as Caesar. "Warren raised wire-haired fox terriers," recalled Colbert. "DeMille frightened him, but then, DeMille frightened almost all his actors." Not Colbert. DeMille planned a seduction scene that would include a strange ritual. "He wanted Caesar to drop rose petals on my feet," said Colbert. "I screamed with laughter when he told me that. I said, 'He can touch my foot. He can even bite it. But if he drops rose petals on it, I'll just burst out laughing.' He finally agreed. That was one of the few times I won an argument with him."

DeMille had been shooting for two weeks when Agnes de Mille arrived. He insisted that she stay at his home with Constance, Richard, and the grown children, John and Katherine. During her first visit to Paramount, Agnes saw DeMille shoot a scene of Gertrude Michael as Calpurnia trying to stop Caesar from going to his death. Agnes also met Roy Burns, the production manager; LeRoy Prinz, the studio dance director; and Rudolph Kopp, who was composing the musical score for *Cleopatra*. No one impressed her. "Calpurnia was one of the regulation DeMille cuties," she said, dismissing Gertrude Michael's stage accomplishments. Burns was "an ex-waiter." Prinz was "LeRoy

Prince, a fibrous toughy." And the gifted Kopp was "Rapp, cheap and commonplace." Agnes wasted no time communicating her plans. "I want to do dances for the camera and not for the proscenium arch," she told DeMille.

"What's the difference?"

When he asked that, Agnes thought that she was one up on him. But he had no need to answer a foolish academic question. He had stacks of concept paintings, knew every shot in his head, and had a small army of assistants. He had to. There were a total of sixty-four departments at Paramount. Agnes did concede the enormity of his responsibility. "Uncle Ce amazes me," she told her mother. "The energy he gives out is that of a general in full battle. No wonder his staff calls him 'Chief.' He insists on

ABOVE: Choreographer Agnes de Mille came to Hollywood to help her uncle Cecil create a dance sequence featuring a bull. In the process, she was photographed on the set of *Cleopatra* with her uncle and her cousin Katherine DeMille, who was acting in Mae West's *It Ain't No Sin*. West would be a victim of the new Code. Agnes would be a victim of politics.

okaying every single item from hairpins to still photographs. He must be shown everything finished out and completed: every eyelash drawn on his costume sketches, every muscle, especially muscles. He has the unflagging zeal, the undivided strength of the prophet, the fanatic—or the absolute monarch."

DeMille was not the only monarch. Colbert had her scepter in hand, too. She was rejecting more costumes and was frequently late to the set. "Claudette had everything DeMille wanted in an actress," says Cecilia de Mille Presley. "Besides being magnificent-looking, she had sex appeal, smarts, toughness, and real acting ability. He told me that she could be difficult. She was often late. Time equals money on a set. She made him wait. And wait he did. He knew her worth. He also liked her. After all, he cast her three times."

A childhood accident had left a slight bump on the right side of Colbert's nose, and cameraman George Folsey said this was why she photographed poorly in her first films. She was determined to prevent this. She required that she be photographed only from the left side. Thanks to *It Happened One Night*, she was becoming a huge star. She began to act like one.

Wilcoxon was merely trying to be friendly when he broached the subject. "I told Claudette between setups that it was all a lot of nonsense," said Wilcoxon, "She was beautiful no matter what the angle. She took great offense at my statement and informed me that she, unlike me, had been doing movies for years, and that people in Hollywood knew a great deal more about these things than people from London."

"I'd become good friends with Whitey Schafer in the stills department," Wilcoxon said. "One day I asked him to flop the negatives on some photos of Claudette and me." Schafer printed the negatives reversed and Colbert's good left side suddenly became her bad right side. These "proofs" were sent to Colbert for her approval. Seeing her "right" side, she mechanically rejected all the poses, not taking time to notice that the sets were backward—*and* the numbers inscribed on the edges of the stills. Wilcoxon went to her dressing room. "Why, I don't understand this, Claudette! Every single one of these proofs has been rejected. There must be some mistake!"

"They know better than to photograph my bad side," she snapped.

"Then why haven't you recognized your left side?"

"That's not left! It's right!"

"No! Look at the numbers on the edge of the pictures. They're backward! They simply turned the neg over when they printed these! You see, I'm right! There is no difference between your right and your left!" Wilcoxon strode out of the dressing room. He had made his point. Colbert would make hers. "I recall her muttering things like 'You're hurting my arm' through clenched teeth as we kissed on camera," wrote Wilcoxon.

On April 7, DeMille was shooting a mob scene on the steps of the Roman Senate. "It was a hot, a blistering hot day," wrote Muriel Babcock of the *Los Angeles Examiner*. "On a raised platform high above a mob of five hundred people was Director DeMille. Below him were men in leather pants laced up the sides, and in sandals—and nothing else. There were ladies of the street in flimsy Roman rags that I doubt would be permitted on

ABOVE: The British photographer George Hoyningen-Huene, who was covering Hollywood for *Vanity Fair* and *Vogue*, took these images on the *Cleopatra* set: DeMille and his concept art; a bull dance rehearsal; Victor Milner ready to soar over hundreds of extras.

Main Street today without arrest. In sharp contrast to this sweltering, half-naked mob, there were actors and actresses in velvet capes and embroidered gold and silver costumes. Horses with leopard-skin saddles and peacocks fanning huge white tails were about. The whole scene was colorful, spectacular. Somewhere in the distance I heard the rumbling roar of a leopard."

Among the extras working that day was a young Englishman who would later gain fame as the debonair David Niven. "I was one of a thousand extras naked except for a loincloth," wrote Niven. "For two days I saw DeMille, on a high platform between two columns, issue instructions for the shoal-like eddying of our vast throng. With his aristocratic face and a fringe of hair at the base of his shining skull, DeMille looked like a benevolent bishop. He did not sound like one."

"That goddamned murmuring behind my back is a hideous conspiracy!"

"You know when you come here how DeMille works! Why does God send me the curse of the child mind?"

"What I want is quiet! Quiet behind the camera! Intelligence in front of it! I know I can't have both! Let's see if I can have one or the other!"

The next day, Agnes de Mille, who had found herself pushed to the perimeters of the stage and ignored for two weeks, finally got an audience with DeMille. She and Ralph Jester wanted to show him a dress made of Lastex that would be worn by a chorus of "African" girls standing like a living frieze behind her as she danced. "Well, Uncle Ce didn't like it a bit," wrote Agnes. "He knitted his brows; he gnawed his fist; he rocked back and forth in his chair; then suddenly he yelped, 'Ouch!' The leopard which lay beside Cleopatra's bed playfully closed his jaws on Ce's calf. Only the thick leather puttee saved Ce's leg. Even so, the teeth grazed his skin." Agnes was sent back to the drawing board.

"The name of this movie is *Cleopatra*," said Colbert a day later. "Why is Mr. DeMille always over in a corner with Harry discussing battle armor and sword designs?" Before her rhetorical question could be answered, stress caught up with her. "Do you know what the temperature on this set is?" asked Colbert. "Eighty-six! It can't be one degree cooler or these purple ostrich feathers will moult! I look as though I have almost nothing on, don't I? This veil weighs seventy-seven pounds, with the jewels!" On April 1, she went home with a fever. She stayed home. The film fell three days behind schedule. "She may be sick," said DeMille, "but I'm the one that's dying." Agnes was losing sympathy. "Well, now Colbert is playing sick, or so C. B. claims," Agnes wrote her mother. "Indeed she may not be playing. In fact, the poor girl may be gravely ill, but the entire company has to lay off until she is ready to work again. This illness involves a possible loss of $10,000. As C. B. crossly and ungallantly expresses the situation, 'She always was a bitch.'"

DeMille was making a sexy movie. He could. In spite of Breen's aggressive management of the SRC, the spring of 1934 saw more skin on screen than ever before. In Leisen's *Murder at*

the Vanities, chorus girls sitting atop huge cacti during a musical number called "Marahuana" were topless except for hands coyly crossed on their chests. *Search for Beauty* had male athletes running naked through a locker room. *The Scarlet Empress* had several scenes of topless women. Breen suppressed a nude swimming scene in M-G-M's *Tarzan and His Mate*. That was his only victory. It was obvious why Joy had thrown up his hands and quit. However, Breen only appeared helpless. He was working behind the scenes, and there was lightning on the horizon. From Chicago came the announcement that a Legion of Decency was being organized.

So what? DeMille was cooperating with the SRC. He even had a censor visiting the set on a regular basis, usually Islin Auster or Geoffrey Shurlock, just to show he was abiding by the rules. Yet no censor heard what Agnes overheard one day. "To a member of his staff Uncle Ce described the dance with the bull as 'an orgasm, a copulation between an animal and a girl.'"

While Colbert was away, DeMille could have resolved the question of what the bull dance would include. Oddly, Agnes could neither get through to her uncle nor get anyone to help her. She could not get rehearsal space, rehearsal time, or dancers to rehearse. All she got were sessions with a bull, photos of herself, and a screen test that caused DeMille to say that she was photogenic only if she looked straight ahead and did not smile; neither her nose nor teeth looked right.

On April 16 Colbert returned. On April 20, Agnes got her chance. A performance of her dance was set for eight thirty. A crew of cosmeticians, including the famous Wally Westmore, worked all day on her, interrupted only by orders from DeMille. "Pull out her eyebrows," he yelled into the phone. "Grease her hair black." The makeup artists were rushing, so they made mistakes. "The body makeup is streaked," said one. "My God, if DeMille sees that! Strip her and do it over!" The costume presented more problems. "The wide, flat Egyptian collar had to be rendered immovable," wrote Agnes. "It was affixed to me by surgical tape, but it slipped repeatedly. Three times the

OPPOSITE: Henry Wilcoxon brought both authority and pathos to his portrayal of Marc Antony. Photograph by Ray Jones.

dressers wrenched the jewels off my resisting flesh. Gouts of blood sprang out all over my back and shoulders. They wiped the blood away without apology."

When Agnes arrived at the small throne room set, she found an audience of fifty waiting. "Cecil sat in Cleopatra's great black marble throne at the top of a flight of steps, the Sun of Horus behind his head. On his right sat Claudette Colbert. On his left, the censor." At a signal from DeMille, Agnes performed her lyric ode to the bull, who was mercifully not present. At the end of her dance, she presented her uncle with a lotus and waited for applause. Out of deference for the boss, there was a moment of silence. "Oh, no. Oh, no," said DeMille slowly. "I am so disappointed! This has nothing. It may be authentic, but it has no excitement, no thrill, no suspense, no sex." He turned to the censor. "Would that rouse you?"

"It sure wouldn't."

"It wouldn't rouse me," said Cecil, "nor any man." He paused, not noticing that Agnes was flushed under her makeup. "What I would like is something like the Lesbian dance in my *Sign of the Cross.*"

"Boy!" chortled the censor, "If you hadn't had the Christians singing hymns like crazy all throughout that dance, you never would have got away with it."

Agnes had heard enough. "That dance was one of the funniest exhibitions I ever saw," she sneered.

DeMille rose and walked past her. "That is precisely the kind of humor we are after, babe." His cast and crew followed. "We'll have to be very careful about the press," said DeMille, trailing off. "This could be awkward," he called back to her. "Try not to talk until I do. You can hurt yourself."

Agnes's contract was abrogated, and she left DeMille's home. A few days later, she talked to Roy Burns. "I came here in

all eagerness." She wept. "I was mad to please, adoring my uncle and believing in him. I have been flouted and cut off on every side. Deliberately. I go back without a foot of film shot. Figure out what I have cost all around and what you got for it—and you tell me if that's good business."

DeMille called in Theodore Kosloff to create a dance. When they were filming it, the bull apparently wished to convey his solidarity with Agnes. He made a big mess on the black marble floor. Twice. As if on cue, two articles appeared in the *Times*, reporting discord in the DeMille clan and sympathizing with Agnes. This embarrassed DeMille. William reached out to him. "Very sorry you and Agnes could not see eye to eye," he wrote. "Of course there is no artist as positive as a young artist, unless perhaps it is an old artist. I am sorry. I had hoped she could be of real help."

Cecil would not yield. "I was not greatly amused by Agnes," he wrote William. "Apparently in her mind, motion

OPPOSITE: DeMille gave his staff a goal: "This entire barge sequence should be the most seductive, erotic, beautiful, rhythmic, sensuous series of scenes ever shown."

ABOVE: Rudolph Kopp's exquisite score makes this sequence a masterpiece of pure cinema. It was also an exercise in eroticism. Because of community standards, no critic wrote directly about it.

OVERLEAF: Fifty years later, when Claudette Colbert was being honored by the Film Society of Lincoln Center, this scene was planned as the last film clip in a compendium of scenes from her career. As she was about to go onstage—and the clip was about to roll—she peremptorily told the director to stop the film. "Don't show that," she said. "It's vulgar." Then she walked onstage. Henry Wilcoxon was more good-natured about the scene. "And, yes," he said, "Claudette and I are doing what you think we're doing behind those curtains."

picture companies are just great big foster-fathers created for the purpose of furnishing little girls with funds gratis. The 'relative' angle put me in a rather foolish light with the company."

William tried to soothe Agnes. "Ce can be tough," he wrote her, "particularly with family. I've had some dealings that weren't pretty. Now you know. The pressures on that man are overwhelming."

On April 28, the Legion of Decency incorporated. Within a month, the Legion collected 300,000 signatures in each of the dioceses of Brooklyn, Philadelphia, and Los Angeles, 500,000 in Cleveland, 600,000 in Detroit, a million in Boston, and a million in Chicago. In itself this meant little to Hollywood. But there was something else to consider. For all its power and influence and wealth, the American film industry was selling a product that was not considered art. Just as photography was the bastard child of painting, the movie was the poor man's theater. "Making pictures is not like writing literature or composing music or painting masterpieces," wrote Edwin Schallert. "The screen story is essentially a thing of today and once it has had its run, that day is finished. So far there has never been a classic film in the sense that there is a classic novel or poem or canvas or sonata. Last year's picture, however strong its appeal at the time, is a book that has gone out of circulation."

This was simply not true. *The King of Kings*, *Ben-Hur*, *The Sign of the Cross*, and numerous other films were in circulation, if not in reissue. Yet even foreign films were considered more worthy than Hollywood films. "DeMille's *This Day and Age* combines recognizable elements from the Russian picture *Road*

to Life and the German picture *M*," wrote Philip Scheuer in the *Times*, as if to justify his praise of DeMille's technique. The Hollywood film was not art; hence, it was fair game for censorship.

The climax of *Cleopatra* was the queen's suicide scene. It was also Colbert's day of reckoning. She was sitting in her canvasback chair, wondering what kind of reptile her director had in store for her. DeMille appeared at the edge of the set. There was a buzz of comment. A snake was wrapped around his left arm. It was shiny and scary-looking. He advanced toward the throne. "No! No!" screamed Colbert.

"Yes," said DeMille. "You said you'd do the scene."

"Don't! Don't come near me with that thing! I wouldn't touch it for a million dollars!"

DeMille continued forward. Then he stopped. The snake's head was resting on his hand, its eyes staring impassively at Colbert. Then she noticed that he was hiding his right hand behind his back. What could be *there*? Something worse? He quickly brought his right hand forward. In it was a small snake,

CLAUDETTE COLBERT

"DeMille's films were special. Somehow, when he put everything together, there was sincerity—and a special kind of glamour."

OVERLEAF, LEFT TO RIGHT: To match Harold Miles's concept art, DeMille stood on a platform in the wee hours of the morning, giving orders with a microphone. "Move that black horse forward. Put one of those red generals between chariots five and six. Bring that Egyptian in front of the tree. Look at Antony! There's no sweat! Where in the Sam Hill is the sweat?" A makeup artist with a large flit-gun sprayed Henry Wilcoxon with the mineral oil Nujol until he glistened—and shivered. • A portrait of Claudette Colbert by George Hoyningen-Huene.

OPPOSITE, TOP: Every prop and piece of jewelry in *Cleopatra* had to be designed and made at Paramount.

OPPOSITE, BOTTOM: Colbert was afraid of snakes, so DeMille played a trick on her to get the last scene in *Cleopatra*.

CECIL B. DeMILLE

"Claudette wanted to do something different with *Cleopatra*, not make her lofty or fussy or superstitious. Nothing like that. She set out to give her humor and humanity, and she stamped her own personality on the role. She emerged from it most vividly, I thought."

perhaps six inches long, like a sand adder. "How about this one?" he asked.

"Oh, that little thing." She sighed. "That's just a baby." She dressed for the scene and did it without a hitch.

DeMille finished *Cleopatra* on May 2 but still had to work with William Cameron Menzies on montages and title art. It was during this period that Wilcoxon was injured. The first incident occurred while DeMille was shooting a sequence for Menzies to use in the war montage. "One of the bit players was supposed to charge me," recounted Wilcoxon. "As he was coming at me, he tripped over an extra who was lying on the ground, acting dead. This man, instead of coming in high, where I was expecting him and had my shield, came low. I couldn't get my shield low enough in time. He ran his sword through my knee. I was taken to the hospital. The injury was serious."

Weeks later, when Wilcoxon returned, the scene had to be completed, and with the same player who had injured him. The man was nervous. He overcompensated. "Instead of aiming for the center of my head," said Wilcoxon, "Bill hit the hilt of my sword and cut the top of my little finger off." A doctor saved Wilcoxon's finger.

Cleopatra had to be submitted to the SRC. Breen was not there; he was in Chicago and Philadelphia, lending support to the Catholic crusade. On May 20, Philadelphia's Dennis Cardinal Dougherty took to the pulpit and exhorted his parishioners to boycott not just immoral movies but *all* movies, and that this was a "positive command, binding all in conscience, under pain of sin." The Legion of Decency, which had collected three million pledges, held its first rally. Addressing 50,000 people, Cleveland bishop Joseph Schrembs roared: "Purify Hollywood or destroy Hollywood!"

In one week, box-office receipts fell 40 percent. In two weeks, the Stanley Theatre chain lost $350,000. *Variety* dropped its insouciant tone. "Need Prompt Action to Avert Drastic Penalties on Picture Industry—Real Danger." Harry Warner called Hays. "Will," he pleaded, "you've got to save us.

I'm being ruined by the hour. If anybody else does this thing, we're out of business." Ordinarily the studios could go to the Giannini family at the Bank of America. This recourse was suddenly unavailable; the Gianninis announced that they were not lending money for immoral films. Only a year had passed since the bank crisis. No studio had enough money to continue production for more than three weeks. "Hollywood knew it was licked," wrote Father Lord, "but to its own salvation." Hays turned to Breen. "Joe, look! For the love of God, come over here! What can you do?"

"I've been telling you guys it's coming," Breen answered.

On June 22, it arrived. The board of the Motion Picture Producers and Distributors Association (MPPDA) assembled in Will Hays's New York office to learn that a Catholic constituency had wrested control of a Protestant market from a Jewish-controlled industry. The content of films would henceforth be dictated by Joseph I. Breen, using a new Code and a new agency. On July 11, the SRC would become the Produc-

———— CECILIA DE MILLE PRESLEY ————

"DeMille knew that the censors were going to take over and enforce their Production Code. DeMille was determined to tweak their noses, to put something provocative in a scene that they would totally miss. This is what he did. Claudette Colbert was lying on a couch. She was wearing a negligee that was virtually transparent. Harry Wilcoxon was sitting next to her, kissing her hand and forearm. DeMille shot the scene through the strings of a harp. He knew that the hands of the harpist on the strings would look like he was caressing her body. Anyone who really understood what he was doing would enjoy it. It was a wonderful scene, and it worked. The censors did not catch it. The audience did. And Grandfather loved it."

OPPOSITE, TOP TO BOTTOM: An uncredited concept painting for *Cleopatra*. • DeMille composed the scene so it would flout the censor.

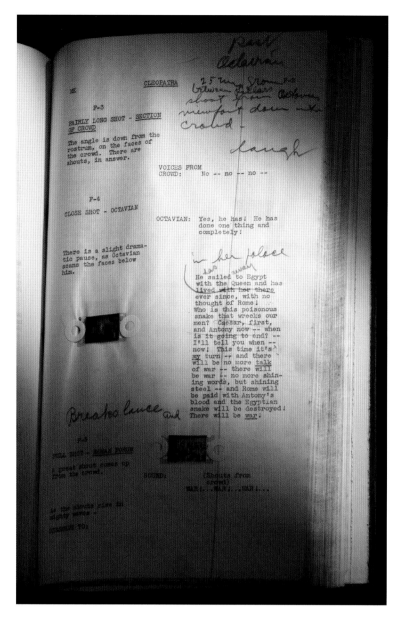

ABOVE: Octavian's speech at the Senate ran afoul of the PCA. "He has sailed to Egypt with the queen and has lived there *with her* ever since," says Octavian. Photograph by Mark A. Vieira.

OPPOSITE, CLOCKWISE FROM TOP LEFT: DeMille aimed the camera at the crowd from Octavian's point of view. • As DeMille shot this mob scene in early April 1934, similar scenes were brewing in the Midwest. • This scene was trimmed to comply with the new Code. • DeMille did not want the censor to cut scenes from *Cleopatra*.

tion Code Administration (PCA). The 1930 Production Code would be reconstituted as "A Code to Govern the Making of Motion and Talking Pictures." This document included "Compensating Moral Values," a requirement that evil be identified and condemned by a major character in every film, and that it be punished by the last reel. Breen had absolute au-

thority. Without his seal on a script, a film could not be made. Without a numbered PCA seal, a film could not be released. If a company tried to release it without a seal, no MPPDA theater could play it. Any attempt to bypass the Code would result in a $25,000 fine. The new Code had teeth. How would it affect *Cleopatra*?

On June 20, DeMille previewed his film at Catalina Island's Casino Theatre. The audience loved it. Once again, DeMille had made a million-dollar movie for less; in this case, $842,908.17. The final cut was locked, and the negative was ready to be printed. But it had to wait for the PCA to open. DeMille got in line. There were seventy-nine films ahead of him. One of them featured his daughter Katherine. She was playing an 1890s vamp in the Mae West vehicle *It Ain't No Sin*. It became the first victim of the PCA. West was made to rewrite and reshoot scenes, and to change its title to *Belle of the Nineties*. The same thing happened to Jean Harlow's *Born to Be Kissed*; rewrites, retakes, and a purified title, *The Girl from Missouri*. Breen had no respect for "glamorous sin-women."

DeMille aligned himself with the new regime by releasing a news item. To meet censorship demands, his next film would be a religious epic called *The Crusades*. Surely Breen would like that. After weeks of waiting, *Cleopatra* was screened and the PCA report delivered. DeMille was shocked. Breen had found things to cut—even though his staff had practically been living on the *Cleopatra* set!

1: There was a line spoken by Octavian (Ian Keith) on the steps of the Forum. "Yes, he's done one thing, and that completely. He has sailed to Egypt with the queen and has lived there *with her* ever since, with no thought of Rome."

2: There was exposure of men's buttocks during a scene with flaming hoops and dancers in leopard costumes, as well as suggestive movements between men and "animals."

3: There were movements suggesting "unnatural practices with beasts" in the bull dance.

Breen wanted these excised, or he would not grant a seal.

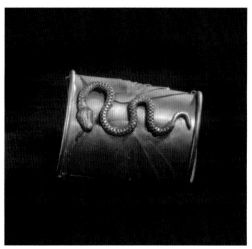

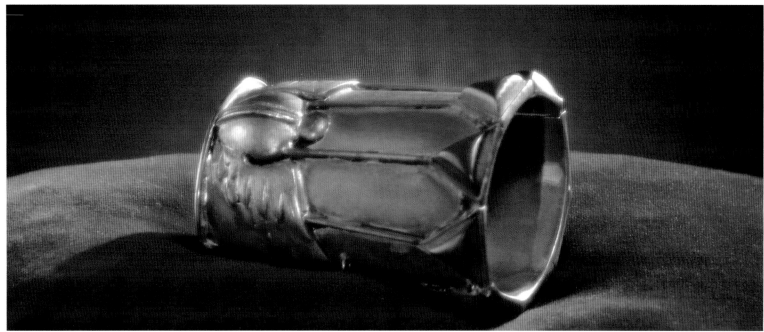

DeMille was furious. There could be no excisions to this film. The negative had been cut. He could not go back and remix three reels. The expense would be staggering. To censor something by cutting the composite negative would result in jump cuts in both picture and sound! Breen did not care. DeMille argued further. He got nowhere. Breen could swear as loudly as he could. He had met his match. "Joe Breen was not a big man, about five foot eight," recalled Vizzard. "He was chesty, with an athletic spring in his legs. When he looked at you, it was as if he was saying, 'You wouldn't like to knock this chip off my shoulder, would you?' He was an intelligent man, so this was no dummy act. He was physically fearless." DeMille had bent producers, extras, and a niece to his will. He could not bend a censor. Cuts totaling twenty seconds were made to the composite negative.

DeMille went to New York for the August 16 premiere of *Cleopatra* at the Paramount Theatre. In spite of three jump cuts, his "epic with sex" was vigorously, rapturously received. It helped that Paramount's sales department had launched a dozen tie-in promotions. It helped that Colbert was the star of the year. And it helped that Americans were still fascinated with Ancient Egypt, especially if it had an Art Deco flavor. These were trimmings. DeMille had built his epic on a sound premise, a woman who wants to save her country from invaders but falls in love with them, destroying both them and herself.

Beyond that, DeMille had accomplished the impossible. He had filmed the idea that Agnes de Mille had heard him describe, an orgasm on Cleopatra's barge. It did not take place between a girl and a bull, but more appropriately, between Antony and Cleopatra. With the confidence of the cinematic artist, DeMille did it in a single ninety-second shot.

It starts at Cleopatra's divan, just as Antony succumbs to her wiles. As the camera pulls back, satin curtains are dropped to give the lovers privacy. The crane lifts the camera. Rose petals fall from the ship's rigging. An immense African guard steps in front of the curtain. A dozen couples sink to the polished floor, embracing. Maidens raise incense braziers. A solo dancer writhes to Rudolph Kopp's seductive theme. The camera continues to pull back, rolling the length of the barge and revealing a row of African galley slaves on each side. As the music hits its first crescendo, an aide signals. The golden oars begin to move. The slave driver (in foreground silhouette) hits a drum, matching the sensual throb of the music. The hypnotic stroke of the oars, the insistent beat of the drummer, the weightless ascent of the camera, and the rhythm of the music all convey one idea—what the Code had supposedly removed from the movies. As the music peaks, the barge sails away from Tarsus. Audiences in 1934 were stunned, mesmerized, or just plain awestruck. No one had ever seen anything like it.

"Motion pictures cannot be made without sex," DeMille declared in a *Film Daily* editorial. "Take it away from films and you take away their very life." There was a lot of life in *Cleopatra*. How would it fare in the new Hollywood?

"At nine o'clock this morning there was a line to the box office of the Paramount Theatre from the Times building," DeMille wired his staff on August 17. "The manager says he hasn't seen a sight like this for a long time." Evading, eluding, and mocking the Code, *Cleopatra* joined the list of DeMille hits, ultimately becoming the best-liked version of the queen's life.

CECIL B. DeMILLE

"Cheapness and vulgarity are not the answer. The public has responded more to Rembrandt and Rodin than they have to the pornographic sketcher who sits in a Paris attic and draws dirty postcards."

OPPOSITE: These adornments helped DeMille tell the story of Cleopatra. Photography by Mark A. Vieira.

OVERLEAF, LEFT TO RIGHT: "Look well for love," says Cleopatra in her final speech. "Look well. And not finding it, give nothing. But if blessed with Cleopatra's fortune, give all." • Paul Hesse used the carbro color process to make this portrait of Claudette Colbert.

THE CRUSADES

The tumult of 1934 softened into the hum of a well-oiled machine as Cecil B. DeMille prepared another epic, *The Crusades*. He began by purchasing *The Crusades*, a popular 1931 book by the historian and novelist Harold Lamb. DeMille wasted no time in bringing Lamb to Hollywood and teaming him with Waldemar Young and Dudley Nichols. This formidable trio came up with a long but well-focused saga.

"*The Crusades* is an example of what I call telescoping history," wrote DeMille. "There were seven Crusades extending over four centuries. It would be impossible to tell the story of them all in 12,000 feet of film. We chose the year 1187 as the focal point for our story, but did not hesitate to bring in elements from other Crusades. The Hermit played by C. Aubrey Smith was meant to embody Peter the Hermit, Bernard of Clairvaux, and all the zealous preachers who stirred Europe."

By 1935, it was standard practice to transcribe story conferences; flashes of inspiration were often erased by dumb ideas during a scripting free for all, so it helped to have it all on paper, even if reading it later was like deciphering what someone had said while going into surgery under ether. At a January 5 conference with executives Emanuel Cohen, Benjamin Glazer, E. Lloyd Sheldon, and Jeff Lazarus, DeMille wanted to know what these execs thought of the first-draft script. The big boss Cohen spoke first, of course. "This is a very important picture and will cost a lot of money," he said, expressing the obvious.

"I think it is a swell picture and a swell job," said Sheldon. "But I am rather anxious to see a stronger spiritual impulse, a stronger underscoring of theme."

"It's terrific stuff," said Lazarus. "But you're right. Whether it grosses one million or five million is going to be decided by how spiritual the thing is. Unless you say, 'Here is the greatest fight that decent people have ever waged,' you won't gross five million."

"We can start with a cross on top of a church," said DeMille. "They throw a rope around and it crashes to the street. We go to a cut of a great bonfire of sacred books and then we go to the slave market."

"We're not spending enough time with the soldiers of the Lord, but with these kings," said Lazarus. "Cecil, you've given them the tar brush. Look at Richard. He had no great purpose."

CECIL B. DeMILLE

"*The Crusades*, in my opinion, is one of the best pictures I have ever made."

OPPOSITE: Cecil B. DeMille used potent symbolism in the advertising art for his 1935 film, *The Crusades*. Portrait of Henry Wilcoxon by William Walling Jr.

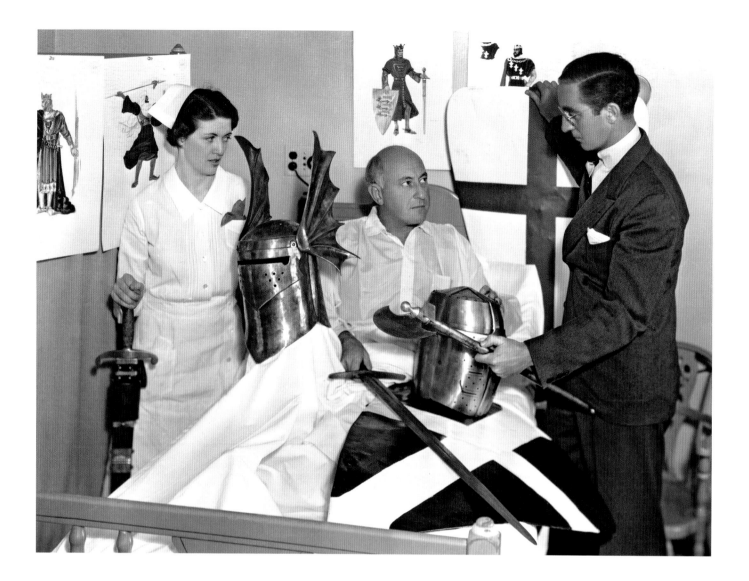

He goes into the Crusade to get out of the way of one wife and to get meat for his men."

"It's awfully important, Cecil," said Sheldon. "Think of these wretched souls that went over there and went through privation when kings were thinking only of another province."

"It sounds like I'm going to have to put back the stuff that was eliminated because of the cost," said DeMille. "The little squire saying good-bye to his old mother. The young boy bidding his sweetheart good-bye. Those shots are what you're missing."

"One group should tell the Crusade story," said Lazarus. "A group that has a great, invincible, clean purpose."

DeMille knew what he had to clarify. "The only way that an audience today will believe that people would give up their lives for the True Cross, for a piece of wood, is to put in a personal story. We have to carry a character like Richard—who is the au-

dience—and show him acquiring spiritual understanding. Then we let the audience take it from there."

Cohen later discussed the budget with DeMille, agreeing only to $1 million. DeMille needed $1.2 million. "Mr. Cohen started to nevertheless proceed with the picture," recalled DeMille. "He said he would take it up later with New York. If

ABOVE: DeMille was hospitalized briefly while preparing *The Crusades*. Ralph Jester submitted designs to the boss as usual.

OPPOSITE, CLOCKWISE FROM TOP LEFT: A Travis Banton costume sketch for Alice of France, who was played by Katherine DeMille. • DeMille did not approve this costume sketch for Berengaria, who was played by Loretta Young. "Mr. Banton, I don't think there will be enough difference between this and the wedding dress and nightgown. CBDM." • The helmet created for Richard the Lionheart, who was played by Henry Wilcoxon. Photograph by Mark A. Vieira.

it was a big success—and we were both confident that it would be—the cost would be forgotten." DeMille had a reputation for extravagance. It was not accurate. He was constantly watching expenses, underbidding, and cutting corners. He was looking for ways to cut the set construction budget by $25,000. He used standing sets from *Cleopatra* and from Henry Hathaway's *The Lives of a Bengal Lancer*, and would use one set twice. First it would be Windsor Castle; three weeks later it would be a street in Marseille. The wardrobe was budgeted at $144,000. DeMille was determined to cut $44,000 from that. Given the volume of costumes needed, he had to employ a large staff. Travis Banton had to oversee Edith Head, Ralph Jester, Natalie Visart, and Shannon Rogers. They were driven to produce. Banton finished 149 sketches—one every two and a half days—at a cost

of $36,400. Head completed 261 sketches—one every one and a half days—at a cost of $10,400.

The role of Richard was promised to Henry Wilcoxon, who had made a splash as Marc Antony. This time Wilcoxon's preparation included a horse named Fouvel. "He was half Morgan and half Arab and all black," wrote Wilcoxon. "He had the strength of the Morgan with the high-strung temperament of the Arabian. It was love at first sight."

At Christmas, Katherine DeMille was hurt when she received no gift from her father. "I purposely bought you nothing this year," he said, "because I want to offer you something

ABOVE: Ann Sheridan was an unknown when she played a Christian girl being sold into slavery.

which I think will do you more good. My present to you this year is the role of Alice of France in *The Crusades*." Katherine had misgivings, but kept them to herself. "One simply didn't refuse a present from Father," recalled Katherine. DeMille could not refuse a gift from Paramount, a budget increase of $40,000. It was not the $200,000 that Cohen had informally promised, but it was timely. DeMille fell ill in January and spent a few days in the hospital. Once he felt strong enough, he resumed his pre-production duties—in his hospital bed. "I pressed nurses into service to model the women's costumes," wrote DeMille, "and I had men from the studio clanging in and out of my room attired as knights, monks, Saracens, and what not."

Filming of *The Crusades* commenced on January 30, 1935. DeMille was shooting scenes out of order, which he preferred not to do, because he was waiting for Loretta Young to finish William Wellman's *The Call of the Wild* for Twentieth Century Pictures. *Photoplay* magazine was not sending reporters to the set. DeMille was irked about an article that caricatured him as mean and fat. He granted access to a *Screenland* magazine writer. James B. Fisher would cover the making of the film from an extra's point of view, and he would be the extra.

On February 2, Fisher was dressed in tights, leather jerkin, peaked hat, and pointed shoes, playing a peasant in the scene

─────── CECILIA DE MILLE PRESLEY ───────

"Henry Wilcoxon was an actor's actor, trained on the English stage. He was successful in America, starring in two pictures for DeMille, but he never became a star. He was so talented in many areas. Henry could do anything: act, direct, write, draw, design, manage, and solve just about any kind of production problem. A career that began with the discovery of a young actor transformed itself into a warm, respectful collaboration. Henry became Grandfather's closest associate. He told me that Henry was one of the most honorable men he ever knew."

where Richard joins the Crusade to avoid marrying Alice. The first thing Fisher heard was not a rich British voice speaking dialogue but a sharp California voice giving orders to a lighting crew. "Hit Richard with that eighteen! Pull those three down harder on the Hermit! Now light that twenty-four and pull it down harder on those monks. Flood 'em all up!"

After the scene was lit, it was time for a rehearsal. And then his first shot of the day. "Knowing nothing of court intrigue," wrote Fisher, "we all shout approval according to the desire of director DeMille, who swings dizzily overhead on the camera boom. An excited 'peasant,' forgetting time and place, shouts 'God bless King George!' DeMille, who forgets nothing, groans. 'You're just eight hundred years ahead of our story! Let's take it again. And please remember that you are in the twelfth century!'"

Filming *The Crusades* was a complicated and arduous process. Every scene was layered with period detail. On February 7, Fisher was fitted in a monk's costume for an upcoming scene. Then he watched Wilcoxon act with Montagu Love in a blacksmith's hut. Love had spent a month learning the trade so he could enact his scenes convincingly. A high school drama class wrote to Love, asking him to recommend the best preparation for acting school. "When I was a young man, the answer to that was Shakespeare," said Love. "Since I've been on this picture, I would say three years as a Boy Scout."

There was no Scout's Honor in Paramount's executive offices. On February 9, Emanuel ("Manny") Cohen was removed from office. The reason was not related to production or expenses; in his obtuse way he had kept the studio going. He had, however, signed a number of stars, including Mae West, Gary Cooper, and Bing Crosby, to personal contracts, effectively cutting out Paramount. This Machiavellian move ended his studio tenure but not his career.

There was more intrigue. On February 13, the *Los Angeles Times* printed the story that Katherine's birth family was in touch with her. A cousin on her father's side in England had read about her in a fan magazine and then tracked her down.

She learned conclusively that her biological father, Edward Lester, had been killed at the 1917 battle of Vimy Ridge. He had still been missing in action when her mother brought her to Los Angeles in 1920. Katherine had been left with an orphanage after her mother died of tuberculosis. Katherine found it stressful to have her private life examined while working for her father. She gained weight and could not fit into her form-fitting costumes, which added to her stress.

DeMille was too busy to comment. He had wig problems. "We had a man right in the foreground of a shot with a dead white part in his wig which was faky," DeMille wrote in a February memo. "We save $80 on a wig like this and then it costs us an expensive retake." He was filming the scene in which Christian maidens are sold as slaves. Fisher was dressed as a "Saracen dandy," and in the foreground with the Christians was Ann Sheridan, a Texas schoolteacher who had come to Paramount a year earlier with the *Search for Beauty* contest. "I was playing this little Christian captured by the Saracens, and I was to be auctioned off," recalled Sheridan. "I had to wear this awful long brown wig—which I thought was going to make me look glamorous, wonderful, like Dietrich. Well, I looked horrible. Like you always do with a wig. So I felt very self-conscious." The scene was already being retaken because of an unsatisfactory performance by the auctioneer. The replacement was doing fine. "J. Carroll Naish was playing the auctioneer with a whip in his hand and looking very oily, and he comes and pulls me by the wrist, and I have this one line to say to this nun, who is also being sold, 'The cross, the cross! Let me kiss the cross!'"

Sheridan was only a year away from her hometown. "Well! Honey! I had this Texas accent, and I said, 'The cwouse, the cwouse! Let me kiss the cwouse!'" Mr. DeMille turned absolutely red with hysterics. "Young lady, where are you from?"

"Denton, Texas."

"How do you say c-r-o-s-s?"

"Cwouse."

"Miss Sheridan," said DeMille. "We're going to take a little respite now and have lunch, and you go with the drama coach here." This time DeMille was more amused than annoyed. "He was giggling. He couldn't stop giggling. I worked on that line for half an hour. It really didn't come out right in the end." DeMille would later have another actress "loop" the lines onto the sound track.

The Crusades picked up steam when Loretta Young arrived on February 25. She was all aglow, in a wonderful mood. Fisher heard gossip that "she has been snowbound for weeks in the Sierra with Clark Gable." Young came up to DeMille with Travis Banton and showed him costume sketches. "This one is lovely," said Young. "I can't wait to wear it."

"There were moments in the past month," said DeMille, "when I wondered if I should ever have the opportunity of seeing you wear it."

On February 27, the Academy of Motion Picture Arts and Sciences, which DeMille had helped to found, held its Seventh Annual Academy Awards ceremony. *Cleopatra* was nominated for Best Picture, Best Sound Recording, Best Editing, Best Assistant Director, but not for Best Director, Art Direction, Costume Design, or, inexcusably, for Rudolph Kopp's exquisite score. Victor Milner won the Academy Award for Best Cinematography. Claudette Colbert won the Best Actress Award for *It Happened One Night*, and Clark Gable won Best Actor for the same film. Loretta Young's cheeriness came to an end when she discovered she was carrying Gable's child. No one was told anything while she pondered her options; this was another of the dramas being played out behind the scenes of DeMille's epic.

In mid-March, DeMille was sick again, but this time he was able to recover after a day at home. It was obvious to every-

OPPOSITE: *The Crusades* was Katherine DeMille's first featured role with her father; it was Joseph Schildkraut's last. "DeMille is always aiming at sweeping theatrical and pictorial effects," wrote Schildkraut.

ABOVE: The Hermit (C. Aubrey Smith) exhorts the masses to join the Crusade.

OPPOSITE: A scene still shows Katherine DeMille as Princess Alice of France, reclining in the cabin of her ship.

one that he was enjoying the production and inspired by the subject. He customarily had guests to the set, even installing bleachers so that groups of visitors could watch him direct. Every journalist found him pleasant and voluble. As much as he yelled at his extras, he knew many of them by name, joked with them, and was proud of them. They were more than daubs of paint on his cinematic canvas. "Don't those people down there look as if one had always known them?" he asked a reporter. "They are an undying type, the lean-ribbed, thin-faced Anglo-Saxons, fond of the outdoors, of horses, of gaiety and danger. Born rebels, preferring activity to thought, and loyal to a leader. They're enamored of change. They never stay at anything long, unless there's danger in it." A child caught his eye, and a dog. "Children, dogs, and horses have reached the peak of evolution," he continued. "They never change from one epoch to another. After all, the Crusades were just 800 years ago—only yesterday."

There was déjà vu on the set one day. Wilcoxon did not feel it because as far as he knew, the incident was happening for the first time. There were DeMille veterans present who could testify otherwise. Wilcoxon saw DeMille lash out at a red-headed extra named Jeanie McDonald. Her infraction was talking when DeMille was directing. It mattered not that she was far away on a balcony. He ordered her to come down and tell everyone what was so important that she would ignore him and keep jabbering. "I watched this little extra girl become Joan of Arc," wrote Wilcoxon. "She took the microphone from his hand and said clearly and resolutely, 'I said, When is that old, bald-headed

ANN SHERIDAN

"Mr. DeMille? Sheer heaven! I adored him! A lot of people said after he died, 'Oh, but I hated him.' Now, I absolutely adored him. He was dear to me."

S.O.B. going to shut up and let us go to lunch?'" Right on cue, DeMille said, "Lunch!" A few extras looked at each other, shook their heads, and went to lunch.

On another day, the DeMille set was visited by the Broadway producer Arch Selwyn, the same man who had fired him in 1913. DeMille was directing hundreds of extras from the boom and appeared not to notice Selwyn. Without a warning, DeMille turned, looked down, and singled out Selwyn. "Well, boss, what you think of things now?" asked DeMille. "How'm I doin'?" There was little that Selwyn could say.

Another visitor saw a deeper purpose in DeMille's film. A religious writer named Charles Woessner was given the grand tour. A book was born, *Cecil B. DeMille: Screen-Prophet and Cinema Apostle*. In it, Woessner went out on a limb. "Cecil B. DeMille is a 'touch man,'" wrote Woessner. "When an idea strikes him, he immediately begins to film the picture that has been created within his mind. It is as if the Creator has pressed a button within him and Divine Intelligence takes hold, with ideas for his 'congregation' of 300 million souls to see, and feel, and live."

It was true that DeMille was encoding *The Crusades* with a message of tolerance. Whether this idea originated with a Divine Button or with experiences of anti-Semitism, no one knew. DeMille charged forth, making a message movie in an industry that eschewed such things. "For over two hours," wrote Woessner, "we heard Henry Wilcoxon pray a short prayer of repentance before Mr. DeMille's camera, yet the prayer lasted for only about thirty seconds on the screen. It had to be repeated and re-said many times before it satisfied this directing genius." DeMille was heading in a new direction, and it looked as if he would find an eager audience. "Seeing his films is to walk into a great art gallery," wrote Woessner. "At each viewing the spectator beholds something new. Some have seen his pictures a score of times. A recent picture was seen 180 times by a single person." Unfortunately, the film was not identified.

Wilcoxon suspected that DeMille had an ethical investment in *The Crusades*. "*The Crusades* presents a strong personal statement of DeMille on the futility of Holy War," said Wilcoxon. "What does it matter how we worship God, so long as each man does it in his own way. The people who insist their way is the only way are the people I have no time for. Their 'intolerance' is what *The Crusades* is all about."

DeMille took the film on his yacht and sailed to San Diego, where he found a working-class, neighborhood theater. "The subjects made a cross section of America," wrote Jeanette Meehan in the *San Francisco Chronicle*. "They were neighborhood folk, transients from an auto-trailer camp, American Legionnaires, shopkeepers, orange growers, a party of St. Louis shoe-factory workers, children, and a sprinkling of Portuguese and Japanese fishermen. As the pageant began to trundle across the screen, DeMille watched the faces of the audience in the reflected light." The audience responded as he had expected. *The Crusades* had come in eighteen days behind schedule and $336,000 over budget. If a world of moviegoers responded as this audience did, all would be forgiven.

The perceptive and clever Andre Sennwald wrote in the *New York Times*: "Mr. DeMille has no peer in the world when it comes to bringing the panoplied splendor of the past into torrential life upon the screen. Once you have granted him his right to exaggerate the significance of Miss Loretta Young and the amorous instinct in the wars of the cross and the crescent, you are his prisoner."

Being DeMille's prisoner displeased *Time* magazine. "The film is historically worthless, didactically treacherous, artistically absurd. None of these defects impairs its entertainment value. It is a $100,000,000 sideshow which has at least three

OPPOSITE: "This portrait was my idea," recalled Henry Wilcoxon in 1975. "I grabbed Bill Walling from somewhere else on the set and got him to take it like this."

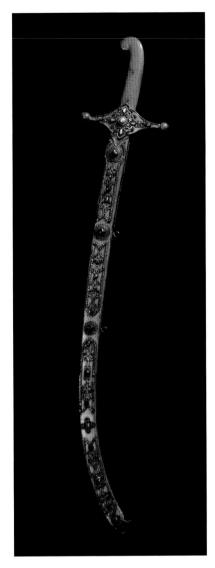

OPPOSITE: Ian Keith made the role of Saladin, Sultan of Islam, an imposing and memorable one. Cecilia de Mille Presley recalls, "DeMille rejected the bloodthirsty image of Muslims that was projected at the time. He portrayed Saladin as a civilized, cultured, chivalrous man. This was the legacy of *The Crusades*. Years later, in Egypt, we benefited from it. The film had been seen there. Its message of respect and tolerance created a red carpet for us."

ABOVE, CLOCKWISE FROM TOP LEFT: This jeweled scimitar and scabbard were made for $150 by a New York company called Becker-Lynch. • DeMille shows the artifact to Ian Keith and an unidentified visitor • This crown was worn by Hans von Twardowski, who was playing Nicholas of Hungary. The cross was bent at an angle because, according to legend, Stephen I had hit it on the lintel of a doorway. Photograph by Mark A. Vieira.

features which distinguish it from the long line of previous DeMille extravaganzas. It is the noisiest; it is the biggest; it contains no baths."

A road show began in late August, general release in October, and British release in January. That last turned out to be crucial. For some reason American audiences did not warm to trundling pageantry. And then, the night before its British release, DeMille's epic was hit by an act of God. King George V died.

"A state of mourning was declared," recalled Wilcoxon. "All movies, theaters, and amusements were ordered closed for three months." This was not just the British Isles. It was the entire British Empire: Canada, India, Australia, New Zealand, Guiana, and the British East Indies. "By the time they reopened,

our publicity was forgotten. The momentum was lost." So was the hope of a profit. *The Crusades* registered a loss of $795,000. This was bad timing. DeMille was about to negotiate a new contract with Paramount.

OVERLEAF, LEFT TO RIGHT: Loretta Young in a scene lit by Victor Milner. • Henry Wilcoxon. Photograph by William Walling Jr.

OPPOSITE, CLOCKWISE FROM TOP LEFT: The battle of Acre as staged by DeMille. • This scene of Richard watching the pilgrims enter Jerusalem was filmed in accordance with a concept painting made by Harold Miles. • The pilgrims enter the Holy City.

ABOVE: A concept painting by Harold Miles.

CHAPTER 6

AMERICAN HISTORY

THE PLAINSMAN AND THE BUCCANEER

n early 1936 Cecil B. DeMille met with John Otterson, Paramount's latest president, to discuss a new contract. DeMille wanted to do another epic, something that would combine the glamour of *Cleopatra* with the grandeur of *The Ten Commandments. Samson and Delilah* could star Henry Wilcoxon and Miriam Hopkins. Otterson was not as rude as Manny Cohen had been, but he had to point out that for all DeMille's hits since his return to Paramount, his flops had cost the company more than a million dollars. He needed to do a modern film, and with bigger stars. Otterson and his colleagues were unanimous on that. They were undecided on what kind of contract to draw up. Nine films? Three? While deciding what to do, they pulled the plug on *Samson and Delilah* and put DeMille on a retainer of $3,000 a week. Retainer or no, DeMille did not appreciate this treatment. "This is their way of getting back at me because of *The Crusades*," he said. "Nobody tells me what pictures I can and cannot make."

DeMille had at one point considered a buyout of Paramount. He had the banking connections to do it, but memories of Culver City stopped him. He momentarily considered retirement. He was fifty-four. He had made sixty films. Constance was not opposed to the idea, but neither was she excited by it. "I just wonder how she would have survived my trying to be interested in nothing but real estate or oil wells," wrote DeMille, "with the

Champion Driver straining to storm the walls of Acre, launch Cleopatra's barge, or chase a pride of lions up the stairs."

DeMille spoke with Samuel Goldwyn about releasing under his aegis. Goldwyn had become the industry's most successful independent producer, with hits aplenty. He was willing to take a chance on his old partner. Excited, DeMille called Wilcoxon. He told him to leave Paramount and come with him to Goldwyn. Wilcoxon wanted to, but there was a problem. "I'm under contract to Paramount," he said. "I'm not even an American citizen. If I walk out, they'll have me deported." DeMille grew angry.

"Excuses! Nothing but excuses! *This* is the gratitude you show me!"

Wilcoxon tried to reason with DeMille, but it was too late. He had said the wrong thing. He had questioned when he should have obeyed. DeMille hung up on him.

Meanwhile, Adolph Zukor heard about DeMille's situation with Paramount. Zukor was chairman of the board, and, though the earth was shifting in Hollywood, he was on firm

OVERLEAF: Cecil B. DeMille expressed the spirit of American achievement through Gary Cooper.

OPPOSITE: Wild Bill Hickok (Gary Cooper) and Calamity Jane (Jean Arthur) talk of love while awaiting death. DeMille thought this scene one of his best.

ground with the stockholders. He saw to it that Cecil B. DeMille Productions was offered a one-picture deal. But the film had to be, of all things, a western. Not just a western, but a super-production, with Gary Cooper as its star. The Goldwyn deal was off. DeMille reopened his office at Paramount. By a strange coincidence, Wilcoxon found himself loaned out by that studio, first to England and then to Poverty Row. Before he was shipped out, he tried to effect a rapprochement with DeMille. "All my calls were rebuked," wrote Wilcoxon. He had definitely said the wrong thing.

If Sam Goldwyn was doing well, Jesse Lasky was not. Of the fourteen films he had produced at Fox Film since 1932, only two had shown a profit. His projects were imaginative, and some were critically admired, but Fox could give him neither star power nor guidance. On May 28, 1935, Fox Film merged with a small company called Twentieth Century Pictures. Lasky joined

CECILIA DE MILLE PRESLEY

"When DeMille was casting the part of a Cheyenne Indian for one scene, he auditioned a young man named Anthony Quinn. DeMille asked him if he could speak Cheyenne. Tony, who was Mexican and Irish, later told me that he burst into a songlike gibberish. DeMille was impressed. In fact, Tony knew nothing of Native American tongues. But when he got the part, he made it a point to learn the proper dialect. He was on his way to becoming a brilliant actor—and for me, one fascinating uncle. He married my aunt, Katherine DeMille."

ABOVE: Dan Sayre Groesbeck made this concept painting for *The Plainsman*.

OVERLEAF, LEFT TO RIGHT: Helen Burgess as Louisa Cody, a character painting by Dan Sayre Groesbeck. • Jean Arthur as Calamity Jane, a character painting by Dan Sayre Groesbeck.

Mary Pickford Productions, where he produced two unsuccessful films. He and DeMille were on good terms but moving in different echelons of Hollywood.

DeMille envisioned his western as a Frederic Remington mural, with all the romance and menace of the Old West. It would be called *The Plainsman*. Since the film was to be a star vehicle, it would include legends like Wild Bill Hickok, Buffalo Bill Cody, and Calamity Jane. The project was too big to be shot by one unit, so DeMille hired a former publicist named William H. Pine to act as associate producer. Pine managed both DeMille's unit and Arthur Rosson's second unit, which went to the Tongue River in Lame Deer, Montana, to film Indian attacks and Custer's Last Stand.

"The cavalry charge has no thrill whatever," DeMille wired Rosson. "It is impossible to get a thrill from a charge coming directly at the camera. Their approach should be diagonal so that we can see the men are galloping. Let me see something that will make an audience get up and cheer, not this Sleepy Hollow scene." DeMille wanted more control, so he devised a ten-foot model of the location, with clay figures of soldiers. Rosson had a corresponding chart at the location. They communicated by telephone so that DeMille could get the shots he wanted.

DeMille was shooting on five acres of backlot in Hollywood; some sets were familiar. "Where the gates of Jerusalem have stood for a year," wrote Katherine Coughlin in *Movie Classic*, "a street in Deadwood City was constructed. The walled city of Acre is now the docks of Leavenworth after the War Between the States. Windsor Castle has become the riverboat docks of St. Louis."

As usual, DeMille was relying on Dan Sayre Groesbeck to pull images from script pages. To aid him, there was a research library of 600 volumes. Groesbeck worked with Victor Milner, Hans Dreier, and Natalie Visart. There were surprises. "Calamity Jane wore that little forage cap because Dan Groesbeck put it in the sketch," said Visart. "And Mr. DeMille loved it. I said to him, 'So do I.' He said, 'Let's use it.' Groesbeck was very good because he always caught the flavor of the person. Unless it was

something that had been established, been okayed, he would just draw it the way he wanted it. If not, he would follow my sketch. It was team work. We were like a big family."

DeMille was often fortunate with actors. Jean Arthur had been in films for thirteen years without becoming a star. Just as he cast her opposite Gary Cooper in *The Plainsman*, she was boosted to stardom by the release of another Cooper film, *Mr. Deeds Goes to Town*. She was shy and found her first day on a DeMille set a bit daunting. "Mr. DeMille was preparing the riverboat scene," said Arthur. "There were 500 people there, stevedores and frontier characters. I felt like a mote in a dust storm—until I saw Satan." This was DeMille's pet canary, the bird that had opened *Madam Satan*. "The poor bird had been left in his cage in the sun by some property man. I carried it into the shade and gave him water. I decided to make him my special charge. Pretty soon people were smiling at me, grips and electricians and actors. Satan broke the ice for me."

Cooper was a major star, one of the top ten box-office attractions. DeMille was not cowed. "No one is to leave the set without my permission," he said one day. A short while later, Cooper assumed a schoolboy manner and timidly raised his hand. "Please, sir, may I leave the room?" This, too, broke the ice. Cooper appeared tranquil, almost drowsy at times. This was a studied effect; his performances were calculated to the second. "Gary is an embodiment of the old saying that art consists in concealing its own artfulness," wrote DeMille. Unlike Josef von Sternberg or Ernst Lubitsch, DeMille allowed Cooper total freedom—except for changing dialogue.

"How in the hell can you read those goddamned DeMille lines?" director Howard Hawks later asked him.

"Well," said Cooper, "when DeMille finishes talking to you, they don't seem so bad. But when you see the picture, you kind of hang your head."

Much was made of the onscreen romance between Wild Bill and Calamity Jane. Never mind that it had not happened. The PCA objected to certain lines of dialogue. When Jane

kisses Bill, he repeatedly wipes his mouth. "You four-flushin' mule," she says. "You ain't wipin' it off! You're rubbin' it in!" The PCA correspondence characterized Bill's reaction as tending to "build up the flavor of her being a prostitute." DeMille argued the lines back in. She was not a fallen woman; she was a new type. "Calamity Jane's virtues were her own," he explained. "Her faults were those of her time. And since she was a real emancipated woman, she was truly natural." Showing just how natural she was caused DeMille some pain. "Jean had to learn how to manipulate a ten-foot bullwhip," said DeMille. "I offered my wrist as a convenient target for the curling end of the whip during Jean's practice sessions. My wrist bore lash marks for days."

More to DeMille's liking was a scene in the Indian tent. "One of the most touching love scenes in any picture I have made is the brief, laconic, almost inarticulate exchange between Wild Bill Hickok and Calamity Jane, when they are awaiting probable death as captives of the hostile Indians." No one played "laconic" better than Cooper. His patented reply to anything was "Yup."

Was Cooper playing Wild Bill or was Wild Bill playing Cooper? "My idea in every picture is to duplicate historical figures as nearly as I can," said DeMille. "Cooper, in general proportions and manner, might be Hickok come to life." Where did the characters diverge? At the point where the integrity of a movie star—or a legend—must be maintained. "As every historian of the Old West knows," wrote DeMille, "Jack McCall killed Wild Bill Hickok by shooting him in the back. First the executives asked me not to kill Wild Bill. I told them I could not remake history to that extent. 'Well then,' Adolph Zukor said finally, 'if he has to be killed, don't let him be killed by that little rat, McCall. At least let Charles Bickford kill him.' But history was adhered to."

Even if he had to be killed by a minor character, Cooper could not die in vain. "While Hickok actually lost his life in a casual poker game," wrote DeMille, "I have found it necessary to imbue that poker game with a patriotic motive." In the scene, Cooper is playing cards to hold the villains until the cavalry arrives.

So that the film would not be attacked for inaccuracy, DeMille inserted a preface after the main title credits. It read in part: "The story that follows compresses many years, many lives, and widely separated events into one narrative, in an attempt to do justice to the courage of the plainsman of the West."

While DeMille was making *The Plainsman*, three momentous events occurred. On June 1, 1936, he directed and hosted the first Hollywood broadcast of Lux Radio Theatre, one of the top five programs on the air. Since the late twenties, radio had assumed a powerful role in American culture. By the midthirties it reached twenty-two million homes. "Greetings from Hollywood, ladies and gentlemen," DeMille said for the first time that night, introducing Marlene Dietrich and Clark Gable in *The Legionnaire and the Lady*, an adaptation of the 1930 film *Morocco*. The weekly series emphasized movie stars and digest versions of recent films. It also made DeMille, who

CECILIA DE MILLE PRESLEY

"*The Plainsman* was the first of six DeMille films devoted to American history. Grandfather's original intention was to make the story equally about Buffalo Bill Cody and Wild Bill Hickok. The finished product was something quite different. The character of Hickok dominated the film. This was not surprising, said Grandfather, as Hickok was played by Gary Cooper.

OPPOSITE, CLOCKWISE FROM TOP LEFT: John Miljan and Gary Cooper await DeMille's interpretation of a scene. DeMille was not afraid to cast Miljan as General George Custer when he usually played lounge lizards; Miljan was convincing as the doomed soldier. • DeMille made the first shot of *The Plainsman* with the Pathé camera he used on *The Squaw Man*. • A torture scene from *The Plainsman*.

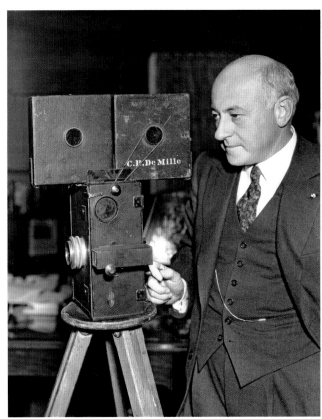

was already a household name, a household *guest*. "It brought me to people not in the mass, but individuals, who did me the honor of inviting me into their homes," wrote DeMille. "These were people to whom I was no longer a name filtered through the wordage of imaginative press agents, but a person whom they knew."

The second event occurred on July 14, 1936, when John Otterson was removed from the Paramount presidency. He was replaced by veteran exhibitor Barney Balaban. This would work to DeMille's advantage. Balaban respected his showmanship.

The third event was a blessed one, the birth of a daughter to Cecilia and Frank Calvin. DeMille's new granddaughter was also named Cecilia. She would figure prominently in his future.

The Plainsman was previewed in December. After the cheers, the most telling comment came in a preview card. "If Wild Bill were not killed," wrote Fred Wendt of New Orleans, "*The Plainsman* would be just another cowboy picture, and the public would forget the whole thing almost immediately." Sure enough, the public treated the film as something more than a western, and it became the hit that DeMille needed. It quickly

ABOVE, LEFT TO RIGHT: William Walling Jr. made this portrait of Gary Cooper and Jean Arthur. • Dan Sayre Groesbeck photographed at work in his office. "Dan was a likable guy," said one of his colleagues when interviewed by historian John Kobal in the 1980s. "But a rough, tough old codger. He worked sloppily. He smoked all the time, always had his hands stained with tobacco."

wiped out the deficits of *Four Frightened People* and *The Cru-sades*. It also established Jean Arthur as a star.

DeMille took no chances with his next film. He cast Fredric March as Jean Lafitte, the controversial figure of the War of 1812. Was Lafitte a privateer, a pirate, or a patriot? DeMille decided to dish him up as all three. He could not make him a saint, but he could make him a hero, however flawed. In February 1937, DeMille went to Louisiana to research the period. He sailed through bayous, bought antiques and archives, and then had a memorable experience. A denizen of the swamps heard his name and approached him. "Oh, Mr. DeMille!" said the Louisiana fan. "We think you're wonderful!"

"Well, thank you, but which picture of mine did you like?"

"What? Does you do pictures, too? We just means you wonderful on the radio."

The Buccaneer would be DeMille's tribute to the pirate-tale illustrations of Howard Pyle and N. C. Wyeth. Dan Groesbeck did not study with either artist, and, while their influence on his work was undeniable, his renderings were unique. He painted concept art for *The Buccaneer* that was bold and startling, yet delicately nuanced, evoking sea air and cannon powder. His pirates were terrifying.

"Caricature is essential in designing for the movies," said Groesbeck. "A belt or a buckle, a kerchief around the head, if scaled to those actually worn by the pirates would look as if the studio were trying to economize on material. That is the effect of the camera—to minimize. The artist therefore scales details of costumes to counteract this effect. Though the players some-times look overdressed on the set, that look vanishes when they appear on the screen. It's good drama."

Groesbeck was not credited for his contributions to set de-sign or costume design; there was resentment from other artists. "When you looked at a Groesbeck sketch, it was hell to convert it into three-dimensional materials," an unnamed designer told historian John Kobal. "It looked great the way he drew it, but

you couldn't tell how the fabric was to be cut or draped, so how could you get what was in his artwork?" Somehow they man-aged, costuming a gaudy, gruesome gang of cutthroats. "When I went ashore on the Catalina Island setting," reported Dorothy West of radio station KPGK, "I found myself in a primitive vil-lage, surrounded by the most villainous-looking men you ever saw outside of a pirate storybook. Most of them wore beards, their faces were slashed with horrible scars, and many were hideously tattooed on their arms and chests. Their clothes were ragged and soiled, they wore wide belts in which hung cutlasses and old-fashioned pistols. After this brief acquaintance, I non-chalantly strolled away."

Groesbeck was right about the camera. It tended to shrink wardrobe accessories. It did not shrink people. It magnified them—and their affectations. Fredric March was known for restraint, but he could also exhibit an overripe theatricality. He was a good judge of both projects and his own limitations, but to play an 1814 pirate with a fruity patois was a bit much. "I'm going to sue this outfit for willful mutilation of a good Middle Western accent," said March, not entirely in jest.

DeMille hired the avant-garde composer George Antheil to write musical scores for *The Plainsman* and *The Buccaneer*. *Photoplay*'s editor Ruth Waterbury, hardly a DeMille proponent, praised him for using Antheil. "I was subtly aware of how the score was contributing to the desired mood of *The Buccaneer*," wrote Waterbury. "It had been composed by George Antheil, that most provocative of composers."

On January 21, 1938, DeMille took his family to Kansas City, Missouri, for the premiere of *The Buccaneer*. The film was well received. That was less important to the family than an event that occurred later that night. Cecilia married the pub-lisher Joseph W. Harper, a longtime family friend. Cecilia had ended her marriage to Frank Calvin in 1937, but he had not left the family. Calvin spent weekends with his son, Peter, and daughter, Cecilia. He also worked as an assistant to DeMille. The

clan gained another member when Katherine DeMille married Anthony Quinn, who was playing a pirate in *The Buccaneer*. Paramount was ready for another project from Cecil B. DeMille Productions. DeMille was ready. He was fifty-six and going strong, partly because of an exercise regimen, but mostly because of his family's support, and, yes, the stimulus of success.

FREDRIC MARCH

"I like to work with Mr. DeMille. He has been generous to me. He made me the Roman prefect Marcus Superbus in one of the four or five top moneymakers of all time, *The Sign of the Cross*."

CECIL B. DeMILLE

"When we are creating film fiction based on fact, we know wherein we err, and freely admit it. Let us not say 'err,' for when we take liberties, we do it necessarily for the sake of dramatic construction. Our characters are substantially true to life, as far as exhaustive research can determine. A motion picture can serve the purpose of bringing before the eyes of pupils in school a vivid impression of events of the more momentous American epochs. In two hours, a panorama can be unfurled which would take many volumes to recount."

OPPOSITE: Groesbeck made this painting to illustrate a scene in *The Buccaneer* script.

ABOVE: This is Groesbeck's impression of the pirate Dominique You. If DeMille had used this as a template, he would have cast an unconventional-looking actor like James Burke or Paul Hurst in this part. Instead he cast Akim Tamiroff, giving the character a comic tone.

UNION PACIFIC

Nearly twenty-five years had passed since Cecil B. DeMille came to Los Angeles and ended up in Hollywood. He held *The Squaw Man* in fond reverence, convening reunions of its cast and crew every few years. (He was in touch with many of them because they continued to work for him.) The Stern-Burns-Revier barn had become a gymnasium on the Paramount lot, but DeMille insisted on hosting his parties there. The luncheon table was usually covered with a red-and-white gingham tablecloth, and decorated with miniature figures of the Old West. Some of the actors and crew had died since the 1935 reunion; Oscar Apfel was one of them. Nevertheless, the twenty-fifth anniversary would be observed, and not only by DeMille. The industry was gearing up for 1939.

Paramount had a new president. When Adolph Zukor retired in 1938, Y. Frank Freeman took his place. "Proudly hailing from Greenville, Georgia, Frank Freeman came up in the motion picture industry through the exhibition side," wrote DeMille. These were the industry members who appreciated DeMille, those who tended the actual box office. They knew what he could do. For the first time in twenty years, DeMille had a sympathetic regime. Freeman would not punish DeMille because *The Buccaneer* lost momentum. He encouraged DeMille

to start another project. The director had toyed with the idea of an aviation film, the sinking of the *Titanic*, or even adapting H. G. Wells's *The War of the Worlds*. He hoped to do a story about the Hudson Bay fur company in Canada until he learned that Twentieth Century-Fox had registered that title. "I am inclined to expounding the theme of Americanism right now, because I think Americanism is far more important than any of the other 'isms' that seem to be receiving attention."

DeMille was undoubtedly referring to the political situation in Europe, where Italian fascism, German Nazism, and Russian communism were vying for headlines. The first few months of 1938 were anxious ones in Hollywood, since Adolph Hitler's annexation of Austria presaged more aggressive action. Both Germany and Italy had been making life difficult for exhibitors, refusing films that in any way questioned their ideologies. The PCA attempted to mediate but there was no talking to their surly representatives. Hollywood depended on Europe for nearly a third of its revenue. It had diminished; it was only a matter of time before it stopped altogether. Every month brought more European exiles to Hollywood. They told stories. Jesse Lasky Jr., who had just started in DeMille's writing department, heard

OPPOSITE: Cecil B. DeMille made *Union Pacific* a romance, an adventure, and an epic. Barbara Stanwyck and Joel McCrea contributed the romance.

some of them. "Gentle elderly Jews who should have been presiding over prayers by the light of religious candlesticks were being made to polish pavements under the delighted scrutiny of brown-shirted, jack-booted bully boys," wrote Lasky. "The horrors related by every arriving refugee were no longer bad dreams—or exaggerations." Germany was pushing these horrors toward England. If England pushed back, there might be a war in 1939.

Box-office receipts were climbing in 1938. The studios upped production to outrace the inevitable. "Twentieth Century-Fox will not curtail production because of possible European losses," said its sales manager Herman Wobber. "The company will seek to recapture business through bigger pictures, and subjects that will have appeal for markets such as South America." Another strategy was to make blockbuster road-show films. These would realize big profits quickly, stockpiling capital and making play-outs in Europe less crucial. David O. Selznick was ballyhooing his superproduction of the bestselling novel *Gone with the Wind*, and paving the way for similar productions. "Production is up about twenty to thirty percent," reported Edwin Schallert in the *Los Angeles Times*. "There is substance to the scope of the new undertakings." This activity was justified, not by fear of war but by a cluster of

ABOVE, LEFT TO RIGHT: "Robert Preston made a big impression in *Union Pacific*," says Cecilia de Mille Presley. "The film was seen everywhere and he was suddenly a hot property." • Natalie Visart shows Robert Preston her costume sketches for his character in *Union Pacific*.

anniversaries. "Motion Pictures' Greatest Year," a campaign of the Motion Picture Producers and Distributors of America (MP-PDA), would honor the hundredth anniversary of photography, the fiftieth anniversary of projected movies, and the twenty-fifth anniversary of Hollywood filmmaking. The spotlight was on DeMille. He had to deliver a blockbuster, something to compete even with Selznick's eagerly awaited epic.

The subject of the film came to DeMille from *Film Daily* publisher Martin Quigley. "Tell the story of the spanning of America by steel, the first transcontinental railroad," said Quigley. DeMille flipped a rare coin to decide whether it should be the Southern Pacific or the Union Pacific. The Union came up tails, but Frank Calvin's father, Eugene, was a retired president of that railroad and could arrange with its current president William M. Jeffers, to facilitate a U.P. project. "I've seen every railroad movie ever made," said Jeffers. "They're all full of discrepancies. This one is going to be correct."

"There will be nothing in our proposed photoplay," Calvin assured him, "in any way derogatory to the history of the Union Pacific." Calvin was sent to research the archives in Omaha, Nebraska. Jeanie Macpherson and Jesse Lasky Jr. began a series of story conferences with DeMille. "How is your father?" DeMille asked the younger Lasky. "We don't see much of each other."

"He's fine," replied Jesse Jr., although Jesse Sr. was in fact experiencing a career slump. He had gone from Mary Pickford's company to RKO Radio Pictures, hitching his wagon to several opera stars, none of whom interested moviegoers. Then he did a

radio show called *Gateway to Hollywood*, which did well but not well enough. Sam Goldwyn was going great guns, with umpteen Gary Cooper films. Cooper was a possibility for the railroad film. DeMille was afire with enthusiasm.

"Sweat, blood, and steel," said DeMille. "That's what built the Union Pacific! Yes, and whisky and sin—in portable hells of corruption following the railroad builders, siphoning their wages away in the saloons, brothels, and gambling dens under the tents that followed the westward-pushing 'End of Track!'" Young Jesse was sensitive, bright, and intuitive, with a well-developed sense of irony. Employment as a DeMille writer was a coveted position, not so much for salary, since DeMille was conservative with a dollar, as for prestige—and the chance to learn from a master. Years later he would tally his gains. "For me it was only the beginning of a relationship," wrote Jesse Jr. "It was strange, productive, remunerative, sometimes inspiring, other times soul-destroying and mind-boggling. Yet while C. B. lived I would seldom manage to escape what he liked to refer to as 'the bondage of great deeds.'"

A sense of irony would be needed if Jesse was to work in a confined space for a prolonged period with DeMille. America's greatest filmmaker believed his own publicity. He had a right to. He wrote it. The director of great stars was as big a star as they. "Greetings from Hollywood" was as well known as "Come up and see me some time." The man who put actors in front of the public was as magnetic a personality as any of them. "An enormously attractive person most of the time," wrote Jesse Jr., "DeMille exuded charm enough to render humans of either sex defenseless, rather as certain insects stun their victims. We could all become his victims, I thought. His victims, his audience, and even, at times, his would-be assassins. He could fall into explosive rages or equally make one feel that the simple achievement of a word combination to be spoken by an actor was equivalent to the conquest of Everest."

Jeanie Macpherson had been with DeMille for nigh-on twenty-five years. She was no longer a font of plot points; she was more of a sounding board. "If that woman doesn't drive you screaming, raving insane," said DeMille, "if you can keep from strangling her with your bare hands, she occasionally comes up with something usable." Macpherson was not barren. She had many thoughts to contribute. DeMille had heard them. "Shut up, Jeanie!" he yelled. "If you have to think of the oldest plot in the world, do it on your own time!" Macpherson would leave the room in tears, vowing never to return. Then DeMille would recall some earlier contribution that might solve the problem at hand, and all would be forgiven. Jesse Jr. was quietly appalled. Then the winds would rise again.

"I want train wrecks," said DeMille, looking into the distance. "I want to see the explosions of steam and bursting boilers! Iron guts! I want to smash through the barricades of mountain ranges of snow and ice!" What were the stars supposed to be doing during these explosions? DeMille had mentioned Gary Cooper and Claudette Colbert. "I want a love story that nobody has ever got on the screen," he continued. "I want human drama! Suspense. Not just 'Will they make it, or won't they make it?' which any damn fool can write. I want a snake under every bed!"

Colbert may have heard that last remark. In August, she wrote DeMille, politely suggesting that her need to control her environment might create problems. She did not want to endanger their friendship. DeMille was genuinely disappointed. Curiously, the film Colbert chose to do, *Drums Along the Mohawk*, had more Indian attacks than the script of *Union Pacific* indicated. It was completed, not by Jesse Jr. and Jeanie, but by a team of writers, most of whom had been at it since the early silents. Walter DeLeon, for example, specialized in repartee, while C. Gardner Sullivan worked from Dan Sayre Groesbeck's drawings and the script synopsis to craft series of shots for action sequences.

What alarmed Jesse Jr. was the interchangeable aspect of screenwriting. "We would be assigned to create sections," he recalled, "then write in tandem, one polishing behind another." Irving Thalberg had originated this practice ten years earlier,

and pride of authorship ceased to exist in Hollywood. "DeMille used writers like a general who counted no costs and spared no feelings," wrote Jesse Jr. "And somehow neither he nor we were ever satisfied. One might rewrite a scene thirty times and still not have arrived at the mysterious ingredient he was seeking. Some writers were quite literally driven to drink, or into massive sulks or sudden resignations." This was Jesse's trial by fire. Did it yield a good script? Was he finally satisfied? Could he sleep at night?

"DeMille took to phoning me at home in the small hours. No hellos. No apologies for having awakened me. Only the cold nocturnal ear-stab of the ringing phone and the rasping voice, slightly nasal, insisting, demanding, 'What does Donlevy do with his hands?'" The villain played by Brian Donlevy was plotting to wreck the Union Pacific, but Jesse Jr. had failed to write any gesture that would telegraph his character to the audience. DeMille was losing patience. He was riding Jesse. "Business is what actors do that I can photograph! Not what they think or feel!" After several wee-hours calls, the half-awake writer came up with a bit of business that intrigued DeMille, if only because it was weird. "He takes a cigar from his pocket, dips the bitten-off end into a shot glass of whisky. Then, then he puts the whisky-soaked end in his mouth. And lights the tip!" The unpleasantness of the gesture was what DeMille liked. Jesse had to get out of bed to rewrite the scene—again. This went on, in various forms and degrees, from March to November. There was, however, a hiatus.

DeMille had fallen ill with rheumatic fever during a trip to Europe in early 1922 but had been healthy ever since. While

OPPOSITE, CLOCKWISE FROM TOP: This script page shows how tricky (literally) it was to synchronize the movements and timing of two live actors performing in front of a rear-projection screen with a herd of buffalo moving on it. • Preston and Stanwyck debate their marriage vows as Indians prepare to attack the train. • This is the scene in which Stanwyck and McCrea had to time their acting to the buffalo behind them. • DeMille liked this concept art so well that he posed with it.

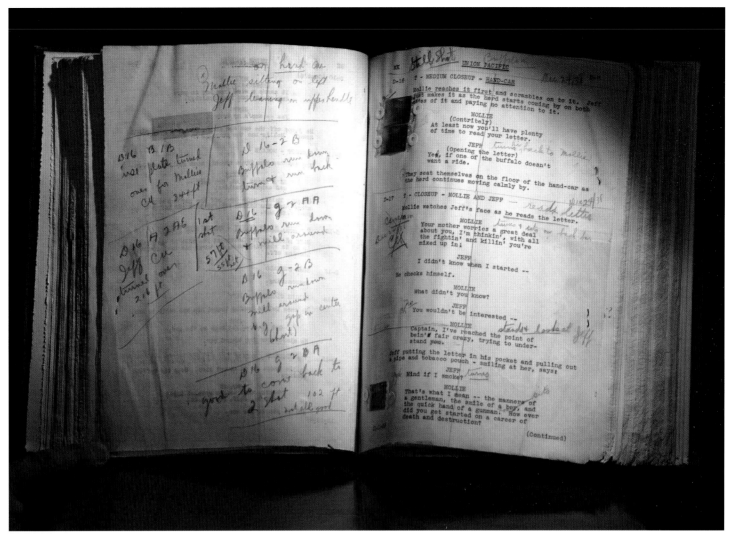

preparing *Union Pacific* he developed prostate trouble. In March 1938, he left his writers to their own devices and went under the knife. The procedure and its aftermath left DeMille medicated and in pain for the rest of the year.

In June, Gary Cooper turned out to be unavailable for the role of Jeff Butler, the railroad troubleshooter, after DeMille had gone to the trouble of creating a distinctive variation of Cooper's "Yup." (Jeff's reply to the most provocative question is a studied "Maybe.") DeMille released an item to the press saying that he was considering Joel McCrea. "I don't know whether to believe what I read in the papers or not," McCrea wrote DeMille, "but I can't think of a type of story or a man I would rather work with. So I hope it's true. Could I talk with you some time?" Way back in the twenties, McCrea had attended school with Katherine, as well as being DeMille's newspaper delivery boy, before signing a contract with him. Since then he had made

a steady climb to stardom, yet was still considered second-best to Cooper. McCrea was good-natured about it. "DeMille never failed to tell me how much he liked Coop, but I wanted *Union Pacific*. I wanted to be the guy who rode off into the sunset, 'right' over 'evil.'"

In September, DeMille offered a contract to Vivien Leigh, who was known solely for an M-G-M-British production, *A*

Yank at Oxford. She also turned him down. His third choice turned out to be a happy one. "I have never worked with an actress," wrote DeMille, "who was more cooperative, less temperamental, and a better workman—to use my term of highest compliment—than Barbara Stanwyck. I have directed, and enjoyed working with, many fine actresses, some of whom are also good workmen; but when I count those of whom my memories are unmarred by any unpleasant recollection of friction on the set or unwillingness to do whatever the role required or squalls of temperament or temper, Barbara's name is the first that comes to mind."

By the time Stanwyck and McCrea started work with DeMille,
in mid-November, James Hogan and Art Rosson had been shooting second-unit footage in Cache, Oklahoma, and Iron Springs, Utah, for a month. Hollywood was sometimes criticized for its portrayals of Indians and for not employing actual Native Americans. DeMille hired hundreds of Cheyenne, Navajo, Piute, and Sioux (some from WPA projects) and brought

JOEL McCREA

"With DeMille, the picture was the thing. He never favored anybody or things like that. He was a wholly professional man. If I was running a studio, I would like a DeMille to make my pictures."

OPPOSITE: This painting by Joe De Yong recalls Thomas Hart Benton.

ABOVE: Here is the scene as it was realized by DeMille, art directors Hans Dreier and Roland Anderson, and cinematographer Victor Milner.

CLOCKWISE, FROM ABOVE: "DeMille drew his sense of scenic composition and balance from such carefully studied illustrators as the great Frenchmen Gustave Doré and Job," wrote Jesse Lasky Jr., who cowrote *Union Pacific*. • Cecilia de Mille Presley recalls: "Grandfather, having put off major surgery, collapsed on the set one day and had to be taken home. After the surgery, he returned to work, weak and angry, because his body refused his directives. He had his crew fix his stretcher to a camera boom so he could swing up or down, to whatever camera angle the shot required." • DeMille, Stanwyck, and McCrea at a working telegraph office. This one was often used to send press releases from the set. • The Native American actor Iron Eyes Cody taught Akin Tamiroff (center) how to use this whip. Cody was a veteran of DeMille's first film, *The Squaw Man*. In 1939, *Union Pacific* was part of a year-long celebration of Hollywood anniversaries. • Barbara Stanwyck brought warmth and charm to the huge canvas of *Union Pacific*.

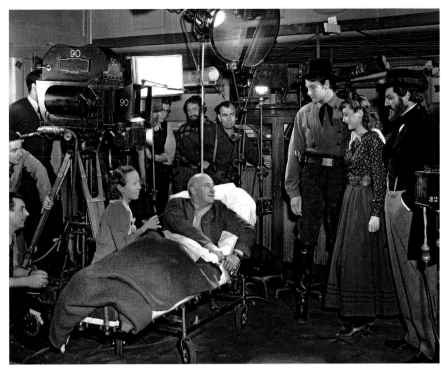

OPPOSITE: DeMille flouted Hollywood convention by having Native Americans portray Native Americans.

THIS PAGE: The attack on the train was one of DeMille's most spectacular and suspenseful scenes derived from Joe De Yong's concept art.

them to location on buses. The Indian actor Iron Eyes Cody worked with Jesse Jr. to check details for accuracy. Cody was another veteran of *The Squaw Man*, and one of many actors, bit players, and extras who petitioned DeMille for work as soon as they heard he was doing a big film. "Whenever DeMille shoots," wrote Gwenn Walters in *Photoplay*, "you get the impression that the whole Paramount lot exists for nothing else but DeMille and his picture." *Union Pacific* needed the lot; it was a mammoth production.

Stanwyck liked working with DeMille. "You certainly knew where his pictures were going," recalled Stanwyck. "Like the girl in the film, he could hear the whistle long before he could hear the train. If there were 500 people up on a mountain, he knew who the hell each one was." McCrea was also impressed. "He was great with lots of people," said McCrea. "He could handle them and make it look right. I think it was showman-

ship, like P. T. Barnum and the circus, you know? He was a showman. A showman on the set, and a showman with the picture." Of course there was the dissenting vote. *Union Pacific* was Robert Preston's third film since being discovered at the Pasadena Playhouse. He found DeMille pompous and distant. "For over two weeks of shooting," said Preston, "Stanwyck and I were alone in the railroad car, and because there were no crowd scenes, no special effects, just two people acting, you'd never have known that the old man was on the set. He didn't

know what to do with us except roll and print. He didn't know what to tell us."

Preston did not know that DeMille was seriously ill. The infection had reasserted itself. He was feverish and in pain. On January 30, he collapsed. He was hospitalized, underwent another operation, and was given massive doses of the new antibiotic streptomycin. He just pulled through. The film lost him for three weeks.

Against the advice of his doctors, DeMille returned to work on February 20. He arrived in an ambulance and was delivered to the stage on a stretcher. "His face a gaunt mask, DeMille, still aboard his litter, was strapped to the platform on the great camera boom," wrote Jesse Jr. "Packed in ice, the invalid could be raised on this contraption, lowered, or whisked to any part of the set in seconds. On this occasion I and everyone else forgave him his irascibility. If ever a man de-

served a medal for courage it was DeMille as he directed from his mobile bed of pain."

Directing even a small film requires strength, stamina, and undivided concentration. Because DeMille, as was his practice, planned the production thoroughly in meetings and on paper,

BARBARA STANWYCK

"I loved DeMille, and he loved me. We only did *Union Pacific* together, but we did lots of radio. We got along great."

OPPOSITE: *Union Pacific* recreated the historic event that occurred on Promontory Point, Utah, on May 10, 1869.

ABOVE: DeMille had replicas of the famous golden spike made to use as mementos of the production.

it could be made when he was not at his best—and made well. *Union Pacific* had something new for DeMille, a plot structure that comprised a series of escalating climaxes: the train robbery, the romantic triangle, the railroad girl's betrayal at the altar, the Indian attack, the collapse of a trestle in the snow, the meeting of the railroads, and the final fight with the villain. The last three reels of the film left preview audiences breathless. It mattered not whether *Union Pacific* was DeMille's biggest, best, or most engaging. This was his entry in the 1939 sweepstakes. It was competing with *Gone with the Wind*.

DeMille had to deliver not only a great film, but also a spectacular presentation. A premiere at Grauman's Chinese or the Carthay Circle (both of which DeMille had opened with hit films) would not suffice. Working with Paramount's publicity department, the Union Pacific Railroad, and the city of Omaha, DeMille mounted a huge event. He and a bevy of stars traveled on a special U.P. train in a whistle-stop tour, arriving in Omaha for the April 28 premiere and a festival called "Golden Spike Days." More than 300,000 people, many dressed in period costumes, crowded Omaha for the event. Three theaters premiered the film simultaneously. *Union Pacific* garnered national coverage. The syndicated columnist (and railroad historian) Lucius Beebe reported the event. "Most of the State of Nebraska dug up grandfather's plug hat and tooled to town for the big doings," wrote Beebe.

"This festival has transcended in magnitude and captured the public's imagination beyond anything that Paramount's high-pressure exploitation staff could have dreamed up. Mr. DeMille, who is accustomed to positively cosmic goings-on, is a bit staggered by it all." Fortunately, DeMille's health held up and he was able to savor his triumph. *Union Pacific* grossed $3.2 million. This put it neck and neck with *Babes in Arms* and *Goodbye, Mr. Chips*—and ahead of *The Hunchback of Notre Dame*, *Jesse James*, *Mr. Smith Goes to Washington*, *The Wizard of Oz*, and *The Women*. Only one 1939 film made more money. *Gone with the Wind* grossed $18 million.

Exhibitors were delighted with *Union Pacific*. *National Box Office Digest* had rare praise for DeMille: "His twenty-five years of picture making have been crammed into one grand prize package." Even critics had to concede that this was a stirring film, an American epic. "DeMille is one of our favorite traditionalists," wrote Frank S. Nugent in the *New York Times*. "We would not have him otherwise."

OPPOSITE: DeMille holds a young Nebraskan as he and his favorite actress bask in the glow of a hugely successful publicity event—not to mention a major hit. *Union Pacific* was one of the top-grossing movies of Hollywood's greatest year.

NORTH WEST MOUNTED POLICE AND REAP THE WILD WIND

Union Pacific was barely out of its road show when Cecil B. DeMille was offered a new producing deal. On June 9, 1939, he signed a four-year contract with Paramount. This provided a cash advance of $100,000 for each film against 50 percent of its net profits. Cecil B. DeMille Productions, Inc., put up 15 percent of the budget—a reminder not to overspend—so DeMille sent Gladys Rosson to the Bank of America to secure a loan. "Whew!" said the loan officer. "That's a lot of money. But you can have whatever you want. You know that."

DeMille's first film under the new contract had roots in his theatrical career. In 1908, he and his brother, William, had written a play called *The Royal Mounted*. It folded after thirty-two performances. In 1939, DeMille dusted it off and told his writers to adapt it. C. Gardner Sullivan and Jesse Lasky Jr. had a new compatriot, Alan Le May. "Alan was lured from short-story writing for *Collier's* and the *Saturday Evening Post*," wrote Lasky. "Lacking any screenwriting experience, he was assigned to collaborate with me. I was supposed to keep Alan from 'going too far wrong.' Alan and I got on well. We learned to cover for each other when one or the other suffered a hangover, making him unfit for DeMille consumption, and we kept the script

moving forward." It moved more quickly when the team added the 1885 uprising that was led by a schoolteacher named Louis Riel. The protracted North-West Rebellion was condensed to provide a background for the bigger-than-life emotions that were DeMille's stock in trade.

Lasky proudly presented the log line to DeMille: "A young nation, threatened by the flames of rebellion, deposits its destiny with a handful of men in scarlet tunics."

"You've just lost me the entire American market," said DeMille. "You'll have to put in an American character. Not just an American star playing a Canadian, but a Yankee hero important enough to be played by a major star." The hero became a Texas Ranger pursuing a murderer who is running guns to the rebellion. Crackling dialogue was needed for their confrontation. "I've never heard such sissy talk outside of a young lady's tatting squabble!" yelled DeMille.

"You won't have to hear any more from *me*!" growled Le May, rising from the conference table.

OPPOSITE: Cecil B. DeMille directs Madeleine Carroll and Gary Cooper in his 1940 film *North West Mounted Police*. He built this sylvan bluff, complete with waterfall, in the middle of a New York street on the Paramount lot.

"Don't you dare get mad at me!" snapped DeMille. "I'm the only one who gets mad on a DeMille picture!" Le May was learning the rules. He adapted and survived. The result was *North West Mounted Police.*

DeMille cast Joel McCrea as Dusty Rivers, the Texas Ranger; Madeleine Carroll as April Logan, a Canadian nurse;

and Robert Preston as her brother, Ronnie, a Mountie with a fatal flaw: His unbridled passion for a "half-breed French and Indian girl" named Loupette Corbeau.

The portrayal of Loupette would require both cunning and abandon. "We considered a half-dozen actresses without finding one who would be exactly right," recalled DeMille. In December, Edwin Schallert of the *Los Angeles Times* wrote that

CECILIA DE MILLE PRESLEY

"One hopes that while working on a set, there's fun to be had for both cast and crew. Because Grandfather prepared his films so thoroughly, there was always time for laughter. He cast Akim Tamiroff, who was Russian, and Lynne Overman, who was from Missouri, as a team. Their antics provided endless amusement, especially when they tried to steal scenes from each other. One day Akim used tiny strings to wiggle his ears behind Lynne's back. Even Grandfather chuckled. On days like this, the set would be filled with visitors from other soundstages who wanted to watch them work. DeMille loved working with both Akim and Lynne and cast them as a team in two films."

OPPOSITE, CLOCKWISE FROM TOP LEFT: DeMille and his assistant Gladys Rosson sift through some of the Canadian archival material gathered by his research and writing teams for *North West Mounted Police.* • Nearly thirty years after making *The Squaw Man*, DeMille posed at his beloved barn, which had been moved to the Paramount lot. • This snapshot of DeMille and his granddaughter Cecilia was taken at his ranch, Paradise, around 1940.

ABOVE LEFT TO RIGHT: Akim Tamiroff and Lynne Overman contributed delightful comic relief in *North West Mounted Police.* • DeMille's fame as a radio host almost surpassed his renown as a filmmaker. Here he is on his Lux Radio Theatre with guest star Joan Crawford.

Marlene Dietrich was the top contender for the "harem-skarem, hot-as-a-firecracker wolf woman, one of the plum opportunities of the year." Paulette Goddard was the glamorous young wife of Charles Chaplin. She had appeared with him in *Modern Times* (1936) and had recently gained attention in *The Women* and *The Cat and the Canary*. She could do even better. "Every actress in town wanted to get into a DeMille picture," recalled Goddard. "Just one could keep your name in front of the public for years." She set her sights on Loupette.

Traveling in the upper echelons of Hollywood society, Goddard had met DeMille, even though he was not given to nightclubbing or parties. Goddard began a campaign. "I look forward to working with you someday," she wrote him from China. Then, as he was casting *North West Mounted Police*, she wrote him: "Aren't you going to give me that part?" He was not. She tried a different tactic. "Loupette means 'little he-wolf,'" she told his assistant. "Shouldn't you change it to Louvette? That's 'little she-wolf.'" DeMille changed the name but kept looking.

One day in late January, DeMille was working in his office. "If you walked into his office," said columnist Hedda Hopper, "you'd find him playing with toy soldiers, moving them all around a model fort with great glee." This was DeMille's new method of blocking scenes. He was creating a battle when Florence Cole knocked at his door. "Louvette is here to see you," she said with a straight face. DeMille was surprised that the highly efficient Cole would play along with an obvious prank. "Florence stepped back from the door, and a dark girl, with eyes that could smolder or melt, came in, made up as a half-breed and costumed as such a girl would dress on the wild Canadian frontier in the 1880s. She gave me one insolent look and said, 'You teenk you wan beeg director, hah? Me, Louvette, show you!' That was enough. Paulette Goddard had the part."

DeMille was ready to start *North West Mounted Police* when Gary Cooper became available. McCrea graciously stepped aside to let DeMille recast the hero. The script, of course, had to be adjusted. "I was called over to do rewrites," recalled Lasky. "DeMille had me devote a lot of time to Gary Cooper. Gary was intensely alert for the false ring of a single word. You had to hit the exact style of his delivery. He was best at delivering a kind of folksy humor. 'I wouldn't jump to conclusions. Liable to be a feller's last jump.' That was a line of mine that he liked to repeat."

North West Mounted Police took longer to prepare than most films because it was DeMille's first in Technicolor. The company had come a long way since he used Dr. Herbert Kalmus's two-color process on *The Ten Commandments*. The three-strip process, introduced to features with *Becky Sharp* (1935) boasted a brilliant palette, but getting the colors on the screen was time-consuming and costly. A Technicolor consultant named Henri Jaffa was assigned to keep the colors in harmony. He told DeMille that it was forbidden to put red and orange in the same shot. "It's too bad the Good Lord didn't have a Technicolor consultant when He created apples and oranges," said DeMille. He shot the colors, they looked fine.

Principal photography commenced on March 9, 1940, as DeMille, wearing a red carnation given to him by Barbara Stanwyck, directed his first three-strip Technicolor scene, a panorama of bright red uniforms. *North West Mounted Police* was completed on May 13 without incident or interruption. Its preview was not so fortunate. The Westwood Theatre was full of rowdy college students. According to Lasky, the film's dialogue inspired catcalls and mimicry.

"I think I eat your heart maybe!"

"Ronnie, a terrible bad thing happen for us."

"I'd come to you if you were on the other side of the moon."

DeMille and his staff were helpless to subdue the students. "They guffawed until they wept," recalled Lasky. "They were

OPPOSITE: This design for Paulette Goddard was made by Joe De Yong. DeMille initialed every costume sketch while preparing a film.

it was darkened by the intrusion of global politics. Madeleine Carroll's sister had just been killed in a German bombing raid on England. When the actress bravely refused to leave the tour, Europe's suffering was conveyed to America. "I have always been glad that *North West Mounted Police* appeared when it did," wrote DeMille, "to give American audiences a warm and true conception of the valor of the British Commonwealth and its peoples." For once, good intentions paid off; the film grossed four times its cost, a stunning $6 million.

Hollywood was booming, even as war raged in Europe. Sam Goldwyn was making one hit after another with Gary Cooper. And DeMille was happy to see his dear friend Jesse Lasky make a stirring return. With the showman's flair that was his hallmark, Jess put together a package of national hero (Alvin York), slick writer (John Huston), esteemed director (Howard Hawks), and superstar (Gary Cooper). *Sergeant York* was released on July 2, 1941, and became Warner Bros.' highest-grossing film to that point—and the third-highest-grossing film in Hollywood history, sitting just behind *Snow White and the Seven Dwarfs* and *Gone with the Wind*. After being written off by Hollywood, Lasky proved that he had not lost his touch.

still laughing when the film faded out, and we faded into the night." What triggered the chaos was not the overripe repartee but gossip about Goddard. The filmmakers had not heard it. The students had. One night that week she and director Anatole Litvak, while dining and drinking at Ciro's restaurant, had supposedly slipped under a table to make love. As preposterous as it was, the story gained a malevolent currency. Fortunately it stayed in Los Angeles. When DeMille previewed *North West Mounted Police* in Santa Barbara, the film captivated its audience. How could it not? Goddard's eyes in Technicolor were worth the price of admission.

The premiere was held at Regina, Saskatchewan, on October 21, 1940. It should have been a festive occasion, but

OPPOSITE, CLOCKWISE FROM TOP: Dan Sayre Groesbeck made this concept painting for *North West Mounted Police*. • DeMille contrasted the saintly nurse (Madeleine Carroll) with the sinful "half-breed" (Paulette Goddard). • Robert Preston, Paulette Goddard, and Gary Cooper.

ABOVE: Paulette Goddard campaigned and schemed for the role of Louvette Corbeau in *North West Mounted Police*.

The next DeMille project was another epic "torn from the pages of history," as the Hollywood cliché goes. He found his pages in the *Saturday Evening Post*, where a short story by Thelma Strabel gave him all he needed to get his writers going. "In 1840 America's lifeline was the sea," wrote DeMille, "when sailing ships linked the Eastern seaboard with the rich Mississippi. *Reap the Wild Wind* told of the salvage masters of Key West who reaped the wind's harvest, fighting hurricanes to save vessels wrecked on reefs." Since DeMille was committed to Technicolor, he needed scenes that would justify its use. "What I want are storms and sinkings and salvage," he told his writers. "I want broken skulls and skullduggery! I want to see the teeth of a reef bite through a hull! I want to contrast it with the tinkle of teacups in Charlestown drawing-rooms. And I want two love stories. The first—ending in

death and drowning. The second—a man and a woman finding, and losing, and then finding each other again. Through hell to heaven!"

C. Gardner Sullivan had gone to M-G-M and been replaced by the British screenwriter Charles Bennett, who had credits like Alfred Hitchcock's *The 39 Steps*. "Charles Bennett would appear wreathed in scarves, draped in a dashing blazer, or dustily booted, fresh from a polo match," wrote Jesse Lasky Jr. "He flew planes, rode like a Cossack, and could on occasion come dangerously near stealing scenes from the Boss." This was

ABOVE: Roland Anderson made this concept painting for *Reap the Wild Wind* (1942).

OPPOSITE: Dan Sayre Groesbeck painted this ghastly scene for *Reap the Wild Wind*.

indeed dangerous, since DeMille considered himself second to none in the enactment of scenarios. "But too often the office performances of our spellbinding Charles were better than the scenes themselves," wrote Lasky. "The written word missed his swaggerings, struttings, and eye rollings." There was one time, however, when Bennett trumped DeMille.

Reap the Wild Wind, for all its spectacle, lacked a climax. DeMille was troubled. "I couldn't sleep last night," he said with dolorous emphasis. "I kept asking myself what we can offer to match the train wreck in *Union Pacific*. The opening of the Red Sea in *The Ten Commandments*. Because until we've got that, gentlemen, we just haven't got a moving picture." Lasky feared he might not have a job. He fumbled for a solution.

"The two divers have gone down into the sunken ship, looking for evidence."

"I know the story," DeMille cut him off. "Get to the point, Jesse. What do they do?"

"The discovery of the girl's body explodes the rivals into violent action, sir."

"That is your great plan, is it? To end this picture, or me? Because it's exactly what everyone expects!"

"But you haven't heard the end of our plan, C. B.," Bennett chimed in.

"Haven't I?"

"No. For in the first instant that the divers start to hack at each other, suddenly you see behind them—rising out of the belly of the dead ship, one great, long red tentacle—and then another. Then, faster than a striking cobra, it sweeps around the body of one of the men. It is—a giant squid! The largest monster of the deep, full of malevolent intelligence. The enemies become

allies against this ink-throwing behemoth, this leviathan with glazed yellow eyes and tentacles thick as pine trees!"

As Bennett acted out the nightmarish scene, DeMille grew silent. Lasky stole an anxious look at the Boss. "He was ecstatic," recalled Lasky.

When DeMille finally said something, it sounded like a prayer. "Wonderful. And in Technicolor."

Only later did Bennett confess that the scene had not been written by him, Lasky, and Le May. "I thought it up this morning," said Bennett. "While I was taking my bath."

An immense tank was built at the Pacific Marine Museum in Santa Monica. A wrecked ship was built in it. It was filled with salt water and stocked with salt-water fish. Last but not least, a mechanical squid was installed in it. The monster was made of red sponge rubber and mechanized by electric motors. Its fourteen-foot tentacles were made prehensile by cables and hydraulic pistons. All these functions were operated from a keyboard that comprised twenty-four-buttons. DeMille directed the underwater scene from a diving suit, using a special tele-

phone system. He even directed on his sixtieth birthday, August 12, 1941.

The cast of *Reap the Wild Wind* said much about DeMille's stature. When Robert Preston dared to question his role in the film, DeMille called him an "ungrateful bastard." Joel McCrea did the unthinkable and turned down the lead. He could do this only because he was such a big star that he had a percentage in his next film, *Sullivan's Travels*. To DeMille, McCrea was foolishly choosing to work for Preston Sturges, who was nothing more than "some writer," in a film that would soon be forgotten.

Paulette Goddard was grateful to be in another DeMille film, but she knew what to expect. "After *North West Mounted Police*, Mr. DeMille swore he'd never have me in a picture again," recalled Goddard. "Then he asked for me in *Reap the Wild Wind*—and we went through the same thing." Ray Milland saw

ABOVE, LEFT TO RIGHT: Paulette Goddard as Loxi Claiborne and John Wayne as Jack Stuart in a scene from *Reap the Wild Wind*. • DeMille and Jesse Lasky Jr. help Jeanie Macpherson celebrate a birthday.

"ripples of discord." Hedda Hopper saw arguments. "There were some days when they went at it hammer and tong," she wrote. "DeMille actually used to invite people to come and watch him 'direct Paulette Goddard,'" the actress recalled. "Then he'd give me a loud Belasco treatment. He thought the way to get the best work from me was to break my spirit. I never realized that I had any!"

Reap the Wild Wind was being prepared for a preview when the "foreign" war suddenly hit home. On December 7, three-quarters of the United States fleet stationed at Pearl Harbor was destroyed by a surprise Japanese attack. Within twenty-four hours, America had joined the greatest armed conflict in the history of the world. DeMille and Paramount were unsure when to release the film. The preview went well, except for the comments of a publicist named Theodore Bonnet. "You're going to cut the squid scene out, aren't you, Mr. DeMille?" asked Bonnet anxiously. "All the women around me hid their heads when they saw it!"

Reap the Wild Wind opened with a war benefit premiere at Radio City Music Hall on March 19, 1942. Before the critics could print their opinions, word of mouth caused a stampede. "Everyone who has the price of admission runneth to the Music Hall," wrote Richard Griffith, "and causeth the gilded rafters to ring with laughter, sighs, and applause." Even as soldiers were being shipped overseas, the film was becoming a phenomenon. "*Reap the Wild Wind* broke the record for Paramount box office

CECIL B. DeMILLE

"My sixtieth birthday came while we were shooting *Reap the Wild Wind*. I summed up my feeling about Paramount, and especially about Frank Freeman, at the luncheon that day. 'Now, for the first time, I am being *helped* to make a picture instead of being *dared* to make one.'"

held by *The Ten Commandments*," wrote DeMille. Of course he expected the usual jibes. "Strange to say," wrote Griffith, "Manhattan's film reviewers are among the enthusiasts. For years they have condescendingly panned his pictures and dismissed his box-office record. But this Technicolored hoking up of Thelma Strabel's novel is apparently to their taste. One wonders. To some of us, the maestro's florid films have always been justified by their elementally human characters. They achieve drama through action, not talk. In other words, they belong in the movies. There isn't anyone like DeMille, the only veteran of pioneer movies to survive intact."

CECILIA DeMILLE PRESLEY

"John ('Duke') Wayne was my favorite of all the actors that I have known. In later years he became a good friend. Duke was complex and highly intelligent, a man of many appetites. He was all business on the set and a lot of fun off it, one tough, rugged man, speaking his mind, but always a gentleman. He was a wonderful guy, a lonely guy. I was one of the few women he could talk to. Among my fondest memories are the times we sat swapping stories. His favorite one about DeMille was from the making of *Reap the Wild Wind*. Grandfather offered Duke the part of Captain Jack, a good guy caught in an evil web by the bad guys. Ray Milland was to play the hero but he came off as a Southern dandy. (This was before he won an Oscar for *The Lost Weekend*.) Duke was being asked to play second to him. Duke agreed to take the part, but told C. B., 'On one condition: I will not play a weakling to that milquetoast Milland.' Grandfather agreed. Duke became the strongest man in the film. 'Your grandfather was a man of his word,' Duke told me. They became friends."

RAY MILLAND

"Cecil B. DeMille was unquestionably one of the greatest showmen the movies ever had. He could utilize a camera better than anyone. He had no peer at manipulating mobs or armies. He could stage and plan a battle better than Clausewitz. At spectacle he was the master."

CECILIA DE MILLE PRESLEY

"DeMille asked Ray Milland and John Wayne to wear this antiquated diving apparatus and go down into a huge tank. They weren't too keen to do it. So he got into the gear, put on the helmet, and went in. It was ostensibly to show them how to move underwater and play the scene, but what he really was doing was showing them that if he could do it, they could, too. I dove with Duke Wayne off his yacht the *Wild Goose* many times. He told me that he did not like to dive deeper than thirty feet because working in the tank had damaged one of his ears."

OPPOSITE: DeMille celebrated his sixtieth birthday at work.

ABOVE: "There is no dearth of action in *Reap the Wild Wind*," wrote Richard Griffith. "DeMille's giant octopus is uncomfort-ably alive. Men drowning look like men drowning, not like actors acting. This is genius of a kind, and it is matched by a broad feeling for beauty."

THE STORY OF DR. WASSELL

With three major hits in a row, Cecil B. DeMille was in a position to generate numerous projects, even if he could shoot only one at a time. His subject matter had to reflect the times. The Second World War was raging. DeMille's directorial peers were being recruited for the making of propaganda films, most of which would ultimately involve filming under fire. John Ford was the first to go. He was followed by Frank Capra, George Stevens, John Huston, and William Wyler. Directors who stayed in Hollywood because of age or other deferments also had to make propaganda films. Even if they were not literally about war, these films were part of the war effort, and hundreds were mandated for the duration.

There was speculation about box office. Would it be hurt by the absence of sixteen million troops? Would film production be hurt by the absence of seven thousand workers, a third of its force? And by the necessity of propaganda films? The answer was a resounding, coin-jingling "No!" Hollywood was embarking on the most prosperous period in its history since the golden days of 1929. Weekly attendance rose to 82 million, and films were held over so long that features waiting to be released faced the problem of dated costumes. One solution was to make films about exotic lands.

On April 28, 1942, President Roosevelt's "Fireside Chat" included a tale of valor. A Navy doctor named Corydon Wassell evacuated fifteen wounded soldiers from Java after being ordered to leave them to the mercy of invading Japanese. "The men were suffering severely," said Roosevelt, "but Dr. Wassell kept them alive with his skill, and inspired them with his own courage."

DeMille was listening to the broadcast. "We had no sooner clicked off the radio," wrote DeMille, "when my telephone rang. It was Ted Bonnet. Did I see what a great picture could be made of that story? I did!" Sensing correctly that there would be competition for the rights, DeMille tracked down Frank Freeman, and the two men drafted telegrams. One went to Washington. The other went to the Motion Picture Producers' Association to register the title *The Story of Dr. Wassell*.

"I want Dr. Wassell and the United States Navy," said DeMille the next morning to Frank Knox, the Secretary of the

OPPOSITE: In *The Story of Dr. Wassell*, Cecil B. DeMille shows a hero (Gary Cooper) who is so desperate to save his patients that he prays to a statue of Buddha in a Javanese jungle. His prayer is promptly answered. "This is absolutely DeMille," says Cecilia de Mille Presley. "It's his whole philosophy. Once again DeMille is taking the great religious philosophies of the world and showing that every philosophy—Christian, Moslem, Jew, Buddhist—has a great meaning and should be embraced. DeMille tried to put that idea in every film he made, whether it was an adventure, a drama, or a comedy."

Navy. DeMille explained that the proposed film would benefit the Navy Relief Fund.

"You can have Dr. Wassell," said Knox. "As for the Navy, they're rather busy right now."

Wassell was delivered to DeMille with all due haste, and without being told the reason for his transfer from Australia. He agreed to participate and was soon enduring hours of interviews. Jeanie Macpherson wrote a first treatment, which was expanded by Alan Le May and Charles Bennett. (Jesse Lasky Jr. had gone to war.) DeMille's staff also interviewed most of the soldiers saved by Wassell. "The research was mainly just talking to Dr. Wassell," recalled Bennett. "We met at lunch a lot. He was a very simple and delightful character, a simple soul. He found all the interest in him very unexpected. I don't think he cared about the film."

With Lasky away, Bennett and Le May perfected a system. "We used to have these long conferences with DeMille," said Bennett. "A court reporter was taking down everything in shorthand. DeMille was not a writer. And not a construction-

ist. When he did try to write something, it was awful. He would come up with a line of dialogue, what Alan and I used to call a 'DeMille Stinker.' And it was so awful! He'd say to the reporter, 'Circle that in red!' Then Alan and I would whisper, 'How the hell are we going to get this line out?' And we'd manage to get around it somehow, 'forget' to put it in. When the script came into his hands, he'd read it and say, 'Yes, yes, very good, very good. Hey! Where's that line we wrote?'"

The Story of Dr. Wassell started shooting on July 6, 1943. "I like Mr. DeMille," said Wassell after a week on the set. "He's a polished gentleman. He has to lay down the law on the set, but then, I don't wonder at that. He's so liberal about visitors that there's bound to be a lot of disturbance. He has to enforce discipline." The legendary routine in which DeMille chastised a

ABOVE: Dan Sayre Groesbeck made these concept paintings for *The Story of Dr. Wassell.*

OPPOSITE: Cooper in one of the many suspenseful scenes. Photograph by G. E. Richardson.

CECILIA DE MILLE PRESLEY

"Grandfather called Gary Cooper an affable, modest American gentleman, and an accomplished artist of his profession. Grandfather made four films in which Gary played the lead; he liked his quiet strength. You felt that whatever Gary said, whether he was acting or not, you believed it. He was straight and to the point. I thought that he and Duke Wayne, although very different as actors, had much in common, both on-screen and off. They both told wonderful stories, loved to laugh, and were fun to be with."

heedless extra and then called lunch had been revived on *Reap the Wild Wind*; if not performed on this film, it was sure to recur on another.

Because DeMille was involved in so many aspects of the production—which was bigger and more costly than even the last—he delegated more duties. "Mr. DeMille was pleasant to work with," recalled Laraine Day, "because we never really worked with him. An assistant did all the rehearsing, and then he'd come in, run through it once, and shoot it. The only time he really directed was in the crowd scenes. Then he was in complete control."

The Story of Dr. Wassell premiered in Wassell's native Arkansas in April 1944 but was released on June 6, the historic D-Day, a major turning point in World War II. "Imagine a DeMille war picture in New York on D-day!" wrote Bosley Crowther, film critic at the *New York Times*. "Mr. DeMille's press agents will have to be forcibly restrained." It was not the publicity department that had to be restrained, but the critical fraternity. Every reviewer conceded that DeMille was imparting a true story, and every reviewer objected to his method.

"Mr. DeMille has screened a fiction which is as garish as the spires of Hollywood," continued Crowther. "He has telescoped fact with wildest fancy in the most flamboyantly melodramatic way. And he has messed up a simple human story with the cheapest kind of comedy and romance." Louella Parsons, who usually gave a rubber stamp to every film she reviewed, wrote: "This picture is too ornate for the saga of a great doctor." Edwin Schallert cited "some of the inevitable DeMille hokum" in the comic relief scenes set in the Javanese hospital.

It was these interludes and the contrived love interest between Cooper and Day that set off the distinguished James Agee. Writing in the *Nation*, he said, "This story is one of the great ones of this war. Cecil DeMille's screen version of it is to be regretted beyond qualification. It whips the story, in every foot, into a nacreous foam of lies whose speciousness is only the more painful because Mr. DeMille is so obviously free from any desire to alter the truth except for what he considers to be his own advantage."

Both Wassell and DeMille were stung by these reviews. "Mr. DeMille is doing some things differently from the way they happened, perhaps," said Wassell, "but his changes are legitimate. He has to have a picture that will appeal to audiences. Furthermore, there are a lot of little incidents that were seen by

others but kept secret from me. Oh, I had a bird's-eye view, all right, but no closeups."

"Not one critic has mentioned that the Borobudur," said DeMille, "a Buddhist temple, is in Java, which is not a Buddhist country. They call our actor Philip Ahn Chinese when he is Korean. They overlook things like that and then attack me on points on which they, not I, are wrong. If these critics are right, then the taste and intelligence of the public must be getting worse every year." *The Story of Dr. Wassell* survived the critics and grossed a jaw-dropping $6.4 million.

CECIL B. DeMILLE

"The critics lambasted *The Story of Dr. Wassell* for departing from the facts, though of course to the critics that was only one of its vices. But Dr. Wassell himself said in a radio broadcast from Little Rock that it was ninety-eight percent true. Such statements, of course, do not affect critics. What, indeed, can affect the affectation of omniscience?"

ABOVE, TOP TO BOTTOM: In *The Story of Dr. Wassell*, Cooper imbued scenes of introspection and prayer with quiet conviction. • DeMille rode an extra high camera crane to film a scene of wounded soldiers being unloaded from the U.S. cruiser *Marblehead* at the Indonesian port of Tjilatjap (now spelled Cilacap).

ABOVE: This dye-transfer print shows how the scene looked in the finished Technicolor film of *The Story of Dr. Wassell*. We may assume that the Unit Stills photographer G. E. Richardson had to take his three-plate camera up in the crane to make this picture. It is also likely that DeMille, as was his practice, sat next to the still camera and posed the actors. This accounts for the studied, painterly quality of the stills shot on every DeMille film.

UNCONQUERED

As Cecil B. DeMille prepared his last film on American history, the Second World War was coming to an end. The Axis powers in Europe would surrender in May 1945, and Japan would surrender in August. Sixteen million Americans had served. More than 400,000 had died. Returning soldiers would have to adjust to civilian life. Maybe they could take up where they left off, with the same wife and the same job; maybe not. Jesse Lasky Jr. had served in the South Pacific. He corresponded with DeMille, as did Henry Wilcoxon. Lasky was reminded of his boss one night on a troop ship when the officers in charge of entertainment chose to screen *North West Mounted Police*. No one in the troop audience knew that Lasky had cowritten the film. "As we moved below decks," recalled Lasky, "it suddenly seemed important to tell someone." He turned to the nearest soldier and modestly explained his contribution. The soldier was skeptical, to put it mildly. "You sayin' you wrote down them words they talked up there on the screen? You tryin' to tell me you wrote down what Gary Cupper said?"

"Much of it," replied Lasky. "Often I'd even be called to the set to give Gary new words to say."

"Ain't no man tells Cupper what to say."

When Lasky got back to Hollywood, he did not resume his marriage, but he hoped to resume his job. He got an interview

at Cecil B. DeMille Productions. "How was the war, Jesse?" DeMille asked him.

"The Japanese weren't as terrifying as working for you used to be, sir."

DeMille hired him back.

Alan Le May and C. Gardner Sullivan had left. Charles Bennett needed help with the Boss's latest concept. "One Sunday afternoon I was reading a work on colonial history," said DeMille. "In the eighteenth century, on American soil, white men and women were bought and sold as slaves. These were convicts from England, shipped to the American colonies to be sold by private transaction or at public auction." The work he had read was a novel, *The Judas Tree* by Neil H. Swanson. It was DeMille's practice to buy a literary work and then have a fresh work created from it so that the resulting film would have an impressive pedigree. This also discouraged plagiarism suits. Swanson was hired to write a book called *Unconquered*, but from the script in development. DeMille wanted to treat "the birth of freedom, and the beginning of the death of slavery, in Colonial America." Lasky, Bennett, and a new writer named

OPPOSITE: Cecil B. DeMille and Paulette Goddard pose for a publicity photo on the set of the 1947 film *Unconquered*. There were no bubble baths in 1763, but the Production Code required that Goddard be covered.

Fredric M. Frank tackled the script so that Swanson could use it to write his book.

Jeanie Macpherson had done the first breakdown of *The Judas Tree*. After thirty years she was still working for DeMille, but she was no longer writing scripts. She was not looking well. In early 1946, she borrowed money from DeMille to pay for undisclosed treatments in a hospital. Since she was away from the office so much, DeMille hired two research experts, Donald Hayne and Henry Noerdlinger. They would provide him peerless service on succeeding projects, all of which were layered with historical detail. DeMille hired the journalist Phil Koury to manage publicity in the frenetic postwar press. As did most people encountering DeMille, Koury saw several people. During their initial interview, DeMille was by turns charming, imperious, and mesmerizing. "DeMille's eyes narrowed in open appraisal," wrote Koury. "I could feel their power and penetration." What really impressed Koury was DeMille's research.

"Did you know that Pittsburgh was once in Virginia?" DeMille asked. "Ah, you didn't, did you? I thought so. Did you know that a Scottish regiment lifted the siege of Fort Pitt, after marching through the forests and encountering Indians? Think of it—a Scottish regiment fighting Indians in America. Only time it ever happened. Those are the things we get for $100,000 of research."

DeMille warned Koury that he did not want a yes-man. "I like to pick a man's mind," said DeMille. "I know what I know. I'm interested in what *you* know. If you don't tell me what you think, if you yes me, the picture is hurt. If you tell me what you think, we'll have no problems." For the most part, Koury found DeMille intriguing—and witty. "My assistants think I'm an insane poodle," said DeMille with a twinkle in his eye. "They never know who I'm going to bite next."

As the new employees were feeling their way around, a veteran of the Lasky-DeMille Barn showed up at the office. Wilfred Buckland had been retired for years and was living with his son, Bill, a childhood friend of Jesse Lasky Jr. Hollywood was not

CECIL B. DeMILLE

"One of the lines in *Unconquered* is 'These men is possum hunters,' spoken by a sergeant bragging of what deadly sharpshooters his militiamen are. I could only bow in merited shame before the letters which came in after the film was released, pointing out that opossum are not shot, but trapped."

OPPOSITE: Dan Sayre Groesbeck made all the concept paintings for *Unconquered*.

ABOVE: In painting details on canoes and Indian blankets, Groesbeck drew on the research of DeMille's staff.

France. Artists got neither medals nor pensions. The Bucklands were destitute. "The old gentleman made a shuffling appearance," wrote Lasky, "He blinked at the models of sets and the sketches which he might himself have prepared long ago, when he had been the first art director in Hollywood." Buckland's visit was propitious. DeMille was lacerating his writers for not being able to finish a scene.

"As usual," droned DeMille, "my writers have failed to find me anything—anything at all—that will enable the hero and her-

oine to survive the redskins." This was true—to a point. DeMille was concerned with topping himself. He had used every kind of plot device. He had to do something that he had never done before, that no one had done before, and put his stamp on it. He was fascinated by the mechanics and driven by the need to excel. He had exhausted his writers. They had run dry. Buckland looked at the sketches and models. What could be done for two attractive people escaping Indians in a canoe?

"Send 'em over a waterfall," said Buckland. DeMille's eyes narrowed. Lasky and Frank exchanged glances. Buckland sketched. "The canoe goes over. Like *this*. Then, just as it plunges down, your boy grabs a tree limb, which happens to be stretched across the falls—here. With one hand he seizes it. With the other arm he holds the girl. Their weight makes the limb swing. Right through the downpour of water, and then . . ." Buckland paused. "It whips them into a cavern! Here, behind the falls."

It sounded so easy, hearing the distinguished artist tell it. Lasky had his doubts. "Will the audience believe it?" he asked.

CLOCKWISE FROM ABOVE: Goddard and Cooper in a scene from *Unconquered*. • Boris Karloff watches as DeMille shows him how to menace Goddard. • DeMille was often visited on the set by Anne Bauchens, who had edited his films since 1915. • Quiet moments were few and far between in *Unconquered*. • Iron Eyes Cody awaits his turn to torture Goddard. Paramount wags dubbed the film "The Perils of Paulette."

"An audience will believe what it sees," said DeMille. Within hours, Dan Sayre Groesbeck was painting, Wilfred Buckland had a check, and his son, Bill, had a job on *Unconquered*. DeMille would, of course, have helped Buckland even had he not contributed an idea, but this made it better.

DeMille wanted the British actress Deborah Kerr to play the bondswoman in *Unconquered*, but her agent's asking price was too high. Gary Cooper was already costing $300,000. Paulette Goddard could be had for $100,000 and was still a top star at Paramount. As DeMille completed casting and writing, there were distractions. Macpherson missed work and then had to be hospitalized. She was diagnosed with cancer. After visiting her in Good Samaritan Hospital, DeMille received another message.

Bill Buckland had become afflicted with mental illness. Wilfred was eighty and infirm. Fearing that he would leave his son to the degradation of a state hospital, he crept up on him while he was asleep and shot him dead. Then Wilfred killed

himself. DeMille got the news on July 18 while eating lunch in the Paramount commissary. Eleven days later, he started filming *Unconquered*. On August 26, Jeanie Macpherson died, aged sixty. DeMille's reaction was stoic.

Like DeMille's last three films, *Unconquered* was shot primarily on stages, a concession to Technicolor, and to the studio system. By 1946, the studio-made film was a marvel of engineering, a purring machine whose whisper-quiet mechanism gave no hint of its complex innards. This was the peak of the Hollywood studio system, the perfection of its glossy product, the apotheosis of its stars. Never again would so much skill be devoted to so much artifice. Movie snow looked like real snow. Movie sets looked like real places. Movie stars looked like real people, only better. Technicolor, however, did not look like real color, which was the point. Why would anyone want real color if one could

ABOVE: Paulette Goddard in Technicolor.

have heightened, enhanced, "supernatural" color? By the same token, why would anyone want reality when the Hollywood movie was presenting a cleaner, clearer, more beautiful version of it? This attitude was exemplified by the musicals of Twentieth Century-Fox, the comedies of Paramount, and anything made by Metro-Goldwyn-Mayer. Wartime receipts had confirmed this. Paramount's latest profit was $39.2 million, which put it where it had been in the golden twenties, far ahead of its competition. The "Paramount glow" of the thirties had hardened to a lacquered sheen. Other than a few Billy Wilder and Preston Sturges films, Paramount's output was irony-free. This was the environment in which DeMille was creating his last American history film.

History or no, Technicolor or black-and-white, stars sold tickets. Gary Cooper was playing a Virginia militiaman named Captain Christopher Holden. DeMille had spent months polishing the dialogue, only to have Cooper decide it was unspeakable. Lasky was summoned to the set. "One scene had to be rewritten over and over again," said Lasky. "When I finally thought I'd found a simple version that suited Gary, he drew a line through two of my best speeches. Opposite one he scrawled the single word 'Yup.' By the other he scrawled 'Nope.' I thought that these were meant as his comments on my lines, but not so. He'd reduced his dialogue to two terse words."

A similar crisis occurred with Paulette Goddard, who was playing a bondswoman named Abby Hale. "I know it's too much to expect from writers," said DeMille, "to supply usable words for actors and actresses to speak. I am not asking for the soliloquy of Hamlet or the Song of Solomon! Just something short and fresh that a real person might say!" No one dared say that there was not a real person in the script. After all, if DeMille made films about real people, no one would want to see them.

Having suffered three union incidents and the loss of two colleagues, DeMille was absorbing himself in his work. He would brook no interference. "I am running a set that costs fifty thousand dollars a day," he said through his microphone to two assistants who were chatting on the sidelines. "If you are not

quite up to this whole thing, may I suggest that you find yourself another picture. Think what fun it will be not having to put up with the bad temper of an evil director!"

The climax of *Unconquered* was the siege of Fort Pitt. Once again, DeMille needed to bring a new twist to an old cocktail. "There is nothing more boring than a siege," he told his staff. "An audience doesn't give a damn about it. And it's been well done in *Drums Along the Mohawk*. Fairly well done in *The Howards of Virginia* and *The Last of the Mohicans*. Each has something to its credit, and each one bored its audience. An audience is not interested in a fight over a stockade. So when we take that on, we take on something that has to be done differently than before—because it's been a flop before."

DeMille envisioned the siege as a tidal wave of fiery brutality, the Battle of Acre on a more intimate and searing scale. The scene was budgeted at $300,000 and required nearly eight hundred extras. There were numerous kinds of incendiary devices: three hundred pounds of dynamite, fifty pounds of flash powder, fifty flintlocks, and three hundred fireballs. The fireballs were fashioned from dried moss and birch bark, and marinated in kerosene. They were tossed into the fort by extras or by special workers wearing asbestos gloves. Phil Koury was on the set when the fireballs started landing. "The players had more to fear from DeMille than from the Indian braves who were lobbing fireballs into the fort," he said. "In the course of that scene's shooting, we watched the Boss driven to new heights of wrath."

"You're about to be scalped alive," came DeMille's voice through the loudspeakers that ringed the stage. "Then suddenly you hear bugles and drums in the distance and you know you're going to be saved. You jump up and down! You cheer! You grab someone and dance! Have you given me that kind of reaction? No! From the way you're acting, I assumed you've just read the market reports and your favorite stock has gone up a couple of points. Now, listen to me! God damn it! I'm giving you the chance of a lifetime to act in a DeMille picture! *I want everything you've got!*"

According to Lasky, DeMille tried for hours to get a shot of fireballs sailing over the walls of the stockade. Every take was spoiled by something, whether an extra looking into camera, a technician missing a cue, or a stuntman falling the wrong way.

Goddard came to the set. Her stand-in was shivering as fake fireballs were hurled at her in rehearsal. Goddard looked at DeMille. "Is that where you want me to stand?"

"Yes, right there," he answered.

"Exactly where do you mean?"

"Right over there."

"Me? With those fiery things?"

"You."

"Oh, no, I'm not," said Goddard.

DeMille was livid. Was she really refusing to do a scene? He lit into her, trying to shame her for her cowardice. She was adamant, even though she burst into tears. "Get her out of here!" yelled DeMille. "Get her out before I kill her!"

"And here's a postscript to the story," said Goddard later. "My stand-in became my double for that scene. She was wearing a wig—and in the scene it caught on fire! I took the hint and headed for New York. Mr. DeMille wouldn't speak to me for years."

Unconquered ran nine days over schedule and (shades of Erich von Stroheim) $394,000 over budget. It ended up costing $4.3 million; it would have to be a huge hit just to break even. It was not. Released in October 1947, it lost over a million dollars. DeMille may have overspent because of the various tricky elements in the production, or because he was hoping to vitalize the material, or because he was distracted

and sad. For whatever reason, he was not able to make a wide-reaching hit. Not one to dwell on failure, the Champion Driver prepared his next project, turning to a source that had never failed him.

CECILIA DE MILLE PRESLEY

"*Unconquered* would have been a bigger success but they made two mistakes. One, they went over budget. Two, they made a waterfall scene that didn't work. I went to the premiere with Grandfather in Pittsburgh. When that scene came on, with Gary Cooper and Paulette Goddard going over the waterfall and then miraculously escaping by swinging underneath on a branch, the audience laughed. Grandfather had to go back, reshoot, and recut before the film could be released. He never really found a way to make the scene plausible.

OPPOSITE: DeMille spent his own quiet time in the company of his granddaughter Cecilia. This photograph shows them in the breezeway that connected the two wings of the DeMille home.

OVERLEAF, LEFT TO RIGHT: Two dramatic Groesbeck paintings for *Unconquered*. • DeMille piled on the thrills in *Unconquered*, and Bosley Crowther of *The New York Times* apparently enjoyed them. "Laugh as one may—and one does laugh—at such accumulated old stuff as Indian fights and a canoe going over a waterfall—and hoot as one may at such brave lines as 'This is greater than you or me or both of us'—*Unconquered* is a picture worth seeing, if for nothing else but laughs."

The Ten Commandments

CHAPTER 7

BLAZE OF GLORY

SAMSON AND DELILAH

n 1948, Cecil B. DeMille was approaching the thirty-fifth anniversary of his arrival in Hollywood. As he looked around him, he saw disturbing changes. Movie attendance was slipping. The weekly high of 82 million had slid to 60 million. Theaters were closing. Something was wrong with the industry. Perhaps it was the recent publicity. An ambitious senator named Joseph McCarthy had decided that the film capital was infested with subversives. Communism was on the move in Europe, so McCarthy was able to grab the attention of the House Committee on Un-American Activities (HUAC). When hearings commenced in October 1947, ten prominent screenwriters were accused of putting communist propaganda into their scripts. The writers refused to testify, and they were thrown in jail. DeMille agreed to testify, but when the committee learned that he planned to use the witness stand as a podium for an attack on it, the appearance was canceled. The furor turned to hysteria. Edward G. Robinson and John Garfield were accused of being communists. McCarthy could not prove his charges, but he did cow the studios into blacklisting these stars, along with 1,500 other film-industry employees. Hollywood was a house divided.

In the days of Famous Players-Lasky, Adolph Zukor's great achievement had been to create a vertically integrated monopoly, one that controlled production, distribution, and exhibition. Not everyone liked his system. "Block booking" forced theaters to take a group of ho-hum B pictures in order to get an eagerly awaited A. The Federal Trade Commission alerted the Department of Justice. In 1938, an antitrust suit was filed against the eight major film companies, *U.S. v. Paramount*. On May 4, 1948, the Supreme Court handed down a ruling that declared the five major studios in violation of antitrust laws. The ruling abolished

CECILIA DE MILLE PRESLEY

"When DeMille suggested to Paramount that his next picture should be *Samson and Delilah*, there were the expected misgivings. 'Put millions into a Sunday school tale?' was one comment. Anticipating this familiar chorus at the next meeting, Grandfather had Dan Groesbeck make a simple sketch of a brawny, athletic man, and, looking at him with a seductive eye, a ravishingly beautiful, young girl. When the executives trooped in, ready to save Paramount from financial ruin, DeMille showed them Dan's sketch. 'Gentlemen,' he said, 'this is the subject.' They reacted to it: 'Oh. That's what you mean. Great!'"

OVERLEAF: Cecil B. DeMille posed with the VistaVision camera for a portrait by Karsh of Ottawa.

OPPOSITE: Delilah (Hedy Lamarr) deprives Samson (Victor Mature) of his strength.

block booking and ordered these studios to divest themselves of their theater chains. The timing could not have been worse.

The movie industry had managed to coexist with radio, even sharing talent like Bing Crosby. Television was not so benign. The average moviegoer could not be at the neighborhood theater and at home watching TV at the same time. At first it looked like a no-contest. How could wavering charcoal images on a little round screen compete with Betty Hutton in Technicolor? Then there were four television networks and more hours of programming. If watching a movie was dreamlike, sitting in front of a TV was hypnotic. TV sets were selling. Box office was slowing. What was the answer? "Hard hit as Hollywood has been economically," wrote Edwin Schallert in the *Los Angeles Times*, "it is mapping a plan of action. Spectacular films retain their place." Ingrid Bergman as Joan of Arc might be the tonic for an anemic box office. DeMille had other ideas. "There was a man named Adam who looked like Errol Flynn," he told his writers one day. "This Adam was lonely. So he complained and God did something to the man's side. Lo and behold, there was a lovely thing lying on a pallet of straw." DeMille fixed his gaze on Jesse Lasky Jr. "What would you say, Jess, is the greatest love story ever told?"

"Romeo and Juliet?"

"Thalberg made that!" said DeMille impatiently, and then he lifted a curio that looked like an animal's jawbone.

"The jawbone of an ass," said Lasky. "Samson. Yeah! Samson and Delilah!"

If Paramount executives were indifferent to a movie about Samson and Delilah in 1935, they were hostile in 1948. They told DeMille to stick to American history. Except for the colonial-era *Unconquered*, it had done well. DeMille was determined to get their approval. He invited them to a meeting and unveiled a provocative concept sketch by Dan Sayre Groesbeck—*Delilah Eyeing Samson*. The project was approved.

OPPOSITE: On the back of this artwork by Dan Sayre Groesbeck DeMille wrote a simple statement of fact: "This sketch sold Paramount on making *Samson and Delilah*."

A sketch is one thing. A screenplay is another. DeMille began with a broad plan, a list of plot points, which he pinned to the wall of his office. "1. Brawl at wedding feast. 2. Fight with Lion. 3. Fight with Wrestler. 4. Jawbone Fight. 5. Falling Temple." Once the broad strokes were done, it was time for his writers to run the gauntlet. Lasky knew what to expect. "Every weekend," he recalled, "DeMille would mull over the sins of his writers, how they degraded drama, frustrated common sense, and multiplied his labors. He would descend on Monday morning in a fine wrath, spitting little balls of cyanide." Transcriptions of the story conferences captured evidence for both sides.

DeMille: This is the best piece of writing thus far, gentlemen, but I'm still a little puzzled by the motives. I don't know what Samson is thinking. He starts out by saying, "You're a vicious little bitch," but I don't know how he feels when he finishes. You don't reach any climax. You ring the curtain down only because you've run out of breath. They're exactly at the point where they came in.

Writer B: Well, his whole feeling has changed.

DeMille: Where do I get that—except from you? All he says is, "You're not going to do anything to me. I'm getting out of here." What progress has been made?

Writer A: She breaks him down in the course of the scene.

DeMille: Where? How? Where does she break him down?

Writer A: Page 100.

DeMille: Nuts! I don't get that on this page. He hasn't changed a bit. There's nothing here that changes

CECIL B. DeMILLE

"In bringing the Samson episodes to the screen, we were dramatizing a story that has been a bestseller for 3,000 years. What book has sold more copies than the Bible?"

him. You have to show me why he changes. He doesn't just look at the moon and start to drool. What is his emotion?

Writer B: He starts out by being very suspicious of her. Then she doesn't give him any reason to be.

DeMille: Is he falling in love with her? Is he suspicious of her? It's a rambling scene. There's no point of construction.

Writer A: The objective of the whole scene is when he takes her in his arms and tells her where he is going to be.

DeMille: He tells her his hiding place? Why would he do that? If he does, he's a goddamned fool. He's suspicious of her! He'd never in God's world tell her that. He's a judge, a hunter, a canny Jew. I don't like this. I don't believe it. If you had three reels leading up to it, perhaps. But to walk into this room with all its finery and say to her, "I'll tell you all my secrets because you have pretty legs." No. Why did you think I'd believe it? *You* don't! To ask the secret of his strength here is just nuts. I know she's going to find out the secret of his strength. I've read the Bible. It's no great surprise that she's going to cut off his hair. You have to be clever enough to make me believe that cutting his hair off will destroy his strength. I gathered she was going to get this guy to a state of imbecility over her and then do what women have been doing for ten thousand years. The main way that women hurt men is to drain them dry. He betrays his people, his trust, everything in the world because of this woman. But the way you have it, there's no possibility of his falling for this girl. He sees a good-looking dame and he's perfectly willing to go to bed with her. That's about all we have now.

The problem DeMille was addressing is a common one. Dramatists who have spent time with their characters forget that the viewer has not. To care about a character, the viewer needs exposition. Then there has to be a struggle. "Conflict is the only thing that will keep an audience awake," DeMille told Phil Koury. "Jesse's father lost a fortune when he became engrossed in a series of individually charming pictures but forgot to build up a clash of characters."

While Jesse Jr. and Fredric Frank labored over the characters, DeMille was casting them. "Casting was risky," wrote DeMille. "If it turned out that my two leads had nothing to give the story but the appearance of male strength and female beauty, the real point would be lost." DeMille used binders full of typed entries. "Nancy Olson—On April 27, 1948, Mr. DeMille screened test of her with George Reeves in a scene from *A Farewell to Arms*. Comments: 'She is extremely interesting, has amazing timing. She is awfully good.' On May 6, 1948, She auditioned the Pavilion scene with John Bromfield. Comments: 'The girl is terrific. She has authority, timing.'" Olson was a front-runner for the part of Delilah. But so were Rita Hayworth and Jean Simmons—until May 25. That was when DeMille screened Edgar Ulmer's *The Strange Woman*. It starred Hedy Lamarr, who had coproduced it. After watching her in the mildly torrid film, DeMille said one word: "Delilah." He met with Lamarr the next day.

—————— CECILIA DE MILLE PRESLEY ——————

"I thought Hedy Lamarr the most beautiful woman I had ever seen. She was also very nice. On the set she and DeMille were having communication problems. The atmosphere was tense. One day Grandfather complimented her on a scene. She burst into tears and said, 'Why do you always say such terrible things to me?' Grandfather was at first perplexed, then realized that when he spoke rapidly, Hedy had trouble translating, as she thought in her native tongue, German. He slowed down, and was always careful to convey a kind expression. Near the end of her life, she wrote of DeMille as 'the most delightful man, charming and kind.'"

OPPOSITE: The tranquility of Samson and Delilah's time together gives no hint of their ill-fated passion.

"I was won over the moment I entered his office and saw the extent of the research that he had done," said Lamarr. "He has documents and evidence to support everything." On June 9, he screened the very torrid *White Cargo*. On June 10, he signed Lamarr.

Henry Wilcoxon had stayed in touch with DeMille during the war, writing letters from the destroyer on which he was a gunnery officer. He had hoped that all was forgiven. When he came back to Paramount, he was disappointed that DeMille gave him nothing better than a minor role in *Unconquered*. Wilcoxon was patient, available, and in top physical condition. He was called to DeMille's office for an interview. "DeMille looked at me admiringly," recalled Wilcoxon. "But, alas, no one remains thirty forever." Still, Wilcoxon was awarded a substantial role, that of Ahtur, the Philistine commander. A more important role was gestating, that of right-hand man to the Boss. DeMille was sensitive to everything occurring in his orbit. He overheard Wilcoxon's comments on numerous production problems. DeMille, who was customarily slow to make a decision, began to listen to Wilcoxon. This was necessary, given the size of *Samson and Delilah*.

Casting Samson was difficult, since Groesbeck's sketches made him look Neanderthal. DeMille needed a muscleman who could act. Wilcoxon thought Burt Lancaster would make the ultimate Samson. DeMille was not convinced. He had recently screened two Victor Mature films. On June 7, DeMille screened the Lancaster film *All My Sons*. "Lancaster and Mature seem the best possibilities," DeMille dictated to his assistant. On June 2, he did an interview with Victor Mature, who had been a star for five years. "DeMille had an extensive knowledge of my entire career," recalled Mature. "That's how thorough he was. When the interview lasted four hours, I knew I was in."

On June 12, DeMille announced Victor Mature as Samson, and assigned Wilcoxon to create an exercise regimen for the actor, who lacked both shape and definition. Wilcoxon was mildly resentful; this would not have been necessary with Lancaster. DeMille kept his own counsel, but there were rumors—never substantiated—that Lancaster was a communist sympathizer. In those nervous times, lies were believed as readily as they were invented. When interviewing Olive Deering for Miriam, similar rumors were whispered. Lasky cited the war record of Deering's husband to prove that she was neither a Red nor a Pinko.

DeMille cast his two remaining principals from one film, Albert Lewin's *The Private Affairs of Bel Ami*, which was the kind

CECILIA DE MILLE PRESLEY

"Victor Mature drove DeMille mad. The rumor was that he hated Victor. Not true. Victor was too nice to hate. It was that Victor did not want to act with a real lion. Grandfather, who was sixty-seven at the time, showed Victor what he wanted. C. B. got on the set with Jackie the Lion and wrestled with him. Victor did not care that DeMille would do it. He would not. Grandfather called him a physical coward. Victor smilingly agreed. Enter the stuntman. In the end, DeMille was pleased with Victor's performance and all was well. The picture was a great success."

VICTOR MATURE

"Mr. DeMille hired the best people in town for his films, and since we were all professionals, he didn't feel he had to direct us too much. He figured we knew our jobs. He'd say a few words to us and then shoot the scene. But he didn't miss a trick. In a scene with eight hundred extras, if one guy in the back was picking his nose, Mr. DeMille would spot it and stop everything to chew him out."

OPPOSITE: After besting a lion and a giant, Samson meets the ruler of the Philistines. From left to right: the chariot driver (Henry Wills); the Saran (George Sanders); Delilah (Hedy Lamarr); Semadar (Angela Lansbury); Ahtur (Henry Wilcoxon); and Samson (Victor Mature).

of film that could be made at United Artists in 1947—clever, adult-themed, well-mounted—and which would fail because of the changing marketplace. This adaptation of a Guy de Maupassant story featured George Sanders and Angela Lansbury. DeMille had already cast Phyllis Calvert as Semadar when he saw it, but Sanders would make a perfect Saran. "I would have cast Lansbury as Semadar if I'd seen this before," he said. He

got the chance to fix his mistake a month later when Calvert bowed out because of illness. "DeMille really was considered an icon of the business," recalled Lansbury. "He thought of himself as a very special person and demanded special treatment and was prepared to play the role of the great Hollywood director to the hilt." If DeMille appeared lordly and his casting process

OPPOSITE, CLOCKWISE FROM TOP LEFT: The unidentified assistant acting as DeMille's "chair boy" makes sure that the Boss connects with the furniture. Photograph by John Florea. • DeMille, who supposedly never demonstrated business for his actors, is seen here demonstrating business for his actors. Photograph by John Florea. • DeMille reviews concept art as he shoots the scene based on the art. Photograph by G. E. Richardson. • Hedy Lamarr reportedly did not care for Victor Mature, but she convinced millions of moviegoers that she did. That's why they call it acting.

ABOVE: Samson interrupts the wedding night of Ahtur and Semadar.

HENRY WILCOXON

"I am often asked what Cecil B. DeMille was really like. My answer is to take a look at the character of the Saran in *Samson and Delilah*. He was modeled after DeMille by the writers, and it is an accurate portrait. A great deal of the Saran's dialogue is practically from DeMille's mouth—most especially the 'Ant Farm' scene in the Saran's chamber when everyone is wondering how to make the tribes of Israel suffer for visiting Samson upon the kingdom. If I were asked to describe DeMille in one sentence, I would have to say that he was a coldly fair man. His thoughts were calculated; his words to the point."

dragged on, there was good reason. *Samson and Delilah* was budgeted at nearly $3 million.

In a meeting with thirty staff members, DeMille laid down the law. "Economic conditions in this industry make it necessary for us to materially change the way we make motion pictures," he said. "If we do not, we may be forced to stop making pictures altogether. If you stay in the groove where you think I'm kidding, this will happen. You cannot give me a $50,000 set when all I ask for is a column and some drapery. Drapes can save us the expense of building half a set, unless buying drapes becomes more expensive. I certainly do not want to cheapen production. I want to cheapen the cost of production. We did it with *The Sign of the Cross*. We can do it again." Various ways of holding down costs were discussed. Shooting second-unit scenes overseas was one. "It's gotten to the point where it's

cheaper to send a unit to Morocco than to Chatsworth," said DeMille.

The script called for Samson to fight a young lion. Would it be better to shoot this in Paramount's outdoor "arena," with the area dressed with boulders, using direct sunlight? This was 1948, not 1913. "There'll be too much airplane noise to record lines if you do it that way," said Roy Burns. "We've had to cancel some Saturdays recently because of the racket."

"Actors react to noises," said production manager Richard Johnston. "They flub lines."

"What about the lion?" asked DeMille. "An ordinary animal wrestle won't do for this scene. I want a scene like no one has seen before, a big effect. I'm prepared to spend money on it."

"We were thinking of getting Jackie," said Gordon Jennings, the special effects manager, referring to the former M-G-M lion.

"Don't talk to the SPCA until after Joe Breen reads the script," said DeMille, calculating what the Production Code boss might require in terms of animal safety.

As concerned as he was with details, DeMille's primary focus was on his five big scenes. These could be advertised. These would prompt word of mouth. These had to be showstoppers, played by bigger-than-life stars in eye-catching costumes. Edith Head had worked around DeMille since the early 1920s, when she was an assistant to Howard Greer. Her first DeMille job was creating the Candy Ball costumes for *The Golden Bed*. When they melted under the arc lights, she almost lost her position. She retained no great affection for DeMille. "He was known around the studio as the Great Man," recalled Head. "He was a great man, an incredible moviemaker. Everyone was in awe of him." Everyone but Edith Head, who was head of the Paramount wardrobe department—and offended by DeMille's lack of deference. "I didn't really feel like a designer," she wrote. "I was just one of the flock. He used seven or eight designers. He even had a designer for the plumes on his chariot horses. And

ABOVE: Delilah drugs Samson's wine.

it was never five sketches. It was thirty. Nobody ever went into costuming with such an insistence on detail."

When Head brought him sketches for Delilah's final costume in the film, DeMille at first drew back and then spent moments of silent contemplation. Head had designed a cape festooned with peacock feathers. "*That* I like very much," said DeMille. Having pleased her boss, Head faced a technical consideration. "There wasn't any place in America," wrote Head, "where we could buy peacock tails." After looking everywhere and finding no peacocks who were willing to be plucked, Head ruefully advised DeMille. Of course he had a solution. His Paradise ranch was home to flocks of peacocks. Competing legends sprang up, either that DeMille collected the feathers or that Head collected the feathers. Who did walk around molting peacocks and pick up their feathers? "I watched wardrobe people carrying bushels of feathers onto the lot," recalled then-publicist Herb Steinberg. "They were collecting them at the ranch at Tujunga." In the end, 1,900 hundred feathers were sewn and glued onto the cape.

DeMille's staff had spent the spring of 1948 writing and casting. The summer was spent in set construction and rewriting. In September, Paramount raised the *Samson and Delilah* budget to $3.5 million. On October 4, DeMille brought his granddaughter Cecilia to Stage 8 and began shooting. Scenes between Sanders and the DeMille repertory company went swimmingly; veterans like William Farnum, Harry Woods, and Julia Faye did not "go up" in their lines. These were the troupers, Hollywood's salt of the earth, unceasingly loyal to DeMille.

On October 9, Lamarr began earning her $10,000-a-week salary. "The spectacular face and figure were enhanced by a miraculous grace," wrote Lasky. "DeMille said she was like a gazelle, incapable of a clumsy or wrong move. She filled the eye of the beholder with such breathless beauty that her acting hardly mattered." It mattered to DeMille. When she did well, he took pains to compliment her, even if her limited understand-

ing of English created a momentary quarrel. She could also be vague and unengaged, which infuriated DeMille, and amused Edith Head. "I can still see that indefatigable old goat riding his camera crane, booming out over the stage, 'Miss Lamarr! Please! God DAMN it! Come out of that MASK!'" Lamarr ignored him. "Mr. DeMille has knowledge and charm such as few people have," said Lamarr for publication. "When he gets mad, I do not listen."

Victor Mature looked up at DeMille. "Geez, look at him. He's a genius, that kid."

Lamarr ignored Mature as much as possible. "She was not exactly a ball of fire," he recalled. "She just seemed to be loping along. But we got along okay, worked well together, and the camera picked up her mystique. George Barnes, who photographed the picture, said to me, 'You can shoot her from any angle. She has no bad angles.'" Lamarr confided to friends that she did not like Mature. He appeared to like everyone. "Jeez, this is a wonderful pastime," he told *Life* magazine. "I didn't want to be Samson at first. You know, more beautiful-hunk-of-man stuff. I figured to hell with it. Then I read the script. Jeez, what do you want to bet it won't make ten million bucks?"

Samson and Delilah could only gross that much if all its scenes made it to the screen. Mature was having second thoughts about wrestling a lion. (Jackie was not the original M-G-M lion. That was Slats. Jackie was his successor, having worked there since 1928, when he dubbed the roars for the silent footage of Slats, which the studio preferred to use. Jackie's contract with M-G-M terminated in 1935, at which time he went freelance, taking calls at Gay's Lion Farm in El Monte.) Jackie was, by all accounts, docile and agreeable. Mature informed DeMille that he would prefer to wrestle a stuffed lion. "I never use stuffed animals in my pictures if it can be helped," replied DeMille. "And I'll tell you why. They always look stuffed. You have to work with a live lion."

"Look, C. B. There's only one Mature and I would hate to see him go this way."

"I am not going to press the matter," said DeMille, "but I can assure you it will be perfectly safe. Jackie was trained as a cub and fed on milk."

"I was raised on milk, too, but I eat meat."

"The animal has no teeth. He can't bite you."

"Mr. DeMille, I don't even want to be gummed."

In mid-November, the time came to shoot the scene. Mature walked from his dressing room to a stage where the lion rocks had been built. There was Jackie, teeth and all. Mature refused to do the scene. He had already been spooked by an errant wind machine. It was time for a DeMille tirade. According to Edith Head, it went like this: "I have met a few men in my time. Some have been afraid of heights, some have been afraid of water, some have been afraid of fire, some have been afraid of closed spaces. Some have even been afraid of open spaces—or themselves. But in all my thirty-five years of

picture-making experience, Mr. Mature, I have not until now met a man who was one hundred percent yellow."

The same thing happened on an exterior set. When faced with an aged, indifferent animal, Mature would not budge. When pressed for a comment, he said, "I wouldn't walk up a wet step." DeMille had to send a second unit to shoot alternate angles of the fight with Mature's double, Kay Bell. The fight was excellent, except for the anachronistic telephone poles at the top of the frame. Time was running out. Mature was filmed with a stuffed lion. A grip moved a stuffed paw across Mature's face. When Anne Bauchens edited the sequence, she did not have enough coverage. DeMille was shooting more lion angles right up to the premiere, and past it, up to the general release. The scene did not work. Likewise, there was a lack of sympathy between the sheepish strongman and the indifferent diva. DeMille tried to reassure Hedda Hopper (and himself) that there was

OPPOSITE: A bracelet worn by Henry Wilcoxon in *Samson and Delilah*. Photograph by Mark A. Vieira.

ABOVE: A Ted Allan portrait of Victor Mature and Hedy Lamarr.

OVERLEAF: Samson is betrayed to Ahtur and the Philistines by Delilah.

much more to the film, that he was using it to bring the Bible to the masses. "Now, just a minute, C. B.!" sniffed Hopper. "You're talking to Hedda now. Those Bible pictures of yours have plenty of sex!"

The final *Samson and Delilah* preview was held at the Denham Theatre in Denver, Colorado. "I have been previewing pictures for thirty-six years," DeMille reported. "This is the best audience reaction I can recall. Not a single person left the theater or stirred from his seat until the end title came on the screen. There were seventy-five laughs, and there were handker-

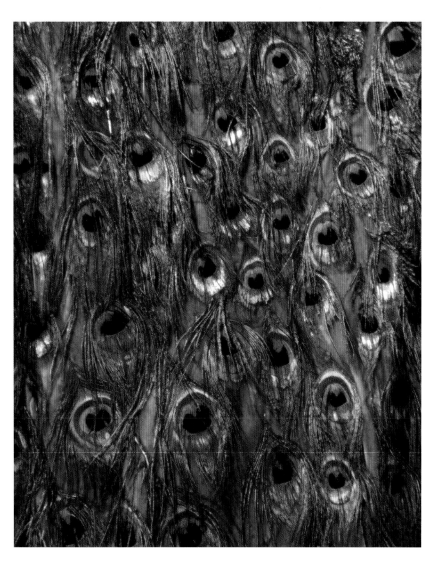

OPPOSITE: Edith Head designed this costume for Hedy Lamarr's final scene in *Samson and Delilah*. Head's work (done in collaboration with Dorothy Jeakins, Elois Jenssen, Gile Steele, and twelve others) was honored with an Academy Award.

ABOVE: Ted Allan made scene stills under DeMille's supervision. The magnificent lighting effects were created by cinematographer George Barnes.

OVERLEAF: This eight-foot-high miniature was used for wide shots in the climax of *Samson and Delilah*.

chiefs aplenty at the end." Mature's prediction about the film's box-office was off the mark. It did not gross $10 million. *Samson and Delilah* grossed $12 million, and reissues and sales to the other media would eventually raise the figure to $25 million. At the time, only *Gone with the Wind* and a handful of Disney features had grossed more. For once reviews were irrelevant. DeMille had fought a depressed economy and won.

THIS PAGE: Critics tried to dismiss DeMille's storytelling, but the primal emotions in *Samson and Delilah* were hard to resist.

OPPOSITE: The special effects supervised by Gordon Jennings created a finale that was literally shattering. *Samson and Delilah* overcame numerous problems, both in its production and in 1948 Hollywood, to become a box-office bonanza. The film remains one of the highest-grossing releases in history.

CECILIA de MILLE PRESLEY

"The scene where Samson brings down the temple on his enemies created an architectural problem. How could moving just two pillars bring down an entire temple? The answer came from the writings of Pliny, the Roman historian of the first century. He wrote the description of just such a building and just such a collapse. Gordon Jennings, the greatly talented photographic effects man, constructed the temple to Pliny's specifications. It produced plausible and spectacular scenes. Ironically, Paramount was collapsing, and this was the film that saved it."

THE GREATEST SHOW ON EARTH

ecil B. DeMille was regarded with awe in 1949, even before the triumphant release of *Samson and Delilah*. This was an anniversary year. Political issues were put aside, and Hollywood honored DeMille for having brought the film industry there thirty-five years earlier. On October 13, 1949, Paramount observed the anniversary of *The Squaw Man* with a party where DeMille had made it. The barn still resided at the front of the Paramount lot, looking like the acorn to the oak beyond. He was joined by Jesse L. Lasky, Winifred Kingston, Blanche Sweet, Pauline Garon, and a few other veterans of the Lasky Feature Play Company.

DeMille and Lasky were honored by the Society of Motion Picture Art Directors for having introduced the first art director to Hollywood, the late Wilfred Buckland. Gloria Swanson presented DeMille and Lasky with one bronze plaque each. "I've known and loved these two gentlemen for a quarter of a century," said Swanson, trimming five years from the imposing total. Lasky had failed to sustain the momentum of *Sergeant York*, but had recently produced a film for RKO release, *The Miracle of the Bells*. As always, he was cheerful and hopeful. Sam Goldwyn was enjoying a run of hits with the Broadway wunderkind whom he had made a star, Danny Kaye. Goldwyn was Hollywood's preeminent independent, emulated by Walt Disney and David

O. Selznick. DeMille was, of course, a monumental figure, the only filmmaker from the beginning of the industry who was still creating hits. There were directors from the early silent era who were still working—Henry King, John Ford, Frank Borzage—but none was in his category. There was only one filmmaker who could be called an equal.

David Wark Griffith had not made a movie since 1931. For years he tried to get work. None of the moguls would hire him. Then he gave up. On July 23, 1948, he died of a stroke in the lobby of the Hollywood Knickerbocker Hotel, where he had been living in shabby isolation. He was seventy-three. "During the quiet months before Mr. Griffith died," wrote the *Los Angeles Times*, "the forgotten father of the film industry strolled Hollywood Boulevard, melancholy and unrecognized by the city of tinsel he had helped create." DeMille, who never failed to praise Griffith, attended the funeral, along with industry figures

CECILIA DE MILLE PRESLEY

"Many children have a dream of running away with the circus. 'For Children of All Ages' was the circus's motto. It was true for both grandfather and granddaughter. We got to run away with the circus."

OPPOSITE: A portrait of DeMille by John Florea.

such as Louis B. Mayer, Mack Sennett, and Charles Chaplin. The eulogy was delivered by Charles Brackett, president of the Academy of Motion Picture Arts and Sciences, which had recently honored Griffith. "What does a man full of vitality care for honors of the past?" asked Brackett. "It's the present he wants. And the future. There was no solution for Griffith but a kind of frenzied beating on the barred doors of one day after another."

In the opinion of the Hollywood community, Griffith was better forgotten, along with the entire silent era. Since the early 1930s it had been fashionable to ridicule the "flickers." Fan magazines ran pictorial features on the "old days," making fun of them as if they were centuries removed. Ruthless in its pursuit of the new, Hollywood had no time for nostalgia. In defiance of this attitude, Brackett and his writing partner Billy Wilder launched a project that would tour the gauzy past, using disenchanted film folk as docents. This odd project, *Sunset Boulevard*, pulled

both Gloria Swanson and C. B. DeMille into its orbit. Who better personified the achievements, glamour, and hubris of silent-film Hollywood? And so Swanson signed on for the role of a lifetime, playing a star who combined the excesses of Nita Naldi and Mae Murray. DeMille played himself for four days in May 1949. Unlike Swanson's character, DeMille—both on-screen and off—was not looking back. He was looking forward, which was one reason for his unparalleled prominence.

DeMille had made sixty-eight features. As of January 1950, these films had sold 1.66 billion tickets in the continental

ABOVE, LEFT TO RIGHT: On the set of Billy Wilder's *Sunset Boulevard*, DeMille bestows one of his rare coins on Gloria Swanson. • This scene still from *Sunset Boulevard* shows that the Paramount publicity department had recently banished 8 x 10 view cameras from the set; from 1949 on, all movie stills were essentially candids. • In real life, Gloria Swanson and Cecil DeMille maintained their friendship.

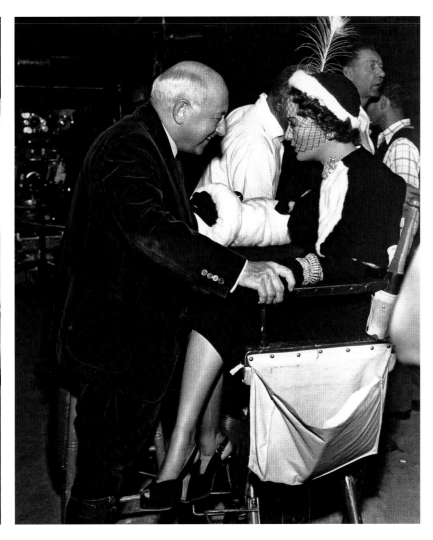

United States and 1.44 billion tickets in the rest of the world. The cumulative gross of the sixty-eight features he had made since 1913 was $600 million (perhaps $12 billion in 2014). He was a boon, not only to a studio suffering the loss of its theatrical real estate, but also to the economy of Hollywood. On the set of *Samson and Delilah* there were nineteen crew members who had been with him for more than twenty years and who collectively had been with him on fifty-three films. There were

hundreds of extras who counted on him for work. There were his industry peers, who shook their heads as he mounted one hit after another. "There has appeared only one Cecil B. DeMille," said Selznick. "He is one of the most extraordinarily able showmen of modern times. However much I may dislike some of his pictures, it would be very silly of me, as a producer of commercial motion pictures, to demean for an instant his unparalleled skill as a maker of mass entertainment."

For fifteen years DeMille had fashioned that entertainment from history, whether American or biblical. And yet an idea he had carried with him since 1923 was fixed firmly in the present. It came from *Under the Big Top*, a book by Courtney Ryley Cooper. "The circus is only the veneer," wrote Cooper. "The circus is a fighting machine waging a constant battle for survival—against adversity, accident, flood and storm—a driving, dogged force which succeeds only through the grit and determination of the men and women who live in the face of fatigue, bodily discomfort, and sometimes in the very grasp of death itself." DeMille was intrigued by the background of a modern circus, with all its color, chaos, and energy. He also liked Irving Thalberg's *Grand Hotel*, which had introduced the formula of a group of characters working out their mingled destinies in one confined setting. Since signing with Technicolor, DeMille had made his films on soundstages, both for control and convenience. In 1948 more films were being shot outdoors, and with excellent results. *Grand Hotel*'s cinematographer William Daniels had just shot *The Naked City* entirely on location in New York, using faster films and smaller lighting instruments. What if DeMille could

C-49
Costume Sketch for SEBASTIAN
in raft in Parade

J L Jensen Jan 24 1951

"There were three different story lines written for the *Greatest Show on Earth*. Arguments ensued over which was the best. To settle this, Grandfather told one of the stories each night to my seven-year-old little brother, Joe Harper, whom we called Jody. The fourth night he asked Jody which story he would like to hear again. 'The Battle for the Center Ring' was Jody's favorite. It was adopted, and it became known as the 'Jody version.' For his insight Jody was given a part in the film.

"His big moment though, was off-camera. A leopard escaped during the train wreck and could not be found—until he tugged at Grandfather's sleeve and pointed to the big cat purring beside him.

". . . In the summer of 1949, Grandfather, his secretary Gladys Rosson, writer Fred Frank, and I boarded Henry Ringling North's private railroad car for the trip of a lifetime, touring the United States with Ringling Bros. and Barnum & Bailey Circus. Grandfather thought I would help him with stories of circus life as seen through the eyes of a child. I was twelve. Instead, he complained, I 'went circus' on him. I was skinny and could wear the showgirls' costumes. I got permission from the circus boss to sub for the girls as long as it was safe. In the Grand Parade I rode horses, elephants, sat in carriages or walked with the acrobats. I carried water for animals and helped anywhere I could be of use.

". . . Grandfather never missed a performance. He and Fred Frank became friends with performers, animal trainers, veterinarians—anyone who traveled with the Big Top—listening to their stories of circus life, and realizing the truly grave dangers some of them faced, sometimes twice a day. The attention to rigging was vital. One oversight could mean injury or death.

". . . The circus folk were some of the most interesting and dedicated people I have ever known. There was Emmett Kelly, the sad clown, Lou Jacobs, the funny clown, and of course, the flyers. The high-wire act was the Alzanas family—the husband, wife, and two sisters—who worked on a wire sixty feet in the air with no net. They became my best friends during our time with the circus.

"Grandfather's reason for traveling with the circus was to meet the people—performers and roustabouts alike—to witness the drama, the sacrifice, and the dangers that existed in their environment. We saw so many incidents that it was hard to decide which to include. When we returned to Hollywood, Fred and Grandfather had to choose from hundreds of worthwhile dramas. The making of this film was great fun for family, cast, and crew. I never saw Grandfather so happy on a set."

shoot on location with an actual circus but with actors playing from a script? It was Selznick who inadvertently paved the way. In April 1948 he entered into negotiations with John Ringling North, president of the Ringling Bros. and Barnum & Bailey Circus, for a profit-participation arrangement in a fictional film. North wanted 50 percent but was offering only the trademark title "The Greatest Show on Earth," the use of circus grounds, and access to circus acts.

DeMille had been compared to Phineas T. Barnum too often not to follow the progress of Selznick's negotiations. When they abruptly ended, DeMille jumped in. He wanted the project badly enough to give North 50 percent of the gross after the film recouped twice its negative cost, an upward sliding scale after that, and a substantial $250,000 adviser fee. For this DeMille got the keys to a wonderland. But first he had to come up with a story as good as *Grand Hotel*. He cabled Jesse Lasky Jr., who was working in Italy, to come back and write for him. "All is forgiven," said the cable. Lasky had done nothing that required

OPPOSITE: John Jensen replaced the ailing Dan Groesbeck as concept artist to create these paintings for *The Greatest Show on Earth*.

forgiveness. To the contrary, DeMille had laid him and Fredric Frank off after *Samson and Delilah*, without warning or severance pay, in violation of guild rules. Lasky declined the offer but Frank was willing to return.

Where Jeanie Macpherson or Henry Noerdlinger would once have prepared stacks of files, Frank, DeMille, his granddaughter Cecilia, and several others did their research in the field. In August 1949, they joined the circus. "Gladys Rosson trouped as wholeheartedly as if she had been to the sawdust born," wrote DeMille. "Her notebook of 135 pages is crammed with incidents comic and terrifying, anecdotes and bits of business, circus slang, and vignettes of life in the 'backyard.'" DeMille celebrated his sixty-eighth birthday on the road, and, in fact in the air. He persuaded the famous aerialist and circus boss Art Concello to send him to the top of the tent in a pulley so he could use his viewfinder to see potential angles. After coming to earth, DeMille suggested that the tent should have openings to let the hundred-degree air escape; his idea was implemented. His vigor was formidable, only slackening at day's end. "At dinner he slipped into a kind of semiconsciousness," reported Phil Koury. "Gladys held up his head to keep it from striking his dish. When he awoke, he went right on with his meal as if nothing had happened."

After three months on the road, it was time to write the script. This proved the most difficult ever. There was too much material to boil down; too many characters. Drafts were prepared. DeMille rejected them. Writers came and went. *Grand Hotel* had not worked as a guide, so DeMille made them use the silent film *Variety*. DeMille sought the advice of his grandson Joseph, who isolated the narrative line. This did not end their travails, but it did unify the quest. In November 1950, after seven writers and $113,000, DeMille finally had a script for *The Greatest Show on Earth*.

Casting the film provided a number of tales for the gossip mills. There were three male roles to be cast: the arrogant aerialist, the circus boss, and the clown with a secret. The three female roles were the iron jaw, the elephant trainer, and the

trapeze star. Wilcoxon was officially hired as assistant producer in May 1950. "I was valuable to Mr. DeMille for many reasons, but mainly for two things," recalled Wilcoxon. "First, I could sketch. This helped him to visualize scenes, sets, costumes, camera angles and that sort of thing. And secondly, I could evaluate things quickly and give my opinion. He wouldn't always act on my opinions, but he did often enough." Wilcoxon again campaigned for Burt Lancaster, reasoning that his circus experience qualified him for the part of the aerialist. DeMille again resisted, hiring Cornel Wilde, a respected star, without finding out if he had sufficient trapeze training. Wilde was an expert gymnast but was unaware that he had latent acrophobia.

The circus boss was based on Concello, but his lines about the circus being all-important could have come from DeMille. In June, Wilcoxon suggested the unknown Charlton Heston for the boss. DeMille screened film of Heston. "He has a sinister quality," said DeMille. "He's sincere—you believe him—he has some power, but he's not attractive in this. Find out if he has any humor." DeMille decided that Kirk Douglas was better, going so far as to visit him on the set of Billy Wilder's *Ace in the Hole* on August 22. DeMille learned that Douglas's agency, Famous Artists, wanted $150,000. DeMille's policy was to cut the asking price by half and then argue. Famous Artists was not interested in arguing. DeMille looked at more film of Heston. "Everything I've seen him in, he's dour," said DeMille. Not long afterward, DeMille was leaving his office. A green Packard convertible drove by. A young man waved at him. "Who was that?" he asked his secretary, Berenice Mosk. "Heston? Really? I liked the way

THIS PAGE: To prepare his shots of the Ringling Bros. and Barnum & Bailey Circus, DeMille had a scale model built. He also fostered advances in photographic technology.

CHARLTON HESTON

"DeMille had a reputation as a man-eater, but I never saw him devour an actor. For one thing, he knew very well that an actor angry at his director, or afraid of him, is not likely to give him a good performance."

CLOCKWISE FROM TOP LEFT: Cornel Wilde and Betty Hutton in a scene from *The Greatest Show on Earth*. • A scene still of Betty Hutton and James Stewart. • Bob Hope and Bing Crosby made an unbilled cameo appearance in *The Greatest Show on Earth*. • A Big Top scene from *The Greatest Show on Earth*. • Charlton Heston and Betty Hutton in one of the finely shaded intimate scenes.

he waved just now. We'd better have him in to talk about the circus manager."

The clown's secret is that he is on the run from the police after helping his terminally ill wife with assisted suicide. DeMille had barely gotten this plot point past the PCA. The doctor becomes a clown to evade arrest, figuring that the police will never recognize him while he is wearing makeup. James Stewart's manager spoke with DeMille, who said, "Naturally I'd love to have Jimmy Stewart, but the part doesn't warrant his usual salary."

"In this instance money doesn't matter," the manager hastened. "He's dying to play the role." Stewart came to visit DeMille.

"Mr. DeMille," he said, "what I've always wanted to play is a clown. Since I was a little boy, I've wanted to run away and join the circus to be a clown. I can't think of anything more fun than being able to make children laugh." DeMille was getting a deal.

Dorothy Lamour was eager for the iron-jaw part. She was cast. In October, the elephant trainer was promised to Lucille Ball, who was finishing a short-term contract at Columbia. On December 18, she came to DeMille's office with her husband, Desi Arnaz. Ball told DeMille that she had suffered miscarriages in the past few years but that she was pregnant again and this time there was hope. DeMille was not moved. He knew that she had just gotten out of her contract with Columbia without telling Harry Cohn, who would have deprived her of $85,000 for dropping out. More to the point, she was interfering with his plans. "You can have a baby at any time," he told her. "How often do you get a lead in a DeMille picture?"

"But you don't understand," said Ball. "Desi and I have been hoping for this for ten years."

There was nothing for DeMille to do but see the couple to the door. As Ball walked off, DeMille looked Arnaz in the eye, "Congratulations," said DeMille. "You're the only man in history who screwed Lucille Ball, Columbia Pictures, Paramount Pictures, Harry Cohn, and Cecil B. DeMille, all at the same time."

Wilcoxon had seen Gloria Grahame in *Crossfire* and *In a Lonely Place*. DeMille looked at a test she had done for *Born Yesterday*. She promised him that the elephant would pose no problem.

The plum role was the trapeze star. Paulette Goddard thought so. She began campaigning for it. "I do hope and pray that I get 'The Part' in your coming film," she wrote him. "I will be a good, good girl. In the meantime I shall be working hard in summer stock. Yours, Paulette. P.S. You can get me from Paramount."

"No one ever walked off a DeMille set and came back," DeMille said to an assistant, who promptly sent Goddard his regrets.

After considering (and rejecting) Patricia Neal, Barbara Rush, and a dozen others for the part, DeMille remembered a conversation he had had some years earlier with the ebullient Paramount star Betty Hutton. "I think you have great emotional power," he said, "if anybody could stop you from screaming and yelling." Hutton was famed for her high-powered, high-volume performances. "Would you like to work for me?"

"I'd give my ears," she said. "I'd love to!"

"Would you do it my way?"

"Sure, Mr. DeMille!"

On October 17, 1950, Hutton came to DeMille's office and told him she had been training on the trapeze. This was DeMille's kind of actor. The film was cast.

The documentary tone of DeMille's project was something new, both for him and for Hollywood. He knew there were technical obstacles. "You cannot light the big top," he was told. "You have to invent a new light." The lighting required for Technicolor film was roughly three times brighter (and hotter) than for black and white. He was determined to shoot in color, so he enlisted the aid of studio technicians and of the Technicolor Corporation. "It was like saying, 'Let's go out and discover oil.' But I would not give the final okay until I had the light," he said. Because it was for DeMille, a new light was devised, a cluster that could be

set on tent poles and remote controlled. Technicolor matched it with a faster film stock. The Champion Driver was on his way.

Location filming was done at the Ringling winter quarters in Sarasota, Florida, from late January through early March of 1951. Although there were the problems of Wilde's freezing up on the trapeze, and the mutual dislike of Grahame and her elephant Min-yak, DeMille got the footage he needed. It was colorful, dynamic, and it captured an environment never before seen in a feature.

"It is a world in miniature," wrote DeMille. "It is independent, self-contained, and self-sufficient. Tragedy and comedy walk the same wire. Life and death swing through the air. The desire to do a 'stream of civilization' picture has always been with me, the story of a world all by itself, of people from all lands, working and living together in a sort of United Nations. I want to put that in bold strokes on a tremendous canvas."

The scenes shot at Paramount from mid-March to mid-May included the intimate interior scenes between Heston, Hutton,

and Wilde, and the aftermath of the train wreck. The scenes between Hutton and Heston were quite different from those between Hedy Lamarr and Victor Mature. They were subtle, coached by Wilcoxon before they were shot. DeMille did get

HENRY WILCOXON

"Mr. DeMille was happiest in the utter chaos of a scene. He reveled in dozens of roaming circus animals, lots of extras, and complicated special effects. He was totally in his element up on the crane."

ABOVE, LEFT TO RIGHT: Betty Hutton on location. • Betty Hutton trained on the trapeze in order to do her own stunts.

OPPOSITE: DeMille's grandson, Jody Harper (at right), appeared in this scene with the world-famous clown Emmett Kelly, seen for once without his makeup

OPPOSITE: The train wreck scene in *The Greatest Show on Earth* was sudden and frightening.

ABOVE: The exterior of the wreck was created on a soundstage. • Gloria Grahame and the elephant Minyak work to rescue Charlton Heston.

Hutton to subdue herself and yet not lose her power. "No one can tell me that Mr. DeMille doesn't exert some kind of magic spell," said Hutton. The scenes conveyed a genuine, almost naturalistic intimacy, something not seen in a DeMille film since the marital dramas of Elliott Dexter and Gloria Swanson, although there were moments in *The Plainsman* and other Gary Cooper films that were tender and underplayed. "Sometimes Mr. DeMille would ask the actors to stay after shooting to run through upcoming scenes to make them smooth," said Wilcoxon. "And then the next morning, everything went easily." These played as beautifully as anything directed by Edmund Goulding or George Cukor.

On the other hand, when DeMille was riding his crane over a set full of extras, his style was exigent. "I have been called a tyrant, a despot, and a martinet," he told *Collier's* magazine. "Yes, I lose my temper when I see somebody playing checkers on a set that costs $50,000 a day, when this fellow should be paying attention to his job." The crew members who had been with DeMille could only chuckle when the old routine occurred again. Heston was unaware that he was watching a vaudeville act being revived, the one that started with two extras chatting while DeMille directed and ended with his calling "Lunch!"

DeMille had appeared in numerous short subjects, playing the irascible director, but no one had ever thought to film one of his operatic scenes. Phil Koury thought one of them amusing enough to transcribe. It took place on the train wreck set, in the sequence where Grahame is trying to get Minyak to lift debris off Heston. The scene was dangerous for Heston and dangerous for Grahame. "No one knows how or why the stars do it," said the Paramount director Leo McCarey. "Not even the stars themselves. But they do it for C .B."

Hey! What have you done with your hands? There are three men and I see only two pairs of hands. Do you hear me? WHAT HAVE YOU DONE WITH YOUR HANDS? DAMN IT! LISTEN TO ME! What have you—there, that's better. You're right, right. There were only two men when I rehearsed it. The elephant was much farther forward. I said the elephant was farther forward! Will someone in this vast assemblage of talented assistants listen to me?

We've only been at this three days now. Not a bad record, you know. If we keep going at this speed we may finish the picture by 1963. Hold that elephant back! He keeps edging forward. Wait. Betty, is it better for you if the elephant starts there? Okay, that's all right with me. All right. Elephant! Action! Hold it! Mel Koontz, take out the kitty. Take away the kitty! I won't be using her on this line.

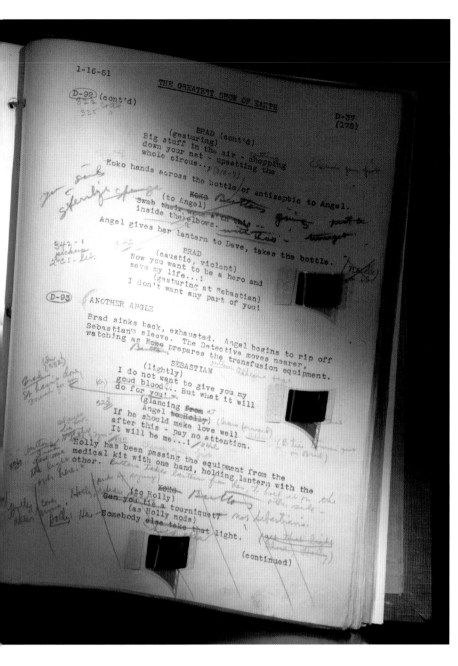

Now, let me see the action from where you drop down. Are there any legs or anything in there? Get your leg there. No! No! Your leg! Do you want me to show you where your leg is! That's it, that's it. You're doing better already. You know where your leg is. You have me to thank for that. You see what you learn on a DeMille picture?

Are there any legs on the other side? Wait a minute. I want to see the spot where he says that. I think . . . I think we should give it a little bit of play. I want to get you in while he's saying his line to you. Betty, do you need a cushion? She can have a cushion if she needs it. It doesn't show. Do that with the entrance once, will you, for me, Betty?

I would keep John's legs right there, to look like he's still pulling on that pole. Here's my—oh, for God's sake, why don't you turn it? All you have to do is turn it. I don't care whether you focus the mike or not. It takes you longer to do that than it does for me to make a motion picture. Eddie, get me a finder. Wait a minute! Wait a minute! We may have to—stop! Everybody stop! DON'T DO ANYTHING!

Fulminations were of no use when it was time to deal with other problems.

Although the PCA had approved the script and the final cut, the Legion of Decency did not agree with the office's liberal interpretation of the section dealing with murder. The doctor had killed his wife. It mattered not that she was suffering from an incurable disease. Euthanasia was murder. The Legion gave *The Greatest Show on Earth* a rating of "B" which meant that it was morally objectionable in part for all persons. DeMille was livid. "It's a lot of hogwash!" he exploded. "Morally objectionable? This is a picture with clowns, elephants, fliers in the air, horseback riders." He paused. "With those Catholics, a little euthanasia goes a long way."

Another surprise awaited DeMille. He had turned seventy on August 12, 1951. *The Greatest Show on Earth* was released on January 10, 1952. On March 19, 1953, the Academy of Motion Picture Arts and Sciences awarded him the Irving G. Thalberg Memorial Award—and awarded the Best Picture Award to *The Greatest Show on Earth*. DeMille was more than pleased. The recognition of his peers had come late, but not too late. And his film would gross more than $16 million. After the ceremony, he made his joy complete by sharing it with his family.

OPPOSITE: The train wreck pits man against nature and makes enemies help one another.

ABOVE: The transfusion scene as it looked after the script clerk marked it with notes from DeMille. Photograph by Mark A. Vieira.

THE TEN COMMANDMENTS

n May 1952, Cecil B. DeMille walked into the executive offices at Paramount Pictures to make a pitch for his seventieth film. He was more than a producer hoping for approval. He was a living legend, renowned for the length of his career, the scope of his achievements, and the complexity of his projects. He was the founder of Hollywood, freshly endowed with two record-breaking hits and two Academy Awards. The project he wanted to make was the life of Moses. He made his presentation to the members of the Paramount board of directors and then waited for a response. There was silence.

"You must be joking, C. B.," said Barney Balaban. The veteran exhibitor had no reason to question the project. DeMille had made him wealthy.

"I assure you, Barney, I would never joke at a time like this. I've received many letters requesting a new biography of Moses. I would perhaps call it *The Prince of Egypt*."

"Surely you can't be considering an old-fashioned historical biography. *The Greatest Show on Earth* was a modern picture. An up-to-date picture. The public is looking forward to more of the same, not this Sunday school stuff."

"I'd like to remind everyone here," said Y. Frank Freeman, "that Mr. DeMille has always known which way the wind was blowing. There's no reason to doubt him now." Freeman was in the minority, interrupted by grumbling and nay-saying. An august voice sounded from the far end of the conference table. It was Adolph Zukor, Paramount's chairman of the board, who had recently turned seventy-nine.

"Cecil and I go back to the very founding of this studio," said Zukor. "Paramount has been saved from receivership more than once by a DeMille production. Perhaps I should remind you about *Samson and Delilah*. While other studios are going out of business, we are in the black." This was true. Hollywood had been hit hard by television. Zukor continued. "I find it embarrassing and deplorable that it takes a Gentile like Cecil to remind us Jews of our heritage! We have just lived through a war where our people were systematically executed. Here we have a man who makes a film praising the Jewish people, that tells of Samson, one of the legends of our Scripture. Now he wants to make the life of Moses. And I have to sit here and listen to you scream and yell about how awful that would be. You should be ashamed of yourselves. We should get down on our knees to Cecil and say 'Thank you!'"

The board members stared at the table. DeMille spoke; "I realize that under the provisions of my current contract, the

OPPOSITE: Cecil B. DeMille's seventieth and last film was *The Ten Commandments*, filmed in Egypt with Charlton Heston in the role of Moses and released in 1956. Photograph by Ken Whitmore.

board of directors has approval. What I have to say is this: I will make this movie. Whether I will make it at Paramount or not remains to be seen, but I will make it."

The project that began in a lackluster fashion turned into a juggernaut called *The Ten Commandments*. Once DeMille got his green light (which he managed to do without presenting a budget), he proceeded slowly, meticulously, and inexorably. He got Jesse Lasky Jr. to join Fredric Frank in writing the screenplay. They worked in collaboration with Aeneas MacKenzie, a veteran whose credits included *Juarez*, and Jack Gariss, who had studied with William de Mille at USC. "Our screenplay was three hundred and eight pages in final draft," wrote Lasky, "fully annotated for source references, detailing props, costume notes, and every camera setup that might be required. DeMille might vary these later, but they had to be there on paper so that

every member of the company would know what was expected of him." This was unorthodox and unprecedented, but it was not done to please Paramount or even the public. It was done to please DeMille.

During the year in which he prepared the script and location trip, DeMille suffered the loss of more associates. Effects wizard Gordon Jennings died in 1953, necessitating the recruitment of Universal's John Fulton. Gladys Rosson, who had come to the Lasky barn from a Los Angeles high school in 1914, died of cancer in 1953. "I would have given a million dollars to save that girl's life," he said. Her last gift to him was the suggestion that they see a play, *The King and I*. DeMille was so moved by Yul Brynner's performance that he went backstage between acts. "I'd never met him," recalled DeMille. "He'd never met me. I told him the story of *The Ten Commandments* from Rameses's point of view in six minutes." Brynner got up and started to walk out of his dressing room. "Do you want to play it or not?" snapped DeMille. Of course Brynner wanted to play "the most powerful man in the world." They shook hands.

Anne Baxter, an Oscar winner for *The Razor's Edge* in 1946, was one of many actresses competing for the role of Nefretiri, the Egyptian queen. Vivien Leigh, Audrey Hepburn, and Coleen Gray had been interviewed. Baxter got the part. "I took a cut in salary to work for DeMille," recalled Baxter. "A lot of actors did. He seemed to expect it as a kind of due."

To advance a casting idea, Henry Wilcoxon found an illustration of Michelangelo's *Moses* in a book and smuggled it under DeMille's nose. The trick was to pretend that DeMille had thought of the idea, while he knew he had not—and knew that you knew. Wilcoxon was ever so off-handed as he turned to the page. His method was convoluted but it worked. "That's Chuck Heston!" DeMille exclaimed.

The exteriors in this *The Ten Commandments* would not be filmed at Guadalupe or some other California location. In October 1954, DeMille took his cast and crew to Egypt. Ever the diplomat, he had made arrangements, first with King Farouk, and then with his successor, General Muhammad Naguib. When DeMille arrived, he was met, not by Naguib, but by another successor, Colonel Gamal Abdel Nasser, and his minister of war, Abdel Hakim Amer. It appeared that negotiations would have to start from scratch until Nasser and Amer laughingly directed their conversation at Wilcoxon. Finally the truth emerged. "*The Crusades* was a very popular film in our Muslim country," said Amer, "due to its fair presentation of both sides and its portrayal of Saladin as a great and holy leader of his people. When Colonel Nasser and I were in the military academy, we saw *The Crusades* perhaps twenty times. The other boys came to call him

Henry Wilcoxon!" DeMille was promised full cooperation.

Shooting began around the walls of the Per-Rameses set on October 14 and continued through the 28th with Yul Brynner's chariot charge. Then DeMille led an expedition to Mount Sinai. The auto caravan could only go so far. "The only way to get to the holy mountain," wrote DeMille, "was a two-hour camel ride or a still more arduous trek on foot. We had to dismantle the cameras and other equipment, load the parts on camels, and reassemble them at the tent camp." DeMille was seventy-three but fit. When Wilcoxon saw DeMille's energy flagging, he chose to blame it on the trip. "There was dysentery, plus extremes of hot and cold, and all the rigors of travel," wrote Wilcoxon. "There wasn't a moment when we weren't being burned by sand, sun, or wind."

The sequence to be captured was the desert exile of Moses. For his first location scenes, Heston had to repeatedly sink to the ground. He found the desert floor more rocky than sandy. "Heston's legs, arms, thighs, and chest are a welter of bruises, and yet the man goes at it," wrote publicist Rufus Blair.

"The truth of the scene was rooted in the rock I stood on," wrote Heston. "It marked my work in the entire film. I have an idea DeMille may have thought of that when he planned the shoot. He wanted me to begin on 'holy ground.'"

"Every day we shipped the precious film back to Cairo," wrote DeMille. "It was packed in ice to keep the desert heat from damaging it. From Cairo it was flown daily to Hollywood to be developed and then flown back to Cairo for us to project at the Misr Studio. Seeing the film made the rigors worthwhile. We were bringing to the screen the very place where Moses talked with God."

The biggest scene to be filmed was the Exodus. Years earlier, Wilcoxon had sat at lunch with DeMille and sketched an angle of the scene, a panorama that would surpass anything DeMille had shot in 1923. "Johnny Jensen did a watercolor of it," wrote Wilcoxon. "We took it to Egypt with the intention of duplicating the shot—precise angle and all—from the top of

the gates." There were also the oil paintings of Arnold Friberg and the storyboard art of William Majors. Because of the grandeur of the set and the expanse of desert at Beni Suef, a huge number of dress extras was needed. "We never really knew just how many people we had," said Wilcoxon. "The estimate was not fewer than 6,000 and perhaps more than 8,000. In addition to hiring people en masse, we searched among what were now the peasants of Egypt for just the right faces for our close-ups. To look upon them was to look back through the millennia."

The big day was November 7. "For hours in the predawn darkness," wrote Wilcoxon, "our legions had been assembling on the Avenue of the Sphinxes with frantic wardrobe people checking every man, woman, and child for anything modern or out of place. Property men moved through the crowd distributing thirteenth-century B.C. tools, carts with solid wooden wheels, and baggage. These thousands of extras knew the story of Mûsâ (Moses), whom the Quran called 'the first true believer.' All of them approached their work with the utmost seriousness. DeMille approached his with something akin to religious fer-

———— CECILIA DE MILLE PRESLEY ————

"Those lunches with Grandfather in the Paramount commissary were some of the most exciting places I've ever been. There were no actors there; well, rarely. Grandfather would usually have Harry Wilcoxon, and the cinematographer, the art director, the production designer, the researcher, and the special effects men at his table. They would brainstorm a part of the picture, and make sure it was historically accurate, and then go around the table to see how each department would contribute to it. You could just sit there and listen to these stories all day. They were fascinating. Of course ninety percent of the books in the Paramount research library came from Grandfather."

vor." When Heston walked through the extras to take his place at the head of the crowd, they regarded him as a reincarnation of Moses. "I was followed by wide eyes," said Heston, "and a soft surf of whispers: 'Mûsâ, Mûsâ, Mûsâ.'"

Cinematographer Loyal Griggs coordinated four newly built VistaVision cameras, one of which was on a Chapman

EDWARD G. ROBINSON

"No more conservative or patriarchal figure than Mr. DeMille existed in Hollywood. And no fairer one, no man with a greater sense of decency. When the part of Dathan was discussed, somebody said that I was ideal but under the circumstances I was, of course, unacceptable—because of the blacklist. Mr. DeMille coldly reviewed the matter, felt that I had been done an injustice, and told his people to offer me the part. Cecil B. DeMille returned me to films. Cecil B. DeMille restored my self-respect."

crane. Forty-five assistant directors awaited DeMille's cue. They had to wait while he rearranged elements of the crowd to his satisfaction. Then it was time.

On a signal from DeMille, Heston raised his staff and spoke his lines: "Hear, O Israel! Remember this day, when the strong hand of the Lord bears you out of bondage!" Then came a prayer: "Bear us out of Egypt, Lord, as an eagle bears his young upon his wings." Heston turned and began walking. Wilcoxon was in costume, working as an assistant director. He heard the

gunshot. "DeMille gave the order," wrote Wilcoxon. "Spontaneously—as one—the entire two miles of our extras shouted: 'Allah! Allah!' and then began to move. They were a nation moving—real people—and the thrill, the feeling that came over us all as we were simultaneously all of one thought can never be described."

The time required to move the column of extras all the way out of the city gates and down to the desert was ten minutes. DeMille let all four cameras shoot an entire film magazine each. The crowds were then brought back and repositioned as crew members cleaned debris from the sand. The sequence was filmed three times. It had looked perfect. DeMille was not sure. To check the camera operated by John Fulton, DeMille

OPPOSITE: John Jensen made this concept painting of Pharaoh Sethi's throne room.

ABOVE: Arnold Friberg made these character sketches to suggest how Charlton Heston could appear as Moses at different stages of the film.

OVERLEAF: Friberg made these oil paintings as concept art of Rameses II.

had to climb a ladder to the top of the city wall, a height of 107 feet. Wilcoxon followed him. When DeMille was half way up, he began to suffer waves of intense chest pain. He had to stop. Fortunately he was able to hold on. Then, with Wilcoxon's assistance, he slowly crept to the top. When DeMille was helped to a chair, Wilcoxon saw that his face was green.

DeMille was moved to a Cairo hospital. The diagnosis was not what he wanted to hear. He had suffered a heart attack. He could not work. This meant that *The Ten Commandments* would not be a movie, but an insurance claim. Millions of dollars would be lost. Thousands of people would lose work. As weak as he was, DeMille would have none of it. "If my motives in making the film were what I thought they were," wrote DeMille, "I would be given the strength to finish it. I was seventy-three years old. That was long enough for a man to have learned something about the ways and power of God; and long enough to make it not so very important if one's greatest effort turned out to be his last. I proposed to be on the set a little after nine o'clock the next morning and to go on with my work." DeMille arrived on the set at 9:20. He deferred some of his directorial duties to his daughter Cecilia and some to Wilcoxon. A few weeks later, DeMille sailed for California, where he could fully convalesce.

While DeMille waited for the rest of the company to return, he was hit with two more blows. Eddie Salven had been his loyal, ubiquitous, and cheerful assistant director off and on since *The Sign of the Cross*. Salven appeased DeMille and weathered his storms as no one else could. In January 1955, Salven disappeared. DeMille, still weak, was frantic. Wilcoxon tracked down Salven. He was in a flophouse, unconscious from a binge and mortally ill with pneumonia. DeMille had barely gotten over Salven's death when word came that William de Mille was dying of cancer. The brothers had their final visit on March 5, 1955, shortly before William died.

A few weeks later, DeMille reopened production on *The Ten Commandments*. It occupied every soundstage at Para-

mount, even the parking lot. Here DeMille would supervise shots of water pouring for the parting of the Red Sea. "We tore down the fence between Paramount and RKO," said Wilcoxon, "and built a tank with eighty feet of curved ramp on either side. Three hundred sixty thousand gallons of water slid down those ramps." DeMille completed principal photography on August 13, 1955, a day after his seventy-fourth birthday. He had worked 161 days, and there had been two more coronary scares, but he was holding up, in spite of the stress. Because of his careful planning, the film was on schedule, but it had nonetheless become the most expensive production to date. DeMille devoted the same kind of ingenuity and care to special effects, sound effects, and editing that he did to his primary images. Every cliché about detail applied to his work, whether he was shooting the obelisk that was supposed to be shot by the second unit, or pointing out a cigarette in an extra's fingers.

MIKE MEDAVOY

"In the '70s, when I was a member of the team that ran United Artists, the "event film" was the thing. But I knew blockbusters were nothing new. Cecil B. DeMille had *Cleopatra* in the thirties, *Samson and Delilah* in the forties, and *The Greatest Show on Earth* in the fifties. The first movie I saw in the American theater was his "event film" *The Ten Commandments*. I'm drawn to films that are rooted in truth or history. That one certainly was. And it passed my criteria. It kept me watching. It struck an emotional chord. DeMille had given his characters a real problem, a struggle for freedom. Watching this event film, I had no idea that the powerful Mr. DeMille had had his own struggle—to get that picture made. When it came time to produce my own films, I had to do what he did: pitch and persuade. I'm glad he succeeded."

OPPOSITE, CLOCKWISE FROM TOP LEFT: Arnold Friberg poses with DeMille. • A publicity photo in one of DeMille's workrooms shows him with Henry Wilcoxon, Kenny Deland, Walter Tyler, an unidentified staff member, and John Fulton. • These Friberg sketches show concepts for the Exodus.

"THE PLANTERS OF VINEYARDS" — EXODUS
A. FRIBERG

"FIRE-BEARERS" EXODUS

A. FRIBERG

KING OF
ETHIOPIA

J.L. Jensen

ETHIOPIAN
GIRL WITH BUNDLES
OF FEATHERS

J.L. Jensen

LISA MITCHELL

"I auditioned for the part of Lulua, the youngest daughter of Jethro, the Bedouin sheik who shelters Moses after he is expelled from Egypt. I auditioned several times with Henry Wilcoxon and different casting directors, among them Buddy Brill and Charlotte Clary. Mr. Wilcoxon really made me feel comfortable. These auditions took place over a period of months in Paramount's casting department office and in a little room called the Fishbowl.

"On July 2, 1955, I went in for a final callback, and this time it was for Mr. DeMille. After that audition, I waited in the same little room. He came in and sat down. 'This is an important part,' he told me. 'It's the teenage flirt. It's the comedy relief. It's something that teenagers can identify with in this very important movie. You have never acted in a picture before. I'll make a deal with you. If I give you this part, you must agree to a few things.

"'Number one: every day after you finish rehearsing your dance, you must come to the set where I am working. I want you to see how movies are made and how I make a movie. I want you to familiarize yourself with all that takes place on a set.

"'Number two: let me yell at you if I want to.

"'Number three: like a lot of youngsters, you slur your consonants. I'm going to give you an exercise. I want you to promise to do it faithfully. You pronounce every CONN-SOH-NAHNT with great exaggeration for one week. Then let go of it, and just speak normally. You will stop the slurring.'

"I did what he asked. It worked."

OPPOSITE, CLOCKWISE FROM TOP LEFT: John Jensen made this costume rendering for the character of the Ethiopian king. • Ralph Jester made this costume rendering for Nassura. • John Jensen made this costume rendering for an Ethiopian girl visiting Sethi's court.

RIGHT: Ralph Jester made this costume rendering for Lulua, who was played by Lisa Mitchell.

OVERLEAF: The city of Per-Rameses that was built for the 1956 version of *The Ten Commandments* looked very much like the structure in the 1923 version, but the topography of Beni Suef was markedly different from Guadalupe. Photograph by Ken Whitmore.

CECILIA DE MILLE PRESLEY

"One of the highlights of the Egyptian trip for all of us was the joint effort of the Americans and Egyptians to see that all went well. People worked longer hours. They worked outside their own jobs to help others. They faced sickness, heat, dysentery, and lack of sleep. Not once did we hear a complaint. That energy and commitment remained until the film was completed. That's why Grandfather took ten percent of his own profit and distributed it to his crew—one hundred in all. I still write those checks, though sadly only a few people remain to receive them."

The young composer Elmer Bernstein had been "gray-listed." DeMille gave him the once-over and hired him for a week; Victor Young was out of town. When Young returned, his health began to fail. DeMille continued working with Bernstein. Then came the test. DeMille brought his secretaries to the recording stage to watch him call out character names and wait for Bernstein to play the corresponding motif from a possible score. Bernstein did well. DeMille's understanding of scoring principles was remarkable. So was his humor. "Mr. Bernstein, do you think you could stand me another six months?"

Postproduction lasted a year, and then it was time for a preview. It took place in Salt Lake City. The preview cards contained more superlatives than a Paramount pressbook. *The Ten Commandments* premiered at New York's Criterion Theatre on November 8, 1956. Once again, reviews were rendered irrelevant, even Bosley Crowther's comment that the giving of the

CECIL B. DeMILLE

"I was not frightened at my first picture but I was terrified at my last picture. You get a little more frightened with each picture you make. You can neither eat nor sleep for about four weeks before you start. After you start shooting, you cease to be frightened. You think about all the things that can go wrong and try to outguess the mistakes that are going to be made. Have a set with about 400 people on it. One makeup on one extra goes wrong. One wig that doesn't fit quite right and everything has to stop until it's cured. That is what you are thinking of constantly. To try and outguess these mistakes. And then someone says, 'You're not in a very good mood today, are you?'"

Law was "disconcertingly mechanical." The juggernaut of a production became a cultural monolith, and a box-office phenomenon. Not even Walt Disney's box office could resist DeMille's power. Only *Gone with the Wind* held its number-one place. *The Ten Commandments* was both a vindication of DeMille's courage and an approbation of his art.

DeMille created a unique profit-sharing plan for the production assistants and crew of *The Ten Commandments*. Since

CECILIA DE MILLE PRESLEY

"*The Ten Commandments*' first shots were to be made in Egypt, showing Moses on the slopes of Mount Sinai. Then we would shoot the huge scene of the Exodus outside Cairo. Accompanying DeMille on the trip were his key crew members, Heston and Brynner, and my mother, father, brother Joe, and I. When our ship landed in Alexandria, Grandfather wanted to go directly to the set. We drove to Cairo, past the pyramids, through the desert. Then we suddenly faced something that took our breath away—the massive gates of Tanis. I saw Grandfather's shoulders relax. We were in Egypt 5,000 years ago."

OPPOSITE, CLOCKWISE FROM TOP LEFT: DeMille was unwell during the filming in Egypt. Photograph by Ken Whitmore. • This scene of Charlton Heston as Moses was shot on the slopes of Mount Sinai. • DeMille inspects the set after a chariot rehearsal.

OVERLEAF: Ken Whitmore made these photographs of the Exodus scene on November 7, 1954.

his 20 percent came from the film's gross instead of the net, he felt he could share 10 percent of that with his studio family. Benefits flowed to these loyal workers for half a century.

DeMille's only sadness at this time of victory was that he could not share it with his wife. Constance had slipped into the early stages of what is now known as Alzheimer's disease. Having endured a mortal illness himself, he was philosophical, but not regretful. "I haven't left *The Ten Commandments* for four years," he told a colleague. "It broke my health for a while. Seriously, it almost killed me. But I haven't left it still because it is the most important thing that I have to give to the world, and the world thinks that. They've expressed themselves so, and that means more to me, really, than life."

CECILIA DE MILLE PRESLEY

"Since making his silent film *The Ten Commandments* in 1923, Grandfather had never stopped researching the life and times of Moses. Paramount's library was full of books devoted to the subject, as was our extensive library at home. Our research was so comprehensive that the University of Southern California published a book, *Moses and Egypt*, which was written by our lead researcher, Henry Noerdlinger, on the missing years of Moses—those young years that the Bible omits. DeMille knew the film had to be thoroughly prepared before the first camera rolled, or the expense would be prohibitive. After *The Greatest Show on Earth*, it was like a military campaign. You had to get it right before the battle, not during it.

HENRY WILCOXON

"To Cecil B. DeMille's everlasting credit, he was always aware of the responsibility that came with recognition. The world judges us by our art, and history judges us by our art. When all's said and done, the only thing that survives of any civilization is its art."

OVERLEAF, LEFT: Henry Wilcoxon directed the scenes shot at the mortuary temple of Queen Hatshepsut in the Valley of the Kings. These frame enlargements show what DeMille and John Fulton accomplished with the help of technicians at both Paramount and Technicolor. Because *The Ten Commandments* was shot in the VistaVision process, the optical printing effects were smoother and sharper than they would have been with conventional 35mm film.

OVERLEAF, RIGHT: Ken Whitmore made this photograph at the Valley of the Kings.

OPPOSITE: The Egyptian army assisted DeMille in the staging of the chariot chase.

CLOCKWISE FROM TOP LEFT: "There was only one DeMille," wrote Anne Baxter, "and there wasn't an actor in the world who didn't want to work for him just once." • Anne Baxter's portrayal of Nefretiri was the last in a long line of DeMille vixens. • Edward G. Robinson was grateful to Jesse Lasky Jr. for his scenes as Dathan. "You gave me the greatest exit a 'heavy' ever had," Robinson told Lasky. "You created a tempest, then an earthquake, then opened a fissure and had me fall into hell. Even in *Little Caesar* I didn't have an exit as good as that!"

—— CECILIA DE MILLE PRESLEY ——

"One night at home in Hollywood, Grandfather was very quiet. I asked him why. He said, 'Pet, so many peoples' lives and fortunes depend on the success of this film. I am just feeling the pressure especially tonight.' He lived to see the 1956 *The Ten Commandments* become one of the most successful films of all time."

OPPOSITE: Yousuf Karsh made this portrait of Yul Brynner as Rameses II.

THIS PAGE: These are some of the custom-made bracelets worn by Yul Brynner and others in *The Ten Commandments*.

CLOCKWISE FROM TOP LEFT: The robe worn by Charlton Heston as Moses resides in the De Mille Estate's archives. Photograph by Mark A. Vieira. • Another photographer caught Ken Whitmore shooting a portrait of Heston off the set. • This is the portrait that Whitmore made.

OPPOSITE: Bud Fraker made this studio portrait of Charlton Heston as Moses. Cecilia de Mille Presley: "Charlton Heston, whom we called 'Chuck,' was a highly intelligent man. I would see him walking on the set, carrying huge books on Moses and the times in which he lived. He trusted Grandfather to give him the best advice. He told me years later that he owed his career to DeMille."

CECILIA DE MILLE PRESLEY

"After Grandfather had a heart attack, he refused to miss a day on the set. It was a serious attack. The pain was bad, and he could hardly move, but he knew if word got out, it would be disastrous for Paramount, a publicity nightmare. He said the attack was only a "bout of dysentery." My mother Cecilia took charge and directed the film with head cinematographer Loyal Griggs, while DeMille sat quietly behind the camera. He went on to regain his strength, finish the shoot in Egypt, and return to Hollywood for more months of work."

CHARLTON HESTON

"Mr. DeMille believed deeply in the message of the film and the power of the man, Moses, to reach across the millennia and move people of every faith, kind, and condition. Held in special reverence by Jew, Muslim, and Christian alike, Moses has become more than an icon. Over the centuries, Moses and the Exodus he led have inspired those who search for liberty."

ABOVE: DeMille had these tablets made to help publicize the film and educate the public. The tablets were hewn from red granite that was brought from the slopes of Mount Sinai. Photograph by Mark A. Vieira.

OPPOSITE: The script for *The Ten Commandments* includes citations from Scripture. Photograph by Mark A. Vieira.

THE TEN COMMANDMENTS

G-16
(301)

G-22A CLOSE SHOT - SEPHORA AND BITHIA - AMONG THE FAITHFUL

Their faces are uplifted with wonder, awe and hope.

> SEPHORA
> (crying out in joy)
> Moses! Moses!

> BITHIA
>
> My son!

G-22B GROUP AT GOLDEN CALF ALTAR

From Lilia's lips breaks the cry:

> LILIA
>
> Joshua!

Unnoticed by Dathan and Abiram whose eyes are upon
Moses in angry amazement, Lilia breaks free and runs
down the steps.

G-22C MEDIUM SHOT - MOSES AND JOSHUA - ABOVE ENCAMPMENT

They appear, outlined against the sky, at the turn
the path above the cleft. Moses' eyes blaze with wrath
above the tablets which he holds. His voice is like
the thunder of Sinai itself.

> MOSES
> You have sinned a great sin
> and become abhorrent in the
> sight of God! You are not
> worthy to receive these Ten
> Commandments!

(cf.
Ex.
32:30)

G-22D CLOSE SHOT - AARON, ELISHEBA AND SEVERAL DOUBTERS

They look from Dathan to Moses in troubled indecision.
Then Aaron and Elisheba move guiltily toward Moses,
followed by some of the others. Another group of
revelers in the disarray of the bacchanalian worship
move toward Dathan.

FULL SHOT - (FROM MOSES' _____ DATHAN AT THE GOLDEN
CALF, SURROUNDED BY REVELERS (AD-023)

Some, with troubled murmurs, start backing away from the

(continued)

EPILOGUE

n late 1956, Cecil B. DeMille was busy with *The Ten Commandments*, both promoting it and enjoying the adulation it brought him. Even before the magnitude of its success became apparent, the box-office reports were wonderful. DeMille was relieved. "I had a frightful responsibility on my shoulders," he said. "I didn't sleep. I worried day and night. I wouldn't have lost a dollar, but it would have killed me if I had ruined Paramount." The film's success was a tribute to DeMille's resourcefulness, but he insisted on sharing the credit, and not only with his colleagues. He credited his earliest teachers. When an interviewer asked him for whom he had made the film, he answered, "For my father and mother."

When DeMille received the Milestone Award from the Screen Producers Guild on January 22, 1956, his acceptance speech reflected the acquired wisdom of a pioneer. "A man is no better than what he leaves behind him," said DeMille. "If we leave behind us an industry broken by greed, or even a commercially successful industry built on filth and false values, distortions of the truth, and glorification of the seamy side of life, then we are no better than those sordid leavings. We are responsible as artists and as molders of men's thoughts. We have a duty to our art, and a duty to the audience."

In December, DeMille took time out from premieres and interviews to participate in a government ceremony. The California State Park Commission and the Los Angeles County Landmarks Committee had realized that the *Squaw Man* barn was the site of the first feature film made in Hollywood. It was decided to designate the barn a state historical landmark. The sturdy structure was still at Paramount, although in use as a set. It was currently dressed as a railroad station for the Hal Wallis production of *The Rainmaker*.

On December 27, DeMille was the keynote speaker for the dedication. "This barn is a symbol of Hollywood," he said to a crowd of dignitaries and well-wishers. "It is not only a landmark of the State of California. It is a landmark for the entire world." Also present were Adolph Zukor, Y. Frank Freeman, Sam Goldwyn, and Jesse L. Lasky. DeMille was seventy-five, Goldwyn was seventy-seven, and Lasky was seventy-six. In another city, in another industry, they might have been relegated to rocking chairs. Here, even in a city that worshiped youth, they were vital and influential. "I don't see myself as an old man who can't do this or that," said DeMille. "Never!"

After forty-five years, the three partners were still friends. "I used to hear my father talking on the phone with DeMille," says Betty Lasky. "He called quite often, and they'd see Sam at

OPPOSITE: Cecil B. DeMille and his granddaughter Cecilia alight from a plane in late 1958.

luncheons and dinners." The camaraderie of their Claridge days was still alive. "When those three got together," recalls Cecilia de Mille Presley, "there was so much laughter. The jokes, the stories. It was delightful." There were reminiscences, of course, but there was also talk of new projects.

Goldwyn was dickering with Ira Gershwin for the rights to the late George Gershwin's *Porgy and Bess*. DeMille was planning a remake of *The Buccaneer*, to be directed by Yul Brynner. Lasky wanted to make a film of his experiences as a high-school cornettist. For four years he and producer Walter Wanger had been shopping a project called *The Big Brass Band*. It was

turned down by NBC and RKO before DeMille stepped in to help Lasky prepare a script. It was slow-going. "I won't let your father talk about bands," DeMille told Jesse Jr. "I won't let him talk about music. I won't let him talk about any of these things he wants to talk about until he has a story. Yesterday was the first day I didn't treat him brutally, because he had the tail of an idea. I treat him brutally for *his* good, not mine. I'm trying to take him

ABOVE: Across the street from the original site of the Lasky-DeMille *Squaw Man* barn there arose the California Bank Building. On September 12, 1951, the partners of the Lasky Feature Play Company dedicated a commemorative plaque.

back to *his* picture." Apparently Lasky still had a problem finding the conflict strong enough to motivate a cinematic premise.

"It is the story that will make or break a picture," said DeMille. "A star is a draw for the first day only. After that, if word gets out that the story values are not there, no star can save that picture." This also applied to action and special effects. "I have never added sensational scenes gratuitously," said DeMille. "Angela Lansbury's death scene in *Samson and Delilah* shows that taking human life is a shocking and fearful thing. There is danger in a casual attitude toward the taking of life. Children are growing up surrounded by television. Cheaply made television westerns show cowboys killing Indians, and Indians killing cowboys. You have 'bang-bang-bang' and three people die. The taking of life is made to appear casual."

DeMille believed that he had a mission. "I am carrying on the work of my father," he wrote. "He studied for the Episcopal ministry but became a playwright because he felt he could reach a larger 'congregation' from the stage." Was DeMille reaching his? In 1957, when he was not traveling to premieres in Europe or having audience with royalty (Queen Elizabeth II), heads of state (Winston Churchill, Konrad Adenauer), or religious leaders (Pope Pius XII), DeMille was in his office, reading fan mail and filing reviews of *The Ten Commandments*. His biographer Art Arthur was helping him. "I don't know if you've seen this letter or not, Mr. DeMille," said Arthur. "It's from a Jewish girl who said that she had a Protestant girlfriend whom she had begun to envy for her faith. The Jewish girl's parents had not been very religious. She saw *The Ten Commandments* and now is very proud of being Jewish. She'll always be proud of it, she writes us. Another girl wrote that she had gone to a synagogue for the first time because of your picture."

There was a letter from the prime minister of Pakistan. "I hope that you latest effort to promote understanding between the three great religions of the world will succeed," wrote Muhammed Ali Bogra. "God has given you a powerful medium for the projection of thought. I sincerely hope that you will under-

take with missionary zeal the task of producing films which will also safeguard a free and democratic way of life."

The reviews were something else. *Time* magazine led the pack with a particularly snide review in which DeMille's film was referred to as "The Sexodus." In self-defense DeMille created a satiric variant of his name: "Colossal B. DeMille."

Another critic said: "*The Ten Commandments* will not send you from the theater spiritually refreshed and uplifted. That must come from within, but the story of Moses will make you walk proudly because of your God-given heritage of freedom and equality."

"He gets the political side perfectly," said DeMille. "The religious side he does not see one percent."

A minister asked DeMille if he attended church services. DeMille was honest. He did not. "A church can be so filled with the mind of God," said DeMille, "that you are almost in heaven. Or it can be so filled with other things that all you smell is cheap perfume." He preferred to enter an empty church—of any denomination—and sit in silence.

"I believe in prayer," said DeMille. "It's the most powerful force in the world. The relationship between the mind of man and the mind of God is a delicate, beautiful drama. It's a powerful experience. It can carry you to heights where nothing else can take you. Only God can take you there. It doesn't happen every time you pray. There are times when He doesn't respond at all. It used to bother me. I would ask, 'Am I right? Am I preaching a phony doctrine?' Then another time He comes and you get so far up. You're so close. It's the most exhilarating, wonderful experience you can have."

DeMille's thoughts on religion were recorded as he worked on his autobiography with Art Arthur and Donald Hayne. He was candid with them about many things, including a sad situation. "Mrs. de Mille is an invalid," he said. "She has lost the power of speech. We've been married fifty-five years. In all that time, I never heard her say an unkind word about any human being. (Although there were occasions where she could have said something about me.)" Seeing Constance in this condition was no doubt difficult for DeMille. Equally hard to bear was the gradual diminishing of his own strength. He was unable to produce *The Buccaneer* with the same energy he had possessed a year earlier. Henry Wilcoxon produced, and, Brynner, instead of directing, starred, with Anthony Quinn directing. The result was a credit to no one.

On January 13, 1958, Jesse Lasky gave a talk about his autobiography *I Blow My Own Horn* to a women's literary club at the Beverly Hilton. He was waiting for his car in front of the hotel when he stumbled and collapsed. In a few minutes, he was dead. The first member of the *Squaw Man* triumvirate was gone. After the funeral, DeMille stayed by the gravesite, apparently talking to the casket. Lasky's widow Bessie was in financial straits and in danger of losing her home to the IRS. DeMille solicited $45,000 in contributions so she could settle the lien.

In June, DeMille had two coronary episodes. While he was in Cedars of Lebanon Hospital, Goldwyn's *Porgy and Bess* sets caught fire and destroyed two soundstages. DeMille sent a sympathetic telegram from his hospital bed. Goldwyn responded, "You remember the experience we had on *The Squaw Man*. That was worse, and we can take it better now than we could then." DeMille left the hospital, and Goldwyn began rebuilding.

"Where there's life, there's hope" is not a cliché to the dying or to their intimates. DeMille was determined to produce another film, if not two. One would deal with the Book of Revelations, with the Four Horsemen transformed into monsters with "chromium heads and jet bodies that scream into the sky." The other film he described to David Niven. "I am appalled by the violence in the world today," said DeMille. "I am going to do something about it. I am going to show that there is something for youth besides street gangs and switch blades. I'm going to tell the story of Baden-Powell and the Boy Scouts. Imagine! The final Jamboree, when the old man is almost eighty, with a hundred thousand youngsters of every race and color from all over the world gathered around him in peace and happiness. It will be my last film, and my greatest."

In December, DeMille traveled to Louisiana to help publicize *The Buccaneer* and to New York, where he was honored by his alma mater, the American Academy of Dramatic Arts. His granddaughter Cecilia called Agnes de Mille and told her that her Uncle Cecil was in town and that he was not well. Agnes hurried to DeMille's hotel room for a reunion that reportedly resolved years of bitterness. As weak as he was, DeMille pushed himself to attend the premiere of *The Buccaneer* at the Classic Theatre in Santa Barbara. While there, he visited the former actor Donald Curtis. After acting in *The Ten Commandments*, Curtis had become a minister of the Science of Mind Church. DeMille was too weak to do anything but sit with Curtis and watch the sun set. "I know I'm made fun of," said DeMille. "I know they call *The Ten Commandments* 'The Sexodus' and what have you. But my ministry has been to make religious movies and get more people to read the Bible than anyone else ever has."

Neither DeMille nor Wilcoxon attended the Los Angeles premiere of *The Buccaneer*. The film did better than it should have, but it came and went. *The Ten Commandments* continued to rumble around the world, smashing records and flouting playout schedules. In its first eighteen months it made $33 million and was seen by 26 million people. In December, DeMille had another heart attack.

By late January 1959, DeMille was too weak and ill to go to his office. He watched films in his screening area until he had another attack. Finally he was too weak to make his nightly rounds and lock up the house. Bedridden, he marked his Bible and made notes in pencil. One of them read: "What am I? I am only what I have accomplished. How much good have I spread?

OPPOSITE: Cecil and Constance de Mille posed for this photograph in the late 1950s.

How much evil have I spread? For whatever I am a moment after death—a spirit, a soul, a bodiless mind—I shall have to look back and forward, for I take with me both."

Cecil Blount DeMille died at 5:05 a.m. on January 21, 1959. Eighteen months later, Constance followed.

Samuel Goldwyn died on January 31, 1974, the last of the *Squaw Man* pioneers.

The films that were supposed to run a few months and then be forgotten have been grandly persistent. Mr. DeMille was right. You don't throw away a Rembrandt or a Renoir after you've looked at it once. He did not throw away what he had created. Fortunately for us, he saved as much as he could store

in his home. It is our pleasure to share as much as we could include here, hoping that what we have learned will both enlighten and entertain.

Seven of Cecil B. DeMille's seventy features have been lost to nitrate decomposition: *The Arab*, *The Wild Goose Chase*, *Chimmie Fadden*, *The Dream Girl*, *The Devil-Stone*, *We Can't Have Everything*, and *The Squaw Man* (the 1918 remake). Roughly twenty of his silent features are available in commercial DVD format. The recent restoration of *The Godless Girl* shows how fine a silent film can look in an electronic medium. Likewise, the Paramount Blu-Ray releases of *Samson and Delilah* and *The Ten Commandments* are high-water marks in digital transfer quality.

In time we hope to see the luminous black-and-white features owned by NBC-Universal, such titles as *The Crusades*, *The Plainsman*, and *Union Pacific* remastered from fine-grain positives for Blu-Ray format; and releases of *North West Mounted Police* and other DeMille Technicolor features. In whatever format or technology his films are viewed, they keep his intention alive.

OPPOSITE AND ABOVE: DeMille was photographed with the film canisters containing *The Ten Commandments* because he had personally inspected each print to be sure it was worthy of exhibition. Whether tending the prints of his films or the deer at his ranch, DeMille was thoughtful and meticulous.

CECIL B. DeMILLE

"Motion pictures have been my life for forty-three years. Every foot of it in film, and every minute of it in time has been adventure which I would not exchange for anything in the world."

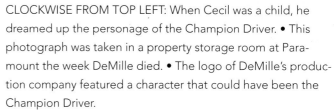

CLOCKWISE FROM TOP LEFT: When Cecil was a child, he dreamed up the personage of the Champion Driver. • This photograph was taken in a property storage room at Paramount the week DeMille died. • The logo of DeMille's production company featured a character that could have been the Champion Driver.

OPPOSITE: Some years after her grandfather's death, Cecilia de Mille Presley returned to the building where his Hollywood saga began.

BIBLIOGRAPHY

BOOKS

Allen, Frederick Lewis. *Only Yesterday*. New York: Harper and Row, 1931.

Arce, Hector. *Gary Cooper*. New York: William Morrow, 1979.

Baxter, Anne. *Intermission*. New York: G.P. Putnam's Sons, 1976.

Baxter, Peter. *Just Watch: Sternberg, Paramount, and America*. London: British Film Institute, 1993.

Berg, A. Scott. *Goldwyn: A Biography*. New York: Alfred A. Knopf, 1989.

Bickford, Charles. *Bulls, Balls, Bicycles, and Actors*. New York: Paul Eriksson, 1965.

Birchard, Robert S. *Cecil B. DeMille's Hollywood*. Lexington, Kentucky: The University Press of Kentucky, 2004.

Black, *Hollywood Censored: Morality Codes, Catholics, and the Movies*. New York: Cambridge University Press, 1994.

Brownlow, Kevin, and John Kobal. *Hollywood: The Pioneers*. New York: Alfred A. Knopf, 1979.

_____. *The Parade's Gone By*. New York: Alfred A. Knopf, 1968.

Byrge, Duane. *Private Screenings*. Atlanta: Turner Publishing, 1995.

Chierichetti, David. *Mitchell Leisen: Hollywood Director*. Los Angeles: Photoventures Press, 1995.

Coffee, Lenore. *Storyline*. London: Cassell Pres, 1973.

Cooper, Courtney Ryley. *Under the Big Top*. Boston, Massachusetts: Little, Brown, and Company, 1923.

Davis, Ronald L. *The Glamour Factory: Inside Hollywood's Big Studio System*. Dallas, Texas: Southern Methodist University Press, 1993.

De Mille, Agnes. *Dance to the Piper*. Boston: Little, Brown, and Company, 1951.

_____. *Portrait Gallery*. New York: Houghton Mifflin Company, 1990.

_____. *Speak to Me, Dance With Me*. New York: Little, Brown, and Company, 1973.

DeMille, Cecil B., and Donald Hayne. *The Autobiography of Cecil B. DeMille*. Englewood Cliffs, New Jersey: Prentice-Hall, Inc., 1959.

De Mille, William C. *Hollywood Saga*. New York: E.P. Dutton and Co., Inc., 1939.

Drazin, Charles. *French Cinema*. London: Faber and Faber, Ltd., 2001.

Easton, Carol. *No Intermissions: The Life of Agnes de Mille*. New York: Da Capo Press, 2000.

Edwards, Anne. *The DeMilles: An American Family*. New York: Harry N. Abrams, Inc., 1988.

Essoe, Gabe, and Raymond Lee. *DeMille: The Man and His Pictures*. New York: Castle Books, 1970.

Eyman, Scott. *Empire of Dreams: The Epic Life of Cecil B. DeMille*. New York: Simon and Schuster, 2010.

_____. *Five American Cinematographers*. Metuchen, New Jersey: Scarecrow Press, 1987.

Fairservis, Walter. *Ancient Kingdoms of the Nile*. New York: Mentor Books, 1962.

Farrar, Geraldine. *Geraldine Farrar: The Story of an American Singer*. New York: Houghton Mifflin Company, 1916.

_____. *Such Sweet Compulsion*. New York: The Greystone Press, 1938.

Fountain, Leatrice Gilbert. *Dark Star: The Untold Story of the Meteoric Rise and Fall of the Legendary John Gilbert*. New York: St. Martin's Press, 1985.

Friends of the Future. *Paniolo House Stories*. Waimea, Hawaii: Xlibris Corp., 2005.

Gabler, Neal. *An Empire of Their Own. How the Jews Invented Hollywood*. New York: Doubleday, 1988.

Gilbert, Julie. *Opposite Attraction*. New York: Pantheon, 1995.

Goldwyn, Samuel. *Behind the Screen*. New York: George H. Doran Co., 1923.

Griffith, Richard, and Arthur Mayer. *The Movies*. New York: Simon and Schuster, 1970.

Gutner, Howard. *Gowns by Adrian: The MGM Years, 1928–1941*. New York: Harry N. Abrams, Inc., 2001.

Hamann, G. D. *Greta Garbo in the '30s*. Los Angeles: Filming Today Press, 2003.

Head, Edith, and Paddy Calistro. *Edith Head's Hollywood*. Santa Monica: Angel City Press, 2008.

Hecht, Ben. *A Child of the Century*. New York: Donald I. Fine, 1985.

Henning, Robert. *Destined for Hollywood: The Art of Dan Sayre Groesbeck*. Santa Barbara: Santa Barbara Museum of Art, 2001.

Heston, Charlton. *In the Arena: An Autobiography*. New York: Boulevard Books, 1997.

Higashi, Sumiko. *Cecil B. DeMille and American Culture: The Silent Era*. Berkeley: The University of California Press, 1994.

Higham, Charles. *Cecil B. DeMille*. New York: Charles Scribner's Sons, 1973.

_____. *Hollywood Cameramen*. Bloomington: Indiana University Press, 1970.

Hopper, Hedda. *From Under My Hat*. New York: MacFadden Books, 1952.

Jacobs, Lewis. *The Rise of the American Film*. New York: Harcourt, Brace, and Company, 1939.

Kennedy, Joseph P., ed. *The Story of the Films*. New York: A.W. Shaw Company, 1927.

Kobal, John. *Hollywood: The Years of Innocence*. London: Thames and Hudson, Ltd., 1985.

_____. *People Will Talk*. New York: Alfred A. Knopf, 1985.

Koury, Phil. *Yes, Mr. DeMille: A Humorous and Candid Appraisal of an Extraordinary Showman*. New York: Van Rees Press, 1959.

Lasky, Jesse L. with Don Weldon. *I Blow My Own Horn*. Garden City, New York: Doubleday, 1957.

Lasky, Jesse L. Jr. *What Ever Happened to Hollywood?* New York: Funk & Wagnall's, 1973.

Lord, Daniel A., S.J. *Played by Ear: The Autobiography of Daniel A. Lord, S.J.* Chicago, Illinois: Loyola University Press, 1955.

Lowrey, Carolyn. *The First One Hundred Noted Men and Women of the Screen*. New York: Yard and Company, 1920.

Maltin, Leonard. *Hollywood: The Movie Factory*. New York: Popular Library, 1976.

Marx, Samuel. *Mayer and Thalberg, the Make-Believe Saints*. New York: Random House, 1975.

McClelland, Doug. *Forties Film Talk: Oral Histories of Hollywood*. Jefferson, North Carolina: McFarland Company, Inc., Publishers, 1992.

McGilligan, Pat. *Backstory: Interviews with Screenwriters of Hollywood's Golden Age*. Berkeley: University of California Press, 1986.

Milland, Ray. *Wide-Eyed in Babylon*. New York: Ballantine Books, 1975.

Moore, Dennis ("Micky"). *My Magic Carpet of Films*. Albany, Georgia: Bear Manor Media, 2009.

Morella, Joe, and Edward Z. Epstein. *Paulette: The Adventurous Life of Paulette Goddard*. New York: St. Martin's Press, 1985.

Niven, David. *Bring On the Empty Horses*. New York: Dell Publishing Co., Inc., 1976.

Oderman, Stuart. *Talking to the Piano Player*. Boalsburg, Pennsylvania: Bear Manor Media, 2005.

Orrison, Katherine. *Written in Stone: Making Cecil B. DeMille's Epic The Ten Commandments*. Lanham, Maryland: Vestal Press, 1999.

Phillips, Kendall R. *Controversial Cinema: The Films That Outraged America*. Westport, Connecticut: Praeger Publishers, 2008.

Ringgold, Gene, and DeWitt Bodeen. *The Films of Cecil B. DeMille*. New York: Citadel Press, 1969.

Rosenberg, Bernard, and Harry Silverstein. *The Real Tinsel*. New York: MacMillan and Company, 1970.

Schatz, Thomas. *The Genius of the System: Hollywood Filmmaking in the Studio Era*. New York: Pantheon Books, 1988.

Schildkraut, Joseph. *My Father and I. As Told to Leo Lania*. New York: The Viking Press, 1959.

Schulberg, Budd. *Moving Pictures: Memoirs of a Hollywood Prince*. London: Alison and Busby, 1993.

Server, Lee. *Screenwriter: Words Become Pictures*. Pittstown, New Jersey: The Main Street Press, 1987.

Shields, David. *Still: American Silent Motion Picture Photography*. Chicago: University of Chicago Press, 2013.

Smith, Ella. *Starring Miss Barbara Stanwyck*. New York: Crown Publishers, 1974.

Sperling, Cass Warner, and Cork Millner. *Hollywood Be Thy Name*. Rocklin, California: Prima Publishing, 1994.

Steen, Mike. *Hollywood Speaks: An Oral History*. New York: G.P. Putnam's Sons, 1974.

Swanson, Gloria. *Swanson on Swanson*. New York: Random House, 1980.

Thomas, Bob. *King Cohn: The Life and Times of Harry Cohn*. New York: Bantam Books, 1968.

Time-Life Book Editors. *This Fabulous Century: 1920-1930*. New York: Time-Life Books, 1969.

Usai, Paolo Cherchi. *L Eredità DeMille*. Pordenone, Italy: Le Giornate del Cinema Muto, 1991.

Van Vechten, Carl. *Interpreters and Interpretations*. New York: Alfred A. Knopf, 1917.

_____, ed. Bruce Kellner. *The Splendid Drunken Twenties: Selections from the Daybooks, 1922-1930*. Champaign, Illinois: University of Illinois Press, 2007.

Vizzard, Jack. *See No Evil: Life Inside a Hollywood Censor*. New York: Simon and Schuster, 1970.

Wagenknecht, Edward Charles. *Geraldine Farrar: An Authorized Record of Her Career*. New York: University Book Store, 1929.

Wagner, Walter. *You Must Remember This*. New York: G.P. Putnam's Sons, 1975.

Westmore, Frank, and Muriel Davidson. *The Westmores of Hollywood*. New York: J.P. Lippincott Company, 1976.

Whitfield, Eileen. *Pickford: The Woman Who Made Hollywood*. Lexington, Kentucky: University Press of Kentucky, 2007.

Wilcoxon, Henry, and Katherine Orrison. *Lionheart in Hollywood: The Autobiography of Henry Wilcoxon*. Metuchen, New Jersey: Scarecrow Press, 1991.

Williams, Alan. *Republic of Images: A History of French Filmmaking*. Cumberland, Rhode Island: Harvard University Pres, 1992.

Woessner, James. *Cecil B. DeMille: Screen Prophet and Cinema Apostle*. Tulare, California: Tulare Times Press, 1935.

Zukor, Adolph, with Dale Kramer. *The Public Is Never Wrong: The Autobiography of Adolph Zukor*. New York: G.P. Putnam's Sons, 1953.

SIGNED ARTICLES

Abend, Hallett. "Old Testament Ways Revived by Players." *Los Angeles Times*, June 17, 1923, p. II1.

Anderson, Antony. "Films: The Whispering Chorus." *Los Angeles Times*, March 18, 1918, p. II8.

Arthur, Jean. "Who Wants to Be a Lady?" *Atlanta Constitution*, September 27, 1936, p. SM3.

Babcock, Muriel. "The Mike at Hollywood." *Photoplay* 50, No. 4 (October 1936) pp. 48-49, 119.

Bainbridge, John. "Samson, Delilah, and DeMille." *Life* 27, No. 23 (December 5, 1949) pp. 138-141, 143, 144, 146, 149.

Barry, Barbara. "Such a Naughty Nero." *Photoplay* 14, No. 3 (February 1933) pp. 46-47, 95-96.

Birkenhead, Peter. "Shifting Sands." *Tikkun Daily*, April 1, 2014.

Blaisdell, George. "A Man With the Bark On." *The Moving Picture World*, March 7, 1914, p. 1243.

Boland, Elena. "DeMille Makes Discovery Satan Was Madame." *Los Angeles Times*, March 2, 1930, p. B9.

_____. "Kay Johnson a Trio." *Los Angeles Times*, September 21, 1930, p. B19.

Brownlow, Kevin. "Lina Basquette." *The Independent*, October 8, 1994.

Bush, W. Stephen. "The Cheat." *The Moving Picture World*, December 25, 1915.

_____. "The Golden Chance." *The Moving Picture World*, January 8, 1916.

Carr, Harry. "Every Little Bit Helps—to Stardom." *Motion Picture* 28, No. 10 (November 1924), pp. 21-22.

Cheatham, Maude S. "Bebe, the Oriental." *Motion Picture* 18, No. 10 (November 1919), pp. 32-33, 123.

Coughlin, Katherine. "Producing *The Plainsman*." *Movie Classic* 11, No. 4 (December 1936), pp. 50, 86-87.

DeMille, Cecil B. "After Seventy Pictures." *Films in Review* 7 No. 3 (March 1956) pp. 97-99.

_____. "The Enduring Art." *The Hollywood Reporter* 142, No. 20 (November 19, 1956).

_____. "Forget Spectacle—It's the Story That Counts." *American Cinematographer* October 1956 p. 7.

_____. "How I Make a Spectacle." *Photoplay* 46, No. 5 (October 1934) pp. 43, 99-100.

_____. "Movie Stars' Secrets." Unsourced clipping, Margaret Herrick Library Microfilm Collection, Fairbanks Center for Motion Picture Study, (hereinafter MHL).

_____. "The Public Is Always Right." *Ladies Home Journal* 44, No. 14 (September 1927), pp. 14, 73-74.

_____. "The Soul of the Circus." *The Hollywood Reporter* 111, No. 22 (October 30, 1950).

Fisher, James B. "Diary of DeMille Crusader." *Screenland* 31, No. 5, pp. 20-21, 67-69.

Griffith, Richard. "New York Critics Praise DeMille." *Los Angeles Times*, April 6, 1942, p. 8.

Hall, Gladys, and Adele Whitely-Fletcher. "We Interview Cecil B. DeMille." *Motion Picture* 23, No. 3 (April 1922), pp. 24-25, 93.

Hamilton, Sara. "The Last of the Veteran Showmen." *Photoplay* 44, No. 5 (October 1933), pp. 32-33, 107-109.

Hopper, Hedda. "Hedda Hopper's Hollywood." *Los Angeles Times*, March 14, 1938, p. A11.

_____. "November Film Menu." *Los Angeles Times*, November 3, 1940, p. D3.

_____. "Roach Eager." *Los Angeles Times*, April 13, 1951, p. 22.

Hutton, Betty. "The DeMille Spell." *The Hollywood Reporter* 116, No. 26 (October 29, 1951).

Jackson, Michael. "We Cover the Studios." *Photoplay* 50, No. 4 (October 1936) pp. 50-51.

Kendall, Read. "Around and About in Hollywood." *Los Angeles Times*, February 10, 1935, p. 9.

_____. "Revenge Dished Up." *Los Angeles Times*, June 18, 1935, p. 19.

Kingsley, Grace. "The Godless Girl." *Picture-Play* 28, No. 5 (July 1928) pp. 50-52, 99.

_____. "Hollywood Moves to the Holy Land." *Picture-Play* 26, No. 1 (March 1927) pp. 44-47, 108-109.

_____. "Universal to Picture World." *Los Angeles Times*, June 3, 1926, p. A8.

Lord, Daniel A., S.J. "Hollywood Treats Own Code as Scrap of Paper." *The Queen's Work* 26, No. 9, (June 1934), pp. 1, 10-11.

Lusk, Norbert. "DeMille Again the Old Master." *Los Angeles Times*, December 4, 1932, p. B17.

Macpherson, Jeanie. "I Have Been In Hell." *Movie Weekly*, August 19, 1922.

Millier, Arthur. "Hush! It Is the Great Fuller Brush Scene in Cleopatra." *Los Angeles Times*, April 13, 1934, p. A1.

Naylor, Hazel Simpson. "Cecil B. DeMille, the Master of Mystery." *Motion Picture* 18, No. 10 (November 1919), pp. 36-37, 126.

Owen, K. "The Kick-In Prophets." *Photoplay* (October 1915).

Peltret, Elizabeth. "Gloria Swanson Talks on Divorce." *Motion Picture* 18, No. 11 (December 1919), pp. 33-34, 74.

Quigley, Martin. "Dr. DeMille on Sex." *Motion Picture Herald* No. 116, No. 7 (August 11, 1934), p. 3.

Schallert, Edwin. "Cecil B. DeMille Meets Censorship Demands." *Los Angeles Times*, July 13, 1934, p. 13.

_____. "English Language on Last Leg, Says DeMille." *Los Angeles Times*, October 21, 1934, p. A1.

_____. "Film Producers Shaken by Clean-Up Campaign." *Los Angeles Times*, June 10, 1934, p. 13.

_____. "Films Can Teach Schools History, Says DeMille." *Los Angeles Times*, January 30, 1938, p. C1.

_____. "Hedy May Play Wire Walker." *Los Angeles Times*, January 22, 1950, pp. D1, D4.

_____. "Hollywood Has No Actors, Declares DeMille!" *Los Angeles Times*, January 28, 1934, p. A1.

_____. "Hollywood Studios Fight the Economic War." *Los Angeles Times*, January 3, 1949, p. 13.

_____. "Inside Story of Paramount Studio Shake-Up Told." *Los Angeles Times*, February 10, 1935, p. A1.

_____. "Irving Thalberg Challenges Cecil B. DeMille." *Los Angeles Times*, April 1, 1934, p. A1.

_____. "Spectacle and Thrill Effects Lend Vivid Interest to DeMille Feature." *Los Angeles Times*, July 21, 1929, p. H2.

_____. "South Sea Lure Holds Java Hero." *Los Angeles Times*, July 18, 1943, p. C2.

_____. "Third Film Based on American History." *Los Angeles Times*, January 27, 1938, p. 10.

_____. "'This Day and Age' Real Film Thriller." *Los Angeles Times*, August 19, 1933, p. A5.

Scheuer, Philip K. "Hollywood Borrows Tricks from Europe." *Los Angeles Times*, August 6, 1933, p. A1.

_____. "How Come Hokum Cited as Opposite of Vices?" *Los Angeles Times*, September 14, 1930, p. B9.

_____. "Old Successes Being Revived." *Los Angeles Times*, May 11, 1930, p. B7.

_____. "A Town Called Hollywood." *Los Angeles Times*, July 15, 1934, p. A1.

_____. "Truth Just Sugar-Coated." *Los Angeles Times*, August 4, 1929, p. B19.

_____. "Wanted! A He-Man Who Can Wear Tights." *Los Angeles Times*, January 7, 1934, p. A1.

Shippey, Lee. "Leeside." *Los Angeles Times*, August 7, 1944, p. A4.

Small, Collie. "Rock of Hollywood: Cecil B. DeMille." *Collier's* 125, No. 8 (February 25, 1950), pp. 13-14, 66, 68.

Spears, Jack. "Mary Pickford's Directors." *Films in Review* 17, No. 2 (February 1966) pp. 71-95.

Slifer, Clarence W.D. "Camera Angles on 3-39." *Screenland* 17, No. 3, pp. 24-25, 92-93.

Smith, Frederick James. "Freddie Takes a Fall." *Picture Play* 48, No.2 (April 1938), pp. 54-55.

St. Johns, Adela Rogers. "The Photoplay Has Its Heroes." *Photoplay* 23, No. 1 (December 1922), p. 31.

Swanson, Gloria. "What My Experiences Have Taught Me." *Motion Picture Classic* 23, No. 5 (July 1926), pp. 18-19, 86.

Towne, Ted. "Calamity Jean." *Movie Classic* 11, No. 5 (January 1937), pp. 31, 84.

Van Ryn, Frederick. "When You See Paramount, Remember DeMille." *Reader's Digest* 41, No. 245 (September 1942), pp. 15-18.

Waite, Thornton. "Cecil B. DeMille's *Union Pacific*." *The Streamliner* 23 No. 1 (Winter 2009), pp. 25-36.

Waterbury, Ruth. "Close Ups and Long Shots." *Photoplay* 52, No. 3 (March 1938), p, 11.

Whitaker, Alma. "Dynamite Marks Debut." *Los Angeles Times*, July 21, 1929, p. B13.

Williams, Whitney. "Under the Lights." *Los Angeles Times*, October 24, 1926, p. H5.

UNSIGNED ARTICLES

"Art Directors Honor Lasky and DeMille." *Los Angeles Times*, September 16, 1949, p. A6.

"Breaking into the Movies in California." *Motion Picture* Magazine, February 1916, p. 110.

"Brickbats and Bouquets." *Photoplay* 34, No. 6 (November 1928), pp. 8, 92-93.

"Brickbats and Bouquets." *Photoplay* 46, No. 5 (October 1934) pp. 8, 14, 16.

"Deadline for Film Dirt." *Variety*, June 13, 1933, I, p. 6.

"DeMille Defends Hokum." *Los Angeles Times*, November 24, 1929, p. 32.

"DeMille Explains How Players Become Stars."

Unsourced clipping, MHL.

"DeMille Finds High School Generation Grown Mature." *Los Angeles Times*, August 20, 1933, p. A3.

"DeMille Hears from Author." *Los Angeles Times*, March 22, 1931, p. 25.

"DeMille on DeMille." *Newsweek* 51, No. 4 (January 27, 1958) p. 13.

"The Dumb Carmen Happy." *Photoplay*, September 1915, pp. 57-58.

"D.W. Griffith Paid Tribute." *Los Angeles Times*, July 28, 1948, p. A1.

"Film Making Means Millions to Los Angeles." *Los Angeles Times*, January 1, 1916, p. III66.

"Gas Turned on to Make Rome Burn." *Los Angeles Times*, October 14, 1932, p. B11.

"Genuine Film Masterpiece." *Moving Picture World*, July 3, 1915.

"Geraldine Farrar Seen But Not Heard." *The New York Times*, November 1, 1915, p. I1.

"Gorgeously Extravagant Production." *Wid's Daily* Magazine 15, No. 28 (January 30, 1921), p. 2.

"Human Touch Injected into Pictures by DeMille." *Los Angeles Times*, February 23, 1935, p. A3.

"In the Motion Picture Swim." *Los Angeles Times*, February 1, 1910, p. III4.

"Kindling." *Variety*, July 16, 1915.

"Lasky Fetes His Success in Film Twenty Years Ago." *Los Angeles Times*, January 14, 1933, p. A12.

"Making a Picture Director." *New York Dramatic Mirror*, January 14, 1914. Fragmentary clipping, MHL.

"Samson and Delilah." *Life* Magazine, December 5, 1949.

UNPUBLISHED DOCUMENTS

Brownlow, Kevin. "Geraldine Farrar: April 3, 1964, a conversation with Agnes de Mille and Kevin Brownlow." Photoplay Pictures Collection, London, UK.

Hopper Hedda. "Interview, December 10, 1951." Hedda Hopper Collection, Special Collections, Margaret Herrick Library, Fairbanks Center for Motion Picture Study, Academy of Motion Picture Arts and Sciences.

Wall, James M. "Interview with Geoffrey Shurlock." Louis B. Mayer Library, American Film Institute.

Zeitlin, David I. "Interview with Anne Bauchens, undated." David I. Zeitlin Papers, Special Collections, Margaret Herrick Library, Fairbanks Center for Motion Picture Study, Academy of Motion Picture Arts and Sciences.

_____. "Interview with Henry Wilcoxon, October 16, 1956." David I. Zeitlin Papers, Special Collections, Margaret Herrick Library, Fairbanks Center for Motion Picture Study, Academy of Motion Picture Arts and Sciences.

AUDIO RECORDINGS

Pratt, George C. "Interview with Cecil B. DeMille." Hollywood, 1958. Unpublished audio tape, George Eastman House International Museum of Photography and Film.

A COMPLETE NOTES TO THE TEXT FOR
CECIL B. DEMILLE: THE ART OF THE HOLLYWOOD EPIC
CAN BE FOUND ONLINE AT WWW.CECILBDEMILLE.COM

INDEX

ACKNOWLEDGMENTS

Writing about Cecil B. DeMille has been a transporting experience. I entered an environment that continues to thrive fifty-five years after his passing. His work lives on. This entrée was made possible by Cecilia de Mille Presley. In the '80s John Kobal began a book for Mrs. Presley, *DeMille and His Artists*. John did not live to finish it. To complete his project became my dream. I thank Mrs. Presley for helping me realize it. To honor Mr. DeMille, his artists, and the *Squaw Man* centennial, I needed access to the De Mille Collection. Helen Cohen of the De Mille Office introduced me to the institutions that house it.

For access to screenplays in the Collection, I thank the Cinematic Arts Library at the University of Southern California; in particular, Ned Comstock, Senior Library Assistant; Sandra Garcia-Myers, Director of the Archives of the Cinematic Arts; and Steve Hanson, Head Cinematic Arts Librarian.

For access to interview transcripts in the De Mille Collection, I thank James V. D'Arc, Curator of the Arts and Communications Archives, which reside in the Harold B. Lee Library at Brigham Young University.

For access to photographs in the De Mille Collection, I thank Linda Harris Mehr, Director of the Margaret Herrick Library in the Academy of Motion Picture Arts and Sciences. I thank Matt Severson, Photographic Services Administrator. I thank his colleagues, Faye Thompson and Sue Guldin. Lastly, I thank Michael Tyler, the Digital Imaging Specialist who made the superb scans.

For the privilege of researching and photographing this material, and the treasures in and around the De Mille Office, I thank Mrs. Presley. I thank Helen Cohen and her associates for a warm, accommodating environment in which to work. I thank our technical staff: Bryce Hirschberg, Jonathan Quiej, Amanda Brooks, Lester Lopez, and Antonio Marroquin.

Our revisionist history of *The Squaw Man* was written with the help of numerous scholars. James V. D'Arc facilitated our research at Brigham Young University, where forgotten sentences in far-flung documents joined existing data to correct a century of apocrypha. Kurt Cox at Western Costume provided information about DeMille's first Hollywood landlords. Richard Adkins of Hollywood Heritage took me to DeMille's first Hollywood office. Robert S. Birchard, the ultimate DeMille scholar, even made sure that my book proposal was accurate. Betty Lasky, the historian of the Lasky family and the Lasky companies, clarified her father's role in the days of the Lasky-DeMille Barn, and recounted her brother's tenure as a DeMille screenwriter. Michael Greco, a historian who specializes in Paramount Pictures, helped us establish a definitive timeline for late 1913. Miles Kreuger and the Institute of the American Musical shared *Squaw Man* photographs that once belonged to Dick Le Strange.

I thank the following individuals for additional imagery and artifacts: Matías A. Bombal, Rob Brooks, Ben S. Carbonetto, Alfred B. Chico, David Chierichetti, Betty Lasky, John McElwee of Greenbriar Films, Rob McKay, Lisa Mitchell, Katherine Orrison, Nancy Pearce, Mark Santamaria, Sue Slutzky, Lou Valentino, and Mrs. Shirley Whitmore. I am grateful to Robert S. Birchard for his kind and resourceful support. His insistence on accuracy and respect for DeMille are exemplary.

I thank these institutions and companies for photographic material: Kirsten Tanaka, Head Librarian and Archivist in the Performing Arts Library of the Museum of Performance and Design in San Francisco; Jamie Vuignier of the Kobal Collection at Art Resource; Marc Wanamaker and the Bison Archives; and Roy Windham, Baby Jane of Hollywood. I thank Victoria Lucai of Sikelia Productions for arranging Martin Scorsese's Introduction, and Brett Ratner for his Foreword.

For expert archival research, I thank Mary Mallory. For assistance with photographic research, I thank Joe Yranski; Mimi Muray, Manager of the Nickolas Muray Photo Archives; Elaina Archer, Director of Archive and Legacy at the Mary Pickford Foundation; and David Shields. For access to rare interviews and documents, I thank Kevin Brownlow of Photoplay Productions; Nancy Kauffman, Archivist of Stills, Posters and Paper Collections in the Moving Image Department of the George Eastman House; Ned Comstock at the USC Cinematic Arts Library; Katherine Orrison; Betty Lasky; and Robert S. Birchard. For advice, I thank Pat Silver Lasky, Peter Betts, and Mark Penn.

I thank the people who saw me through the second computer crash, the one that "could not happen" but did: Brad Hill, Erica Dorsey, and Angel Cortez. For PhotoShop tutelage I thank Frank Coiro, Jonathan Quiej, and Amanda Brooks. For sustenance during writing and editing sessions, I thank my friends at Casita del Campo restaurant: Omar Sandoval, Baldomero Mendoza, Jay Richards, and Rigoberto Benitez.

For manuscript review, I thank David Chierichetti, Katherine Orrison, and Betty Lasky. For helping us reach our public, I thank Jerry Digney of Digney Mario PR; Susan King of the *Los Angeles Times*; Gary Baum, Senior Writer at the *Hollywood Reporter*; Dean Rhys Morgan; Brett Ratner; Mike Medavoy; Deborah Thalberg; Daniel Mayer Selznick; and Jeff Mantor of Larry Edmunds Book Shop.

For generous assistance and support, I am deeply grateful to: Connie Parker, Helen Cohen, David Chierichetti, Jon Davison, Kim Hill, Robert L. Hillmann, Andrew Montealegre, Bruce Paddock, Howard Mandelbaum, Ben Carbonetto, Jonathan G. Quiej, Peter Koch, Darin Barnes, Karie Bible, Cari Beauchamp, Kenton Bymaster, Vincent Estrada, Felix Pfeifle, Marguerite Topping, George Wagner, Leonel and Horalia Way, Dana Sherman, Freddie Tryk, Damon Devine, and P.R. Tooke.

For guidance, I thank Suzanne McCormick, Jann Hoffman, Bill Pace, William Martin, Bryan Potok, L.C.O., Ruben Alvarez, M.D., and the Rev. Dr. R. Scott Colglazier of First Congregational Church of Los Angeles.

In the mid-'70s I photographed Henry Wilcoxon and then Katherine DeMille Quinn. In both cases I was treated to reminiscences about Mr. DeMille. I thank Katherine Orrison for bringing Mr. Wilcoxon's magic to the project. I thank Betty Lasky for unflagging support.

I thank Deborah Warren of East-West Literary for her resourceful, creative work on my behalf. Every writer should be as blessed.

I thank my editor, Cindy De La Hoz, for advocating the project and for bringing it to a grand conclusion. I am truly grateful for her guidance.

I dedicate this book to my parents because they took me to see *The Ten Commandments* in 1956, and introduced me to *The Sign of the Cross* in 1962. I hope this book conveys both my gratitude to them and my enjoyment of Mr. DeMille's artistry. For ongoing encouragement, I thank my family: Beverly Ferreira Rivera, Sue Costa, Dorothy Chambless, Michael Chambless, Lenore Griego, Matthew Griffiths, Guy and Shannon Vieira, and Steve and Janine Faelz.